CULTURE, PLACE, AND NATURE

Studies in Anthropology and Environment

K. Sivaramakrishnan, Series Editor

Centered in anthropology, the Culture, Place, and Nature series encompasses new interdisciplinary social science research on environmental issues, focusing on the intersection of culture, ecology, and politics in global, national, and local contexts. Contributors to the series view environmental knowledge and issues from the multiple and often conflicting perspectives of various cultural systems.

Timber and Forestry in Qing China

SUSTAINING THE MARKET

Meng Zhang

UNIVERSITY OF WASHINGTON PRESS

Seattle

Timber and Forestry in Qing China was made possible in part by a grant from the Association for Asian Studies First Book Subvention Program.

The Office of the Dean of the Bellarmine College of Liberal Arts at Loyola Marymount University provided additional support for this publication.

Composed in Warnock Pro, typeface designed by Robert Slimbach

25 24 23 22 21 5 4 3 2 1

Printed and bound in the United States of America

UNIVERSITY OF WASHINGTON PRESS
uwapress.uw.edu

LIBRARY OF CONGRESS CATALOGING-IN-PUBLICATION DATA
Names: Zhang, Meng (History professor), author.
Title: Timber and forestry in Qing China : sustaining the market / Meng Zhang.
Description: Seattle : University of Washington Press, [2021] | Series: Culture, place, and nature studies in anthropology and environment | Includes bibliographical references and index.
Identifiers: LCCN 2020051268 (print) | LCCN 2020051269 (ebook) | ISBN 9780295748863 (hardcover) | ISBN 9780295748870 (paperback) | ISBN 9780295748887 (ebook)
Subjects: LCSH: Timber trade—China—History—Qing dynasty, 1644–1912. | Timber—China—History—Qing dynasty, 1644–1912. | Deforestation—China—History—Qing dynasty, 1644–1912. | Sustainable development—China—History—Qing dynasty, 1644–1912.
Classification: LCC HD9766.C62 Z43 2021 (print) | LCC HD9766.C62 (ebook) | DDC 338.1/749809510903—dc23
LC record available at https://lccn.loc.gov/2020051268
LC ebook record available at https://lccn.loc.gov/2020051269

The paper used in this publication is acid free and meets the minimum requirements of American National Standard for Information Sciences—Permanence of Paper for Printed Library Materials, ANSI Z39.48–1984.∞

For my parents

CONTENTS

MAPS, FIGURES, AND TABLES

MAPS

FIGURES

TABLES

FOREWORD

The expansion and deepening of scholarship on the environmental history of China and East Asia more generally has enabled detailed treatments of key topics, across different periods. The modern period, where this particular book is situated, has benefited from regional and comparative work examining natural resources management, conservation, and commodity markets in the last centuries of imperial rule in China. Such work has revealed sophisticated production regimes, extensive market integration, and impressive infrastructure for timber economy development by the end of the nineteenth century.

Meng Zhang joins a complex scholarly field, providing a lucid study of timber markets in modern, late-imperial, China. She offers a rare, close examination of the structures and flows through which a vast region was well supplied with wood for all purposes in the two hundred years preceding World War I. Wood was crucial to urban settlement, shipping and commerce, war and state edifices of various kinds, as well as domestic use and small-scale development in this period. Wood was produced, she shows in captivating detail, as well as processed, transported, and utilized across complex market institutions that were but loosely regulated by the imperial government or other state officials.

Not since Conrad Totman's path-breaking work, for Japan, has a study of forest management and commercial forestry in East Asia provided such a vivid account of regenerative and production forestry in the modern period.[1] While Totman, who covers a much longer period, provides a narrative of reckless exploitation followed by state controls and market development, in this book Zhang zeroes in on the particular development of markets and the relative absence of the government in fostering or directing them.

This leads to a wonderfully people-centered account, focused on growers, loggers, transporters, and merchants. It shows how they came to constitute a sustainable and enduring timber economy over centuries up and down the Yangzi River valley. Along the way we get a sophisticated analysis of property rights, futures markets, and credit relations through which forestry developed in southern China. This book is a healthy antidote to tired debates contrasting state control and free markets in a commodity that takes long to mature, is expensive to transport, and has fluctuating demand cycles. Zhang adeptly blends ecological and economic history to consider at once the material properties of trees and forests and the cultural construction of commerce in their products, notably timber. She offers an original analysis of liquidity issues in timber production related, to the extent possible, to a close examination of *Cunninghamia lanceolata* (China fir) ecology to draw out the ecological agency of the tree in shaping financial instruments.

If property rights reveal the production economy, the trading system is unraveled through the study of merchant guilds, financiers, and licensed brokers who matched buyers and sellers, producing the links in the supply chain. Zhang provides comprehensive coverage of all stages of market development for timber in modern China, including state procurement of timber and the private sector economy in large woods, production zones and the routes traveled, as well as the institutions that financed operations and enforced contracts. Regional variations in systems between urban centers and rural frontiers, and the adaptation of the timber markets to growing deforestation as we enter the twentieth century are all accounted for with attention to local diversity and long-term dynamics. An amazing range of historical records are used, from transit tax documents to court filings and rulings as well as the regulations enforced by trade associations.

The many original insights in this book flow from careful documentation of the interlocking relations that emerged between state and private institutions. A prime example, among many, is the self-directed merchant organizations that became part of local commercial taxation structures, thereby gaining legitimacy while sparing government a parallel organization. By the end of the book Zhang leaves us with a tantalizing introduction to the early twentieth-century and interimperial competition in forest products trade between China, Russia, and Japan. This later history has received its own valuable treatment in other work, especially on Korea, that ably complements Zhang's research.[2]

The narrative trajectory of the book blends a compelling story from varied ingredients while distilling a strong argument, well-flavored by salient literature, that will be savored by scholars of China. At the same time this book will enliven more general interest in the history of forestry, sustainable natural resource management, and the relative role of states and market institutions in land control, wood trade, and related environmental outcomes.

K. SIVARAMAKRISHNAN
Yale University

ACKNOWLEDGMENTS

It would not have been possible to research and write this book without the generous support provided by many people. First and foremost, my greatest debts are owed to my mentors R. Bin Wong, Richard von Glahn, and Jean-Laurent Rosenthal, whose sustained encouragement and constructive criticisms have guided this intellectual journey from the beginning. This book bears the methodological imprint of countless meetings of the UCLA-Caltech Chinese economic history group, where assumptions are interrogated, hypotheses are overthrown, counterfactuals are entertained, and historians and economists must make sense to each other. I have also benefited enormously from the feedback of William Rowe, Matthew Mosca, and Larry Neal, who have read through an earlier draft and devoted their time to my book manuscript workshop.

Many others have influenced the evolution of this book. Conversations with Nicholas Menzies, Robert Marks, David Bello, Ian Matthew Miller, and John S. Lee formed my thoughts about forestry and environmental history. I was fortunate to draw on NI Yuping's insight on the Qing domestic customs and commercial taxation when he was visiting UCLA. My understanding of the relationship between Chinese merchant organizations and the local state has been influenced by many conversations with Maura Dykstra through graduate school. Francesca Trivellato, Oscar Gelderblom, and Naomi Lamoreaux challenged me to situate Chinese long-distance trade and economic institutions in a global framework. I thank the following colleagues and friends for their engaging conversations and intriguing questions at various stages of this project: Angela KC Leung, Amy Gordanier, Andrea Goldman, Aurelia Campbell, Bradley Camp Davis, Brett Sheehan, Brian Lander, Boyi Chen, CAO Shuji, Chelsea Zi Wang, Michael G. Chang, Christopher Coggins, CH'IU Pengsheng, Dagmar Schäfer, Dong Yan, Dora Costa, Dorothy Ko, Elizabeth Köll, Eric Tagliacozzo, Ethan Segal,

Evelyn Rawski, Ghislaine Lydon, Guillermo Ruiz-Stovel, Holly Stephens, Huiying Chen, Janet Hunter, Jessica Goldberg, John D. Wong, Joshua Herr, Joshua Goldstein, Judy Stephenson, Karl Appuhn, Kenneth Pomeranz, Lan Wu, Luman Wang, Margaret Wan, Miriam Kaminishi, Nan Jia, Nicola Di Cosmo, Patrick Wallis, Peter Perdue, Philip Hoffman, Shigehisa Kuriyama, Stevan Harrell, Steven Miles, Sudev Sheth, Sunkyu Lee, Tak-Jun Wong, Thomas DuBois, Thomas Rawski, Tobie Meyer-Fong, Xiang Chi, Xiaowen Hao, Yi Wang, You Wang, and ZHAO Siyuan, with no doubt glaring omissions.

I was privileged to join the history faculty at Loyola Marymount University, where I enjoy the warmest welcome and collegiality. My special thanks go to Elizabeth Drummond, Amy Woodson-Boulton, and Carla Bittel, whose intellectual insights, practical strategizing, and mental counseling have been indispensable. Research support provided by the Dean's Office of the Bellarmine College of Liberal Arts enabled me to fund a book manuscript workshop in the early stage, which pointed me in the right direction. A fellowship in the School of Historical Studies at the Institute for Advanced Study supported me during the final stage of the book's production.

The following libraries and archives provided generous assistance, without which I could not have accumulated the materials for this book. I thank the staff and scholars at the Richard C. Rudolph East Asian Library, UCLA; the First Historical Archives of China; the National Library of China; the National Science Library, Chinese Academy of Sciences; Sichuan Provincial Archives; Suzhou Municipal Archives; Shanghai Municipal Archives; Nanjing Municipal Archives; National Palace Museum, Taipei; and the Institute of History and Philology, Academia Sinica.

I appreciate the following platforms of vigorous scholarly exchange and the financial support for travel and research provided by many of them: the Association of Asian Studies, World Economic History Congress, the American Society for Environmental History, the Association for East Asian Environmental History, the International Society for Chinese Law and History, Business History Conference, the All-UC Economic History Group, the UCLA Center for Economic History, the economic history seminar at Yale University, the Wood Age in Asia conference at Yale University, the USC China Studies Group, the Business History Initiative at Harvard Business School, the Caltech Early Modern Group, Utrecht University, the Summer Institute for Chinese Studies at the University of Pittsburg, and the D. Kim Foundation Workshop on the History of Science and Technology in East Asia.

At the University of Washington Press, my heartfelt thanks go to Lorri Hagman and the entire able team, who have patiently shepherded this project through to completion. I was especially fortunate to have two distinguished and perceptive reviewers, who suggested key structural revisions that improved the book immeasurably. I am honored that K. Sivaramakrishnan welcomes this book into the Culture, Place, and Nature series and anchors it in broad themes with his insightful foreword.

Portions of this book were previously published as the following journal articles and are reprinted here with permission: "Timber Trade Organizations in Shanghai: Institutions, Enforcement, and Dispute Resolution, 1880–1930," *International Journal of Asian Studies* 14, no. 2 (2017): 143–70, © 2017, Cambridge University Press; and "Financing Market-Oriented Reforestation: Securitization of Timberlands and Shareholding Practices in Southwest China, 1750–1900," *Late Imperial China* 38, no. 2 (2017): 109–51, © 2017, Johns Hopkins University Press. I thank the Toyo Bunko and the Rubenstein Rare Book and Manuscript Library of Duke University for permission to use historical photographs in this book.

Tracing my debts further back, I thank ZHOU Li'an and DENG Xiaonan, professors at my alma mater Peking University, for sparking my interest in the intersections of economics and history and encouraging me to pursue graduate studies exactly ten years ago—I hope they see this book as a satisfactory periodic report. My deepest gratitude is owed to my family for their unconditioned love. My parents have supported all my endeavors, even though they had to come to terms with a daughter living far away and doing something they could not explain to bewildered neighbors. Our extended family, in the stereotypical Chinese fashion, provides a fanciful combination of solidarity, warmth, meddling, and drama, which I cannot help but miss dearly from overseas. Finally, I must thank my husband, Ye Wang, and our dog, Bajie, who have accompanied me through days and nights of this intense adventure with humor and mischief.

MEASURES AND RELATED TERMINOLOGY

In the business of timber trade, logs were measured by circumference at eye level, based on which they were graded into different classes in a system called the Longquan *ma*. The diameter was sometimes used in official documents but less often than circumference. Throughout the book I have preserved the measurement in circumference so that the classification of different grades of logs in the primary sources is clear to readers. The corresponding diameter at breast height (dbh), the standard measure used today, can be inferred by dividing the circumference by π, which I include when applicable for the readers' convenience. For the unit of measurement, I have used "foot" to translate *chi* (often referred to as "Chinese foot"); 1 *chi* is now standardized as exactly ⅓ of a meter (approximately 1.09 international feet), but its exact length varied in history by region and industry. The "foot" used in the Qing timber trade (*tanchi*) was, with some regional variations, about 34.2 centimeters (1.1 international feet).[1] Furthermore, 1 *zhang* is equal to 10 *chi*, and 1 *cun* is equal to 0.1 *chi*.

Silver, in different physical forms and measured by slightly different units of accounts, served as the standard currency for large-scale transactions during the centuries covered in this book. In Qing China uncoined silver (*yinliang*) and imported foreign silver dollars (*yinyuan*) were both in use and measured in tael (*liang*), which weighed between 33.99 and 37.50 grams by different standards.[2] Furthermore, 1 *qian* is 0.1 tael, and 1 *fen* is 0.1 *qian*. During the Republican period, silver dollars minted by different banks circulated, denoted in *yuan*. For the broad analyses provided in this book, the differences are not relevant. I have provided values and units as they appear in the sources.

CHRONOLOGY OF LATER DYNASTIES AND QING REIGN PERIODS

Tang	618–907
Song	960–1279
Yuan	1279–1368
Ming	1368–1644
Qing	1644–1911
Shunzhi (SZ)	1644–1661
Kangxi (KX)	1662–1722
Yongzheng (YZ)	1723–1735
Qianlong (QL)	1736–1795
Jiaqing (JQ)	1796–1820
Daoguang (DG)	1821–1850
Xianfeng (XF)	1851–1861
Tongzhi (TZ)	1862–1874
Guangxu (GX)	1875–1908
Xuantong (XT)	1909–1911

TIMBER AND FORESTRY IN QING CHINA

Introduction

During his journey along the Yangzi River in the 1870s, British diplomat Augustus Raymond Margary remarked on the curious appearance of timber rafts:

> [The rafts,] seen from a short distance, look like a floating village with a brisk population, and on a nearer view, one cannot help admiring the ingenious construction. The larger lengths of timber are closely massed together, forming a compact raft of no mean dimensions, down the center of which are constructed a series of neat huts for the crew to live in. The head of the raft is shaped off to somewhat of a sharp prow, and at the stern a gallery runs out fitted with steering apparatus. The fast stream of the Yangtze carries them down with sufficient speed, but they are also furnished with enormous sweeps requiring the strength of 10 to 12 men to manipulate. . . . Three or four of these rafts generally come down in company, one behind the other in a long string, and for means of communication, a diminutive raft, rowed by five men, answered every purpose of a boat. It had all the appearance of a long-legged fly shooting across the water in spasmodic spurt.[1]

What Margary had witnessed was the operation of the cross-regional system of long-distance timber trade that spanned over the Yangzi River and its tributaries (figure I.1). As the premodern equivalent of reinforced concrete, timber was literally the building blocks of late imperial Chinese cities. The voluminous timber trade, which brought at least five million logs annually to the lower Yangzi valley by the late eighteenth century, supplied

FIGURE I.1 Rafts on the Yangzi River in Jiangxi, 1930. *Source*: "Chōkō no ikada," *Atō ingashū* 5, no. 79 (1930): 81. Courtesy of the Toyo Bunko.

the construction of theaters, guild chambers, temples, ancestral halls, brothels, restaurants, teahouses, and other iconic architectures of early modern urban life in the hundreds of cities and market towns that dotted this most prosperous region of the empire. Similar processes of commercialization and urbanization featured the middle and, to a lesser extent, upper reaches of the Yangzi River system as well, which also drew from this network of trade for timber supply. Cities built on wood could be easily wiped out by a bad fire, after which everything had to be reconstructed amid the ashes. Top-notch commercial centers, such as Hangzhou, Hankou, and Nanjing, were also the most notorious for hazardous fires, as the flames could spread so easily thanks to the densely constructed wooden structures in the city.[2] In addition to the construction of buildings, other necessities—including coffins, furniture, junks, and carriages—all pressed the market for constant supplies of wood in all sizes and varieties.

In response to such booming demand, an interregional trade structure developed over the course of several centuries and expanded to cover thousands of miles, sustained by a complex system of institutions in production, harvesting, transportation, investment, transaction, and taxation. Map I.1 overviews the structure of the trade when it reached its full extent by the eighteenth and nineteenth centuries. This expansive market, under

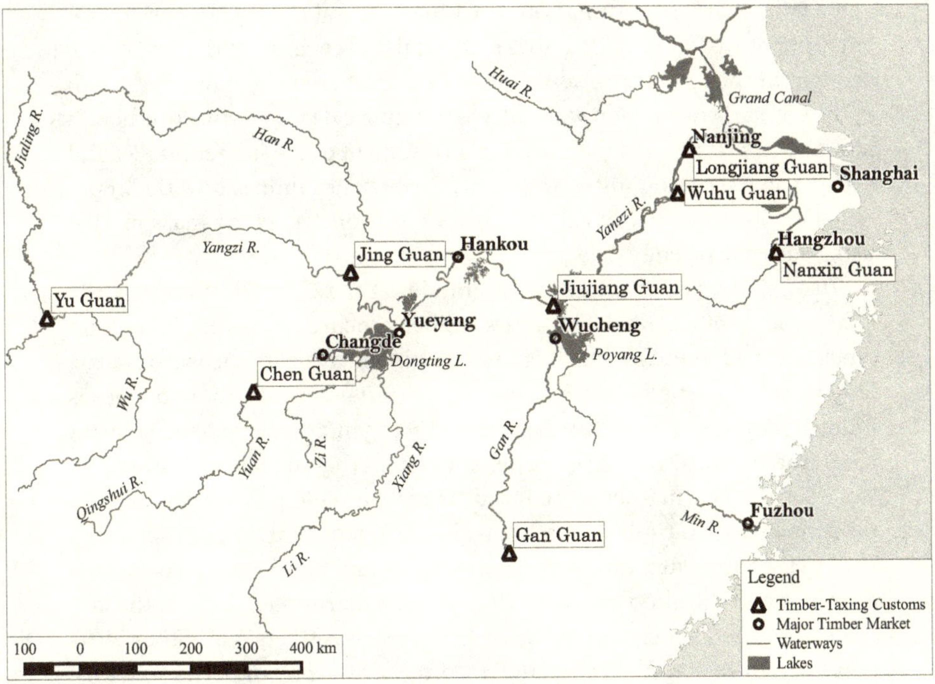

MAP I.1 Timber markets, trade routes, and customs stations.

fairly light taxes and laissez-faire regulations, was able to assure a steady wood supply for the state itself, which was a minor function in terms of volume yet crucial for the timber market to operate the way it did. More remarkably, this system assured a supply of timber for civilian consumption even in the face of population pressure and increased deforestation. In large part, it did so by rewarding patient investment and encouraging market participation so that people all along the supply chain—tree growers, loggers, rafters, sellers, brokers, wholesalers, retailers, and manufacturers—could all profit from it.

The trade of timber has long been recognized as one of the most important interregional bulk trades in late imperial China. Business historians have remarked on the enormous wealth accumulated by big timber merchants. "Licensed salt magnates and timber merchants" (*yanshang muke*), as the set phrase suggests, occupied the top notch of the mercantile community in the markets of Jiangnan (literally "South of the River," the most prosperous region in the lower Yangzi area then and now).[3] Environmental historians have drawn attention to the toll of imperial timber procurement and private market consumption on China's natural forests.[4] However, previous literature has provided little statistical evidence about the systematic changes in the structure and volume of the timber trade, rendering much of the scholarly discussion without a firm empirical foundation. This book's first objective is to trace the historical evolvement of the timber market and clarify some common misconceptions. Chapter 1 examines how the imperial state obtained its timber, and chapter 2 reconstructs the mass market using customs revenue data.

Two related issues are worth highlighting here. The first regards the relative scale of the imperial state's timber procurement, and the second concerns the kind of forests from which timber was cut. The way that the late imperial state obtained logs for imperial construction purposes underwent a significant shift from directly organizing corvee labor to cut trees from the forests to a procurement system that drew readily available timber from the market at reduced prices. In effect, this amounted to taxation levied on timber merchants. By no means limited to timber, this change is congruent with the decline in importance of the state-controlled economy and the almost universalization of a market economy in the late imperial period generally.[5] While memorials, gazetteers, and other writings by Confucian-minded scholars often criticized imperial extravagance and attributed grave environmental and social problems to the emperor's obsession with grand palaces and mausoleums, the actual effect of imperial timber consumption on the forests of central and southern China was rather limited. In fact, direct official logging missions were restricted to a few humanly accessible pockets in the vast old-growth forests of the southwest. Furthermore, by the seventeenth century the majority of imperial timber came not from old growth but planted forests, not through corvee logging missions but via monetary procurement of readily available logs that took away only a tiny fraction of market supply. Timber plantations that developed in many mountainous regions of southern China came to be the most important source of timber supply for mass consumption, and this resource was distributed through the densely connected veins and nodes of an expansive interregional trading network.

SUSTAINABILITY AND INSTITUTIONS

The temporal durability and geographic scope of the timber trading system generate two questions: how to sustain a reliable supply of timber for several centuries, and how to sustain a business network that spanned more than a thousand miles. These two problems found their resolution in a set of underlying institutional mechanisms of "sustainable markets," which aligned the historical actors' incentives toward the direction of resource regeneration, market participation, and fair trading, although such solutions were by no means absolute.

"Sustainability" is a complex concept. Although the general meaning of the term as the endurance of systems and processes is widely acknowledged, "sustainability" takes on different definitions and emphasis in various professions and disciplines. Biologists, economists, sociologists, and ecologists all work with definitions that overlap but have distinct, even conflicting, priorities. Applied biologists and economists focus on the interlinked aspects of the environment and the socioeconomic well-being of the population: applied biology is concerned with sustainable yields from renewable resources (forests, fisheries, etc.), while sustainable economic development requires that current economic activity not disproportionately burden future generations. Sociologists add in attention to the crucial role of social organizations for devising viable solutions to achieving sustainable development. These approaches, despite their differences in focus, are mostly people-centered. With an eye toward the long-term welfare of the people, these approaches promote improved environmental stewardship. Ecologists' emphasis on the sustainability of ecosystem diversity raises a higher bar, however. The requirement that ecosystem diversity not be significantly affected by human intervention puts more stringent restrictions on human activities than what would be required for sustained yield and endurable economic development.[6]

Historian Mark Elvin's famous critique of China's "three thousand years of unsustainable growth" and a line of literature inspired by it have implicitly used the notion of strong sustainability as the evaluation criteria, which this author considers practically unrealistic and intellectually restrictive.[7] Indisputably, much of human behavior ever since the Neolithic Agricultural Revolution has brought irreversible impacts to the flora and fauna in the environment that we live in, but sticking to the notion of strong sustainability inhibits us from appreciating the operational implications of a variety of human practices, with some sustainable over longer periods at lower cost than others. In this book I use "sustainability" in the weaker sense of sustained yields and endurable economic processes. This people-centered approach is built on the understanding that people are the instruments and beneficiaries (as well as victims) of all development activities, and their active involvement is the key to the success of any sustainable regime of resource management.[8]

For timber supply I focus on market-oriented regeneration of forest resources. For timber trade I focus on the sustainability of long-distance business and credit arrangements. These two aspects of sustainability are very much intertwined, and the inseparability of one from the other is a testament to the importance of forestry to the market and the market to forestry. However, this market-based system of timber production and trade was not sustainable in the sense of ecosystem diversity: the planting of timber trees for market sale was largely mono-crop cultivation that did not attain the level of biodiversity in natural forests. Nevertheless, plantation forests provide valuable ecosystem services, including enhancing local water supply, soil conservation, and carbon storage. Such a replanting system was *more* sustainable, both environmentally and economically, than either unregulated clear-cutting or reclamation of the hillsides for the cultivation of maize and other New World crops, which had caused serious problems of soil erosion and river silting in the late imperial period.[9] Therefore, rather than defining an absolute standard, "sustainability" is better thought of as a continuum of different levels of endurance of the interconnected domains of ecology, economics, and politics. Commercialized reforestation was indeed a more sustainable regime of timber harvesting than other prevalent systems that exploited forest resources in the early modern world. This historical episode of successful coordination of natural agents and social actors, if not ecologically ideal, certainly informs our practical concerns with environmental policy and institutional approach.

Sustaining the timber resources and a long-distance trade network was no easy task. All the actors involved in different segments of this system faced distinct challenges. To name a few, a tree planter worried that he would not be able to make profit in time for his son's upcoming wedding, as it would take another five years for trees to become useful timber; an itinerant trader worried about harassment from bribe-seeking government clerks when passing through transit tax stations; a wholesaler was cautious about selling to a first-time customer on credit, who he feared might default and disappear. Without effective measures to deal with these and other problems to a reasonable extent, this timber-producing and -trading system could not have developed into the impressive scale and structure it achieved in the eighteenth and nineteenth centuries.

An intricately embedded system of institutions collectively mitigated these challenges. By "institutions," I mean "the rules of the game," as understood by economists, or more precisely, "the humanly devised constraints that shape human interaction."[10] Written regulations, conventions, codes of behavior, and other said or unsaid rules provide the framework within which human interactions take place by defining the set of choices of individuals and structuring incentives. Of course, any rules, despite their level of formality, can be violated, in which case punishment in some form is in order, from legal prosecution to social awkwardness. An essential part of the functioning of institutions is the costliness of ascertaining violations and the severity of punishment.

Although theorists tend to differentiate between "formal" institutions as those established by state laws and "informal" institutions as more ambiguously defined social norms, the distinction is much murkier in reality. Institutions that defined the market space in late imperial China ranged from permanent state establishments to provisional local maneuvers, from well-defined private-order arrangements to equivocal network-based negotiations. Indeed, the complementarity and interconnectedness of these institutions defy any clear-cut distinction between formal and informal institutions. We can only achieve a good understanding of the forestry practices and business paradigms in late imperial China through a comprehensive examination of how these interrelated institutions shaped each other and evolved over time in an institutionalized, yet not necessarily formalized, market sphere.

SUSTAINING THE RESOURCES: PROPERTY RIGHTS, MARKET, AND REPLANTATION

As the total volume of timber trade expanded over centuries, the natural forests in southern China became increasingly depleted. Market demand for timber was only one factor. Increasing population pressure drove intensified settlement into the uplands of hills and mountains, where forests were felled to open fields to plant maize, potatoes, or other New World crops that were especially adapted to the dry upland ecosystems. Highland deforestation not only led to shortages of timber and fuel but also caused a chain reaction of erosion, silting of waterways, and the danger of flood and drought as water-storage capacity was reduced. In some areas in the nineteenth century, such ecological destruction and the consequent conflicts between highland and lowland communities had become acute.[11]

However, during the late imperial centuries, a noticeable countertrend was the development of tree replantation for market sales, which generated a remarkable supply of timber and also held the hillside soil against erosions. During several business trips across China in the early twentieth century, transpacific timber magnate Robert Dollar encountered big timber rafts that were floated down the Yangzi River from hundreds of miles away. In his memoir Dollar ponders the sustainable source of domestic timber supply in China:

> For a long time, I thought, when they were cutting such small timber that they must be nearing the end of their supply. But on investigation I find that whenever a small tract is cut off it is compulsory to immediately re-forest it by planting the ground over with small plants, and that in a couple of decades a full crop is again ready for cutting. . . . This is the competition we have to meet in the small sizes of Oregon pine, and the reason that the Chinese market for Oregon pine calls for large sizes and excludes all of smaller. . . .
>
> This is quite an improvement on the American mode of cutting everything down and doing nothing to reproduce. This Chinese method of reproduction will give them an everlasting supply of small timber. Would it not be well before it is too late, to take a leaf out of the Chinese book of knowledge, even though we think we know so much more than they?[12]

Dollar's depiction of the Chinese situation is probably too rosy. China's deforestation was precipitating at the very time of his writing. In 1750 about 25 percent of China's land surface had been forested, but by 1950 that had shrunk to less than 10 percent.[13] However, it was indeed true that in some places the reproduction of timber trees was routinely practiced for sales in the market. Admittedly, such practices by no means reversed the general trend of deforestation—a fate that late imperial China shared with many parts of the early modern world.[14] Nevertheless, a close examination of this reforestation regime serves to question the validity of a simplified linear model of change and contributes to a more finely grained history from which we might draw valuable insights from instances of successful attempts at mitigating the often-conflicting demands of environmental preservation and economic prosperity.

Existing literature highlights some successful examples of forest management and tree-planting practices in the mountainous areas of the "Old South" (Anhui, Zhejiang, Jiangxi, and Fujian) as well as the Southwest (Hunan, Guizhou, Sichuan).[15] In all the cases where the cultivation of timber trees developed into an industry of some scale, a common factor was commercialization. With increasing cross-regional economic integration, the high demand for timber from urbanizing areas did not simply wipe out the natural forests in the frontier. In many cases, this demand also provided the monetary incentives for the locals to replant trees when that seemed the most profitable among all alternatives. Less attention has been paid to a practical conundrum, however—that is, even the most economical timber tree species take decades to grow.[16]

The biggest challenge for the tree-planting industry was dealing with the long waiting period before profits could be realized from cutting and selling the trees, with no income whatsoever during the intervening two to three decades. This peculiar cashflow structure of tree planting presented a daunting challenge to premodern rural households. Written contracts for the transactions of timberlands provide a glimpse into the historical solutions to, in modern economics terms, a liquidity problem: the valuable assets possessed by the owner (growing trees) could not be readily converted into cash or other highly marketable (thus liquid) assets. Chapter 3 reveals a property rights framework that solved the liquidity problem associated with the long-term nature of tree growth by the division and securitization of the various kinds of rights over timberlands. The development of active transactions of one's entitlements to ownership and tenancy rights, which were increasingly divided into shareholdings that could be traded independently before the standing crop of trees was harvested, allowed people to transform expected future proceeds into cash flows to match a household's consumption patterns. These practices created a market of proto-futures for a revenue yet to be realized and proved successful in promoting commercialized reforestation in a rural household-based economy.

Cross-regional comparisons reveal a common set of shareholding and tenure practices in forestry across the broad regions to the south of the Yangzi River despite varying local conditions. These market-oriented reforestation practices entailed the following key features: private, instead of state, ownership of mountain lands; rotational planting of timber trees for sale in the market; claims of profits from timberlands based on shares; construction of divisible and tradable shares based on land ownership and labor input; and transfers of shares using written contracts. Such experiences of reforestation based on private property might seem out of tune in the high modernist tide of state-centered environmentalism. However, although twentieth-century environmental policies largely stressed the importance of public planning and government regulation to remedy market failures, scholarship has also questioned the universal validity of the top-down, so-called command-and-control regulations. Economists have expressed concerns over the cost, inefficiency, and rigidity of such policies, while ecologists have pointed out the often-unforeseen consequences of losses of system resilience.[17]

Besides government-based regulatory solutions, scholars have contemplated the alternatives of market-based approaches. Pertinent here are proponents of a property-rights approach to encourage efficient natural resource use through "environmental markets": well-defined and enforced property rights over a certain resource assign the flow of net rents to owners, instilling incentives for stewardship of the resource; transferability of property rights enables flexible responses to new information and values.[18] The property rights regime adopted in the southern China timberlands could be seen as such an environmental market. The effective reforestation system not only provides a historical instance of a successful environmental market but also challenges us to go beyond the abstract debate on the dichotomy of state versus private ownership, command-and-control versus market-based solutions, to examine in detail the specific mechanisms embedded in functional local institutions and base future policy recommendations on what already works well in local contexts.

SUSTAINING THE BUSINESS: ACCESS, INFORMATION, AND ENFORCEMENT

In addition to the question of sustainable timber supply, the other key question concerns the challenges in sustaining the long-distance trade. Although these challenges could take many manifestations, at the core are the interrelated issues of access, information, and enforcement. Was this line of business open to new entrants, or was it monopolized by vested interests? How could an itinerant merchant locate potential trading partners in a strange city, and how could one find reliable information about their trustworthiness and solvency? What were the available mechanisms to enforce an agreement when violations or disputes arose? The capacity of the interregional timber market relied on effective institutions to undergird market openness and fairness, without which many exchanges would not have taken place and the sustainable supply of timber would be threatened first in circulation and further through chain effects on production.

Two institutions defined the late imperial marketplaces: intermediaries and merchant organizations. The business of intermediating transactions was largely dominated by licensed brokerages known as *yahang*, although small unregistered intermediaries also occupied some niche. The late imperial state placed licensed brokerages at the center of its market management strategy, which performed the dual tasks of economic intermediation between traders and administrative intermediation between the state and the market. Whereas state-designated organizations of merchants for different trades traced their history at least to the middle imperial period, the proliferation of commercial organizations that were spontaneously established merchant communities (*huiguan* or *gongsuo*) was a new phenomenon in the eighteenth and nineteenth centuries.[19]

Research on licensed brokerages and trade associations features predominantly in the historiography of Chinese business history. A central question concerns the extent to which they facilitated or prohibited market exchange. Criticisms often derive from the perspective of market access. The limited number of official licenses and the prohibition of unlicensed intermediaries have led to a popular view that the licensed brokerage system increasingly shackled free exchange during the Qing dynasty.[20] Similarly, some scholars view the Chinese merchant associations as monopolistic organizations similar to European guilds. In return for their contributions to the local government, merchant associations were granted considerable autonomy, including such attempts as limiting membership, restricting competition, and manipulating prices.[21] More positive assessments of licensed brokerages and merchant organizations stem from their contributions to the issues of information and enforcement. These perspectives argue that the intermediating and information-sharing functions of both institutions served as valuable remedies for the problems of information asymmetry and searching cost, especially in long-distance trade.[22]

Most of these previous studies either discuss national trends in general terms or look at all the brokerages or merchant organizations in a given locality without much distinction in the specialty of trade. A good account of the dynamics in a particular trade is rarer still. Such an account should include interactions among all the brokerages and merchant associations of this trade within the same city as well as cross-regional interactions, if any, between trade associations in different marketplaces. By focusing on timber-related institutions in multiple localities, I provide such a cross-regional examination. Chapter 4 examines the dynamic interactions among different players in the timber markets and the mechanisms of timber transactions along the long supply chain. Chapter 5 explores the mechanisms of contract enforcement through merchant organizations and the court system. The findings about market access, intermediation, and contract enforcement not only apply to the trade of timber but are generally representative of long-distance, capital-intensive, bulk trades that were largely free from the state's direct interference (unlike the trade of salt or grain, for example).

The market environment lay somewhere between the free-market ideal and a controlled space featuring oligopoly and oligopsony, with higher-level markets approaching the former. The most important functions performed by licensed brokerages and other economic intermediaries alike in the timber trade were informational: the matching of buyers and sellers as well as creditors and borrowers. What made these intermediaries essential to long-distance trade was their exceptional knowledge about sources of supply and demand, market tendencies, and the solvency and history of individual firms and traders. The reliance on licensed brokerages in wholesale transactions was more a result of the indispensability of their economic services than a mere pro forma fulfillment of state requirement.

Similarly, the most appealing economic function that a trade association offered its members was information and enforcement. Without effective mechanisms to fend against default, long-distance timber trade could not have relied on credit as much as it did. At the center of the trade associations' enforcement capacity was reputation mechanisms based on information sharing and collective punishment strategies. Moreover, trade associations and the court system constituted a complementary institution of contract enforcement, which, since the first decade of the twentieth century, was further enhanced by the network of the chamber of commerce that facilitated vertical interinstitutional communication as well as horizontal cross-regional dispute resolution. The formal market regulating apparatus and private-order initiatives by the merchant communities constituted an institutional continuum that collectively defined the business norms in the local marketplaces. These market institutions played a crucial role in the wood supply chain by lowering the entrance barriers to this trade, facilitating the circulation of goods and capital as well as checking speculative and fraudulent behavior.

WOODS AND THEIR ECOLOGICAL MATERIALITY

Human-devised institutions of forestry, property rights, markets, and laws never operate solely in the domain of human interactions; rather, they are motivated, enabled, modified, and constrained by their interactions with the natural environment. In this story the trees are no less of a protagonist than the planters, rafters, merchants, and magistrates. The very practice of tree plantation was dependent on the enabling biology of timber trees, fir (*shan*) in particular and pine to a lesser extent. The Chinese word *shan* corresponds to the genus of *Cunninghamia*, a straight-growing evergreen conifer in the cypress family (*Cupressaceae*). In southern China, *shan* is principally *Cunninghamia lanceolata*, in vernacular use known as "China fir" due to its morphological similarity to true firs (*Abies* sp.).[23] Throughout this book for simplicity I follow the vernacular custom and universally use "fir" for the Chinese word *shan*. Fast-growing, straight, durable, and insect-resistant, China fir has been and still is the most widely used species in plantation forestry in central and southern China.[24] Though slightly less valuable, pine—mostly *mawei song* (*Pinus massoniana*)—was also prized by planters for its rapid self-regeneration.

Commercialized forestry was enabled and conditioned by the biology of these suiting species. The broad region south of the Yangzi River, where commercial silviculture and private timber trade flourished, maps exactly to the geographic extent that suits the ecological requirements of these fast-growing timber species. Without this enabling ecological condition, it would be hard to imagine the human practices working. Although this book's narrative unfolds as a story of how forestry and timber markets expanded to frontier regions via human-devised institutions, it could be told with equal validity as a story of how fir and pine used their human agents to replace the mixture of subtropical broadleaf and conifer forests in southern China and colonize ever greater areas as the dominant species.

It should be stressed that the focus of the book is on timber—woods that are big enough to be used for construction and worthwhile enough to be produced and transported across long distances. Human actors had to base their moves around the materiality of timber woods—its natural cycle of growth, bulkiness, density, morphology, and flammability. Patience had to be sustained in one way or another as nature takes its time through photosynthesis. Human labor had to be spent in logging, pruning, and transportation. Slipways had to be built on trestles in rough terrains to carry large timber out of the forest. Warping, large knots, or other "imperfections" had to be dealt with, whether mechanically or financially. Pine resin had to be extracted to make the logs floatable. Small waterways had to be dredged to bear the rafts, space had to be negotiated with other traffic along narrow canals, and the risks in traversing through dangerous gorges and waves had to be borne.

Technology and energy had to be exerted to manufacture the desired shape and size. When the railway age finally came to China in the early twentieth century, the round logs' resistance to the preindustrial technologies of traditional sawmills rendered the Chinese market dependent on the imports of precisely and uniformly sized railway sleepers from the mechanized sawmills of America and Japan-controlled Manchuria. In these and many other cases, the ecology and materiality of the trees defined the scope of possibilities for human maneuvers. With its focus on timber, this book has inevitably omitted many other wood-related consumptions in the early modern period—for example, tung oil, lacquer, mulberry, and a wide range of food and drugs. Many of these nontimber trees were cultivated in plantations just like fir (although they required less time to mature), with their products intended for national and even international markets. Another omission is firewood, whose production and consumption remained rather local; even with fuel shortages, high transportation cost meant that firewood had never become worthwhile to transport over very long distances to be used as fuel.

The Qing empire encompassed a great diversity of forest ecosystems, for which the mode of access, management, and use differed greatly. This book focuses on the broad areas in southern China connected by the Yangzi River and its tributaries, where private plantations of fir and pine prospered and, with a few exceptions, economic interests rather than political or ideological priorities prevailed for timber access and circulation. This historical legacy carries on to this day: both timber and nontimber plantation forests in contemporary China still concentrate in the areas covered in this book.[25] This could be regarded as one archetype of Chinese forest management and use, but certainly not the only one. If, for example, one hopes to find in China historical precedents that most resembled the ideal type of modern state forestry, even traces of preservationism, the best candidate could be Qing policies toward the forests beyond the Great Wall. A brief discussion of this contrasting case is in order before we delve into the Yangzi model to highlight how intraimperial forestry differences resulted from both material-ideological calculations and divergent forest ecologies.

Beyond the Great Wall, natural forests flourished in several subregions in Manchuria and the eastern end of Inner Mongolia. Although land reclamation and agricultural settlement were encouraged in a few pockets, forests were at the center of the Qing imagination of this region as the nurturing ground for both precious resources and the unspoiled character of its people. Two related considerations, material and ideological, defined the contentions in Qing "imperial foraging" to use historian David Bello's term.[26] On the one hand, the consumption and foraging of a suite of products native to ecologies (ginseng, pearls, sable fur, etc.) in the Northeast were signified as the epitome of Manchu identity. On the other hand, however, expanding consumption, overhunting or picking, and the intrusion of Han commercial capital threatened to deplete the resources and undermine the very identity that these activities were supposed to strengthen. Anxieties about an environmental and identity crisis prompted the Qing state to do everything in its power to cultivate an enclaved nature by restricting access, assigning quotas, establishing monopolies, issuing licenses, disciplining natives and migrants, reforming bureaucracies, and enforcing patrols.[27]

Although illegal woodcutting and poaching were by no means eliminated, the effects of Qing preservation policies in the Northeast were evident in the overall state of its forest coverage by the early twentieth century. Some pockets underwent more serious deforestation than others. For example, to supply construction materials for the Summer Palace in Chengde and provide fuel and food for a large permanent community, trees were cut from the Imperial Hunting Reserve (Mulan Weichang) and surrounding hills, civilians were resettled, and forests reclaimed for agriculture. The nineteenth century increasingly saw forest officials and merchants colluding to cut, steal, and sell timber from the Imperial Reserve. Meanwhile, with the autumn hunt discontinued from the 1820s, the Imperial Reserve was increasingly under pressure to open up for reclamation and settlement due to its close proximity to the disaster-prone North China Plain. Toward the end of the dynasty, the Imperial Reserve had become a largely agricultural zone.[28] The case of the Imperial Reserve exemplified shifted forest policies and the consequent changes in land use in response to shifting national and regional political priorities. The whole of Manchuria would come under the same pressures to open to settlers in the late nineteenth century, facing threats of encroachment from Russian and Japanese imperialists from the outside and subsistence demands from North China refugees from the inside.

If the Qing imagined the Manchus as hunters and the Mongols as pastoralists and strived to preserve the ecologies deemed suitable to such identities against overuse and agricultural reclamation, such considerations were much less relevant to the former Ming territories to the south of the Great Wall: after all, the Han are supposed to be farmers, and they don't need as much protection from the merchants among them. In the grand scheme of the Qing imperial vision of its different constituencies, the distinction between the Han, the Manchus, the Mongols, the Tibetans, and the Uighurs is first-order, while the distinction between the Han and other minority ethnicities of southern and southwestern China—namely ethnic distinctions among former Ming subjects—is second-order.[29] If Sinicization of the Mongols was a grave threat to the dynasty, Sinicization of the Miao or the Yao was certainly not objectionable *in principle* if not celebrated, although most of the time the state would not push too hard for it, and even set up quarantines for *practical* fears of resistance and turmoil. In a nutshell, those material and ideological concerns that prompted the Qing preservation polices in Manchurian and eastern Mongolian forests were not directly relevant for the broad basin of the Yangzi River system, including the minority regions of the southwest. If the state was absent as a preservationist regulator or a conservationist rationalizer, what forces managed the forests and time supply in southern China? To what extent was there meaningful "management" rather than free-for-all exploitations?

What follows is a history of the circulation of people and woods across both time and space as well as an examination of the process through which institutions were negotiated to sustain this circulation. The first two chapters delineate the structure of the interregional timber trade system from the two interrelated angles of state consumption and mass-market development. The remaining chapters pivot around the institutions that underlay the sustainability of the timber market, both by facilitating the regeneration of natural resources and by mitigating the challenges of long-distance trade. The interactions between market, institutions, and forestry must be understood as an intertwined whole. The state's laissez-faire attitude toward forest management, the procurement of tribute timber from the market, as well as the voluntary development of plantation forestry in the private economy were all premised on the expansive interregional market, without which the forms of forest management and mechanisms of timber supply would not have been the same. Toward the end of the period examined in this book, these conditions began to break down one after another. With fierce competition from imported timber, the intrusion of foreign capital, crumbling interregional trade, and the final collapse of transportation networks at the onset of Japanese invasion, the sustainable markets disintegrated and would never return to their prewar forms, as the state started to assume the dominant role in forest management and resource allocation in the postwar era.

CHAPTER ONE

Obtaining Timber for the Court

THE development of the timber trade across the Yangzi River accompanied the late imperial cycles of urbanization, population growth, migration, and deforestation. The source of timber supply to economic core areas of eastern China steadily pushed its geographic boundaries toward the west and the south. China's medieval economic revolution during the Tang-Song transition (ca. 750–1150) had begun to exhaust the forest reserves in the lower Yangzi areas; even the modest development of commercialized forestation in nearby provinces could not keep up with Jiangnan's demand. Over the course of the Ming-Qing period (1368–1911), many mountainous regions in southwestern China were transformed from remote natural forest reserves sparsely inhabited by indigenous groups to sources of large quantities of timber to be consumed in the cities and towns in Jiangnan and along the Grand Canal.

The development and expansion of this interregional timber market was of critical importance to the imperial court. In many ways the court was just like any other consumer: it desired a list of goods with specified features; it worked with a budget and sought the most cost-effective ways to obtain those goods. Other features of the imperial court, however, distinguish it from regular consumers: not only would the amount of the court's purchase daunt any individual consumer, its demands also tilted toward the luxurious end. Although an individual consumer's purchase was limited to what the market had to offer, the court had many nonmarket means at its disposal. To use timber as an example, where the market did not yet exist or when the market could not satisfy the court's extraordinary demand (in terms of either quality or quantity), it had the capacity to mobilize funds and labor to search, cut, and transport the exact varieties of timber it needed. However, if it became possible and more cost-effective to buy timber from the market, the court would not choose the more costly option of overseeing production directly.

An examination on the way in which the imperial court obtained timber and how it had changed serves a threefold purpose: (1) to assess the late imperial state's priorities, capacity, and limitations in managing the circulation of resources; (2) to gain an understanding of the market environment within which imperial procurement operated; and (3) to evaluate how these practices and institutions had affected the forest ecosystems. While tribute timber officials in the early Ming often had to personally organize the labor force to cut and transport logs out of the southwestern mountains, by the Qing official procurement almost completely relied on market purchases, thanks to the increasing incorporation of even remote areas into the interregional timber trade system. To briefly capture this centuries-long process: the state pioneered the extraction of timber resources from the southwest and, through its military actions and administrative incorporation, enabled merchant capital to follow the state's lead and extend the timber market to an area where there used to be none. The state, in turn, could rely on the now expanded market to obtain its timber, largely eliminating the need to manage the forests or oversee the logging process.

A question central to environmental historians' concern is how big an impact the state's consumption had exerted on forest ecosystems. The short answer is, maybe counterintuitively, minimal. The Qing court's annual timber demand from within the Great Wall, once institutionalized into a quota tribute system, amounted to about seven thousand regular-sized logs, the kind that glutted the mass market and came to be routinely produced from privately managed forests, and twelve hundred large-sized logs, which had to be tapped from old-growth forests. The latter presented some logistical difficulties and brought procurement officials to the frontier Miao markets, but even then they could bid for the goods from merchants' hands, albeit at higher-than-desirable prices, instead of having to organize lumberjacks into the mountains. As to the seven thousand regular-sized logs, they amounted to a negligible in-kind levy (in addition to normal monetary customs taxes) on an interregional market that by the eighteenth century was delivering five million logs annually to the lower Yangzi emporium of Nanjing.

LONG-TERM PATTERNS OF TIMBER SUPPLY

Timber has been recorded as an important commodity in interregional trade since very early times. In the Qin-Han empire (221 BC–220 CE),

Jiangnan was a well-forested periphery that supplied timber to the north and the northwest, where the core of the Chinese state was located. Several centuries of disunion and disturbance ensued after the breakdown of the Han empire into warlord regimes. The subsequent conquest of northern China by various nomadic groups forced the refugee Chinese courts, as well as large waves of migrants, to resettle in Jiangnan and thus began the process of the relocation of the Chinese empire with Jiangnan as the new economic heartland. By the medieval Tang-Song transition, forest clearance for agricultural cultivation was complete in the lowlands of the Yangzi delta.[1]

The Song dynasty (960–1279) saw an explosive expansion in timber consumption. The government required timber for official buildings, city walls, hydraulic projects, and shipbuilding, while commoners used timber for houses, coffins, boats, furniture, and fuel. In the eleventh century the timber demand in the Northern Song capital of Kaifeng was satisfied primarily from the forests in the northern Qinling Mountains and the middle and lower Yangzi valley.[2] The loss of the northern territories to the nomadic Jurchen state initiated a new cycle of migration to the south and further advanced the agricultural and commercial development of Jiangnan. Wood and bamboo were the dominant materials for Chinese buildings, palaces, and civilian houses. Fires in the crowded cities of Jiangnan occasionally burned thousands of houses to ash, which remained a serious problem in urban communities until well into the twentieth century.[3] Junks, the main means of transportation through the webs of canals and rivers in Jiangnan and along the coast, required a steady supply of various kinds of wood for construction and maintenance.[4]

The expanding demand for fuel, furniture, and construction materials in the cities and the increasing number of market towns exhausted the natural forests in their close vicinity, and timber imports became indispensable. The Southern Song capital of Hangzhou drew timber from the mountains in Anhui, Zhejiang, Jiangxi, and Fujian. The Hangzhou timber market, which developed outside of the Tide Waiting Gate (Houchao Men), where a branch of the Qiantang River entered the Southern Song city and connected to the Grand Canal, remained active into the Qing period. The shipbuilding industry was also a major destination for timber from Hunan and Jiangxi.[5] Transportation costs constituted a major portion of timber prices in downstream market towns. Rafting was the most cost-efficient means to transport large volumes of timber. Hence the mountains closest to well-connected rivers were deforested first. In the densely populated Jiangnan area, cleared mountain valleys and gentle slopes were converted into agricultural land. In some of these areas, however, low transportation costs and easy access to the consumption market motivated market-oriented tree cultivation. Systematic tree plantations, most commonly of China fir, developed in mountainous prefectures such as Chuzhou in western Zhejiang and Huizhou in southern Anhui, a new development during the Song. In these regions forested uplands were gradually claimed as private properties.[6]

By the Southern Song (1127–1279), fir silviculture in Huizhou and environs had essentially become commercialized, and timber was perceived as a crop in its own right, rather than as a by-product of land clearance or as a secondary product grown to satisfy household needs. Fan Chengda, an official appointed to Huizhou in the twelfth century, remarked that many locals in the hills of Xiuning County made their living by growing trees.[7] Timber produced in Huizhou, Chuzhou, and nearby prefectures was floated down the Qiantang River to Hangzhou, along which timber taxes were collected at transit points.[8] In the late twelfth century, many people from Huizhou made fortunes from this trade route, the first time that Huizhou timber merchants earned national fame.[9] During the Song, timber in transit was assessed a tax at 10 percent to 20 percent, mostly in kind, to meet the material demand of state construction projects. In times of need the state also engaged in direct purchases at downstream timber markets or the upstream logging centers.[10] Fan Chengda lamented about the delays and material costs that Huizhou timber merchants suffered at the tax point in Yanzhou, the passway from Huizhou to Hangzhou, which relied on timber taxes as an important source of government revenue.[11]

Population growth, urbanization, and agricultural cultivation continued to drain the few forest resources in the lower Yangzi area. Tree plantation practiced in western Zhejiang and southern Anhui became increasingly insufficient to meet Jiangnan's growing appetite for timber. Meanwhile, beginning in the Southern Song, patterns of settlement, deforestation, and conversion to agricultural production in the interior frontiers of central and southern China followed a similar sequence as what had already happened in the vicinity of the lower Yangzi area. Migrants from the eastern provinces continued to flood into Hunan and Sichuan during the Yuan (1279–1368) and Ming (1368–1644) dynasties. The establishment of military stations and, later, civil administrations in Guizhou, Yunnan, and Guangxi invited Han settlement in these areas since the Ming.[12] These developments steadily pushed the outer geographic boundaries of Jiangnan's timber supply to the southwest.[13]

Over the course of the Ming-Qing period, many parts of Guizhou, western Hunan, and the mountain ranges surrounding the Sichuan basin were transformed from remote reservoirs of huge timber for imperial use, to the source of luxurious timber chased by adventurous merchants, and finally to suppliers of large quantities of regular timber for the consumption of the mass market. In pursuit of extraordinary timber for palace constructions, the state spearheaded the exploration and extraction in remote mountainous areas. Over time, as commercial capital followed the state's lead and extended the market network to more frontier areas, the state could free itself from the "production" processes; instead, it increasingly relied on monetary purchases from the market to fulfill its demands for timber.

OBTAINING TIMBER FOR THE MING COURT

The third Ming emperor Yongle's decision in the early fifteenth century to relocate the capital from Nanjing to Beijing brought great challenges to the court's timber supply. While Nanjing, sitting at the confluence of the Yangzi River and the Grand Canal, was a burgeoning hub within the timber network that had developed since Song times, the new capital in the deforested North China Plain was farther removed from easy access to timber supply. The general decline in markets and commerce in the first decades of the Ming, which resulted from overlapping crises of warfare, depopulation, and unfriendly fiscal policies, also restricted the state's option of market purchases.[14] The difficulty was further exacerbated by the Ming court's acute demand for massive amounts of extraordinarily large timber to construct the new capital city. The magnificent palaces and temples required timber of the greatest size and quality to be used as weight-supporting pillars and beams. Obtaining large fir was hard enough; the imperial aesthetics of the Ming viewed *nanmu* as the choicest wood for the most important of imperial architectures, a precious rarity that could only be found in some inaccessible pockets of old-growth forests in southwestern China.[15] Such enormous demands presented great challenges for logging and transportation.

The early Ming state obtained timber through two means. It initially collected in-kind transit taxes on commercial timber rafts at some domestic customs stations. Even before these taxes were increasingly converted into silver payments by the late fifteenth century, they did not generate much timber for state use, given the limited scale of interregional timber market in the early Ming. In particular, they could not meet the state's need for large timber. As a result, the Ming court often had to resort to the second method—namely, directly logging large timber from remote forest reserves, most importantly in the southwestern provinces. When a major construction project came underway, a special official commission from the highest level would be dispatched to oversee the full process of labor recruitment, mountain survey, logging, and transportation. In the early fifteenth century, the largest timber used in the construction of the imperial palaces in Beijing was cut from the old growths of Sichuan, Hunan, and Guizhou. The Jiajing (1522–1566) and Wangli (1573–1620) eras saw another peak in the court's search for large timber in these provinces.[16] However, by the late sixteenth century the supply of *nanmu* had dwindled so much that it was no longer possible to construct monumental-scale buildings entirely out of *nanmu*. Even when *nanmu* was still used, it was for the largest and most visible pillars, while most of the structure was built of fir.[17]

During the sixteenth century, the overall economy had recovered from the early Ming reversal and ushered in a new era of prosperity that historians refer to as the "second commercial revolution." This era lasted, with some interruptions, through the eighteenth century and surpassed the previous Tang-Song transition in scale and spread.[18] Steady gains in productivity and the formation of national markets for agricultural and industrial goods stimulated regional specialization. The influx of foreign silver facilitated monetization and expansion of trade. The production, trade, and consumption of timber all developed as a part of this general trend. With population growth, expansion of agricultural settlement, as well as deepening regional specialization of production, wood consumption became less local and more reliant on interregional trade. Translocal timber markets already began to recover to the Song level by the late 1400s, connecting centers of consumption in Jiangnan to the forests of Anhui, Zhejiang, Jiangxi, and Fujian. Timber production also became a specialized regional enterprise. Commercialized tree plantation, which emerged during the Song, expanded to more places. Trees were grown in specialized forest plantations and cut to supply distant consumers.[19] While the plantations supplied ordinary-sized timber, potentially exorbitant profit from large timber attracted commercial capital to expand the timber trade network to more remote old-growth forests. The southwestern mountains, where the early Ming officials searched for imperial timber, came to be frequented by adventurous timber merchants as well.

The active and expansive timber markets offered the court an alternative to direct involvement in the logging process. In the sixteenth century the state increasingly preferred to contract the procurement to timber merchants, who received government funds and were required to deliver timber of specified quantity and variety. By the late Ming the state acquired the majority of its fir logs through market purchases by these commercial agents.[20] The state's shift to market purchases and the expansion of timber trade went hand-in-hand and reinforced each other. Although the state could only begin to rely on the merchants when the market had grown to a certain scale, once the contractual agency was established, the state's orders and funds further facilitated the expansion of merchant capital into the southwest. As the market continued to expand and mature, ensuring reliable supplies of timber to satisfy most of the state's needs, it largely eliminated the need for the state to directly manage forests or oversee the logging process. These trends carried on in the Qing dynasty, which institutionalized the state's purchase of timber from the market into a routine system.

EMPIRE EXPANSION AND TIMBER TRADE IN THE FRONTIER

The incorporation of the southwestern frontier into the interregional timber trade system not only was the result of economic forces but also part of a larger political and social process that accompanied the expansion of the Ming-Qing empire. Initially conquered by the Mongols in their military maneuver to subjugate the Southern Song, the far southwest was gradually brought under firmer administrative and military controls of the empire in later dynasties. The strong drive of the Ming-Qing empire to incorporate the southwest derived from multiple motivations, including security against the Mongols and Tibetans, access to strategic minerals and other natural resources, and relieving population pressure through Han migration and settlement. This vast area—which encompassed what later would become the provinces of Guizhou, Yunnan, the mountain ranges of Sichuan, and the western parts of Guangxi and Hunan—was not "uninhabited lands" but had been settled for millennia by diverse ethnic groups. Although the master narrative of imperial history presents a neat story of assimilation, historians have unpacked how the late imperial state's attempts at centralized domination were constantly resisted, negotiated, and conditioned by the agency of the local groups and the environment.[21]

Following earlier precedents, the Ming state recognized local hereditary leaders through the Native Chieftain System (Tusi) in the southwest to extend nominal state control. Throughout the Ming and the early Qing, the state resorted to a variety of military and political strategies to deal with revolts, divide up large chieftainships, and restrain their autonomies. The Ming state also established garrison towns and agricultural-military colonies throughout the southwest, promoting the migration of Han settlers from China proper. Such efforts culminated in the Qing Emperor Yongzheng's decision in the early eighteenth century to launch an extensive project that sought to abolish the native chieftainships and extend direct bureaucratic administration by state-appointed officials (*gaitu guiliu*), some limited form of which had previously been experimented during the Ming and his father Emperor Kangxi's reign. Emperor Yongzheng's ambitious move, however, ignited pervasive Miao revolts that took the Qing state a decade to suppress.[22] This and other large-scale military operations in the region carried out by the Ming-Qing state over the centuries required considerable investment in building infrastructures and collecting local intelligence. Roads and rivers that were built, repaired, or dredged initially to facilitate the state's military operations later became essential in easing the movement of civilians and commodities. Gazetteers about the local environment, transportation routes, and ethnographies spread from official compilations to commercial publishers, providing guides to itinerants.[23] Enormous economic and environmental transformations of the southwestern frontier accompanied the state's military intrusion, administrative reforms, and intermittent pro-settler programs.[24]

Most relevant to the increasing accessibility of the southwest to Han timber merchants were improved transportation conditions, better knowledge of the landscape, and more familiar administrative structures, which, to varying degrees, were all by-products of state expansion. A case in point is the Yuan River basin in southeastern Guizhou and western Hunan. An area of richly forested hills inhabited by diverse "Miao" groups, the Yuan River basin began to supply large amounts of logs for both state and civilian use in the eighteenth century, after Emperor Yongzheng's military campaign suppressed the Miao revolts.[25] The establishment of subprefecture civil offices in the newly pacified "Miao territories" brought administrative principles that the Han merchants were well versed in, as well as the familiar authority of Confucian-trained scholar-officials, whom they knew how to interact with—although that did not mean they could always get what they wanted.

A significant event in the development of the timber industry in this region was the mobilization of local laborers to dredge the upper end of the Yuan River during the military campaign of the 1730s.[26] An endeavor meant to facilitate the movement of military forces and supplies, the dredging opened the export route for forest resources along the river valley into the larger Yangzi River system. Since then, timber produced from the Yuan River basin, known as "timber from the Miao territories" (*Miao mu*) or "timber from western Hunan" (*xi-Hu mu*), became increasingly important in satisfying the demands from downriver markets and the Qing state's procurement of imperial timber.

THE TIMBER TRIBUTE SYSTEM OF THE QING

With the final suppression of the Revolt of the Three Feudatories (1673–1681) that had ravaged much of southern and southwestern China, Emperor Kangxi's court finally had the fiscal means and secured access to southern forests to reconstruct the Hall of Supreme Harmony in the Forbidden City, which was destroyed by an earthquake in 1679. Although the original reconstruction plan was to use several thousand trunks of *nanmu*, officials who had been dispatched to Sichuan to survey the forests reported the virtual absence of large *nanmu* with reasonable accessibility and the tremendous difficulties of transporting logs out of the deep mountains. In 1686 the emperor decided to forgo the previous dynasty's entrenched obsession with *nanmu* and to use pine and fir instead. Indeed, already in the sixteenth century, fir had often been used as a substitute for *nanmu* in Ming imperial constructions with *nanmu*'s increasing scarcity. This episode in the early years of Emperor Kangxi's reign concluded the last major official attempt to directly oversee the survey, logging, and transportation of imperial timber from southern China.

Thereafter, a regularized timber tribute system based on market purchases of fir in the four provinces of Jiangsu, Zhejiang, Jiangxi, and Hunan became the dominant source of imperial timber from within the Great Wall. It was supplemented only occasionally by official commissions to search for extraordinary *nanmu* in the inaccessible mountains of Sichuan and Guizhou, which were of much smaller scales than the Ming *nanmu* requisitions and were only meant to supply for the few largest structural members in the grandest halls.[27] Following the trends already visible in the late Ming, the Qing procurement of imperial timber more decisively adopted new species of choice and a new procurement method: China fir, a much more common and regeneratable species than *nanmu*, was being purchased from the market instead of directly cut from the mountains.

The regular timber tribute system of the Qing was referred to in official documents as the "annual timber quota" (*e'mu* or *nianli muzhi*) or "timber tribute for imperial construction projects" (*qingong limu*). Colloquially, it was called "imperial timber" (*huangmu*) in the private sectors. This system, under the management of the Board of Works, was finalized in 1687 and lasted until the fall of the dynasty in 1911.[28] By 1687 annual quotas, timber standards, and official prices were set in place for the four provinces of Jiangsu, Zhejiang, Jiangxi, and Hunan. Annual provincial quotas remained the same until the end of the dynasty (except for a minor increase in Jiangsu's quota in 1698).[29] Governors of these four provinces each appointed a timber tribute commissioner, usually a subprefect-level official, to purchase timber at the designated official prices and transport them to the Imperial Timber Storage located in Tongzhou, near Beijing.[30]

China fir was the only species demanded by the timber tribute system. In total, the imperial court was receiving seventy-four hundred regular-sized logs and twelve hundred large-sized logs annually. They were divided into four classes according to the length and circumference of the logs (table 1.1). By matching the required size of each class with China fir's pattern of the annual radial growth, it is possible to estimate the approximate tree ages. There are very few comprehensive studies of China fir's growth pattern by age, however, especially beyond a few decades. The age-diameter pattern used here is that of *Cunninghamia lanceolata* included in a 2012 study.[31] The oldest tree in the sample was around eighty years in age, attending a circumference of about 80 centimeters (2.34 feet—i.e., diameter at breast height 0.75 feet), which, according to the Qing court's standard, would be better than Class 3 but not passable for Class 2, which would be at the very least more than a hundred years old.

Class 1, "mast logs" (*weimu*), referred to long poles that were uniformly thick from top to bottom, usually from trees that had grown for hundreds of years. Although occasionally appropriated by official shipyards to be used as masts, most of the "mast logs" were used as weight-bearing pillars in the biggest halls of imperial palaces, temples, and mausoleums. Class 2, "proper fir" (*shanmu*), were poles from one-hundred-year-old to two-hundred-year-old trees. They were used as pillars and beams of general imperial and official buildings and were sometimes cut into planks for shipbuilding.[32] These top two classes were rarities in the timber market, which was dominated by logs harvested from commercialized plantations after just dozens of years of growth. The bottom two classes, "scaffold logs" (*jiamu*) and "slim fir" (*tongpi gao*), usually from twenty-year-old to forty-year-old trees, were readily available from timber markets. "Scaffold logs" were so named because they were used to set up temporary frameworks for ceremonies or civil examinations. These were usually recycled back to the imperial storage after use.[33] Slim poles of China fir were generally called *shan gao*. *Tongpi gao* was a high-quality variety of *shan gao* that was red

TABLE 1.1 Quota of timber tribute by province

[1]	[2]	[3]	[4]	[5]	[6]	[7]	[8]	[9]	[10]
CLASS	LENGTH (FEET)	CIRCUMFERENCE (FEET)	DIAMETER AT BREAST HEIGHT (FEET)	AGE (YEARS)	HN	JX	JS	ZJ	TOTAL
1. "mast logs" (*weimu*)	60	4.5	1.5	centuries	20	20	20		60
2. "proper fir" (*shanmu*)	30	3.9	1.3	>100	380	380	380		1140
3. "scaffold logs" (*jiamu*)	30	1.5	0.45	30–35	1,400	1,400	2,400*	1,400	6,600
4. "slim fir" (*tongpi gao*)	25	1.3	0.40	25–30	200	200	200	200	800

Source: GX_HDSL, *juan* 875, 877.

Notes: * In 1698, Jiangsu's quota for "scaffold logs" was increased from 1,400 to 2,400. Columns [1]–[4] report the officially required length, circumference, and diameter at breast height (dbh) for each class of logs. If only circumference is mentioned in the sources, dbh is inferred by dividing the circumference by π; and vice versa. Column [5] is the approximate age estimated based on the average diameter growth pattern of China fir. Columns [6]–[9] report the annual quota demanded from Hunan, Jiangxi, Jiangsu, and Zhejiang.

and had a bark similar to that of the Chinese parasol tree; they were usually sawn to make furniture and utensils.[34]

Notice, however, that these usages of the different-sized timber logs detailed refer to imperial and official usages and do not represent how commoners would use them. "Mast logs" and "proper fir" were absolute luxuries in the private timber markets. The most commonly traded poles were sized between 1 to 2 feet in circumference (diameter at breast height 0.3–0.7 feet), ranging from below Class 4 to above Class 3 by imperial standards. In common civilian constructions, "scaffold logs" and even "slim fir" could be used to build the supporting structures of a house. In between Class 2 and Class 3, poles of 2 to 3 feet in circumference (diameter at breast height 0.6–1.0 feet) were good for private shipbuilding—and were later used as utility poles and streetlights in the early twentieth century.[35]

In principle, the Qing state would allocate tribute responsibilities to different provinces according to their local specialties. Both symbolically and substantively, the court was to enjoy the opulence produced by an empire that spanned over multiple ecozones and diverse local niches. In the case of timber tribute, the quotas placed on Hunan and Jiangxi, the two biggest timber-exporting provinces, could be understood along this line. Zhejiang and Jiangsu, however, were included more because of their abundant provincial treasuries and easy access to major timber markets rather than their proximity to timber-producing areas. Zhejiang was tapped initially because of Hangzhou's status as an important timber market along the Grand Canal during the Ming dynasty, but soon it became obvious that its capacity was limited to middle-sized materials cultivated in the mountains of southern Anhui and western Zhejiang. While the other three provinces were required for "mast logs" and "proper fir," Zhejiang was exempt from supplying these large logs from the beginning.

The ordinary varieties of "scaffold logs" and "slim fir" were procured by the four provinces directly from the timber markets within their jurisdiction, usually through the mediation of licensed brokers. Zhejiang relied on the timber market in Hangzhou. Jiangsu had ready access to Nanjing, the largest distribution center for timber shipped down the Yangzi River. Hunan and Jiangxi were both rich in timber resources, so purchases were made close to the sites of logging to reduce costs. In Jiangxi the procurement responsibility fell on the prefect of Ganzhou, a mountainous southern prefecture whose timber was transported northward along the Gan River and into the Yangzi River.[36] In Hunan logs from the timber-producing areas in southwestern Hunan and southeastern Guizhou were transported along the Yuan River and gathered in Changde prefecture before entering the Dongting Lake. A prosperous timber market developed in Changde during the Qing and the subprefect of Changde had usually been delegated the responsibility of purchasing Hunan's timber tribute since the late eighteenth century.[37]

While the lower two classes of logs could be obtained easily from these private markets, the three provinces that were ordered to supply "mast logs" and "proper fir" had to make more efforts to meet the annual quota. Since 1746, a decade after the pacification of the Miao rebellions at the Hunan-Guizhou border area, timber tribute officials in Hunan started the practice of procuring the required large logs from the Miao territories, which soon became the established precedent. Hunan governor Yang Xifu explained in 1747:

> Because it is difficult to find mast logs and proper fir from nearby places, it is necessary to make direct purchases from the Miao territories that are upstream from Chenzhou, including the prefectures of Yuanzhou and Jingzhou [in western Hunan] and parts of Guizhou province. Scaffold logs and slim fir could be purchased from Changde, where timber merchants gather. Once tied into rafts, they are transported through the Yangzi River, the Dongting Lake, then the Grand Canal and the Yellow River. It is also necessary to prepare protection logs to prevent damages to the tribute timber from the bumps and clashes along the way.[38]

Jiangxi and Jiangsu faced more difficulties than did Hunan. By the 1720s at the latest, the Board of Works began to complain about the constant deficiency and inferior quality of the logs supplied by Jiangxi and Jiangsu. Defects in quality were sometimes measured in monetary terms, for which the timber tribute official was required to compensate from his private purse. For example, in the term of 1724, among the 1,400 scaffold logs submitted by Jiangxi, 170 were inferior in quality, for which the responsible official was fined one-third of the official price (0.067 tael per log, 11.4 taels in total).[39] For the required large logs, shortages and defects were not allowed to be resolved by financial payment; rather, the deficit had to be made up in future terms. The number of delivered logs was first discounted by any defect in length, thickness, or texture to generate the account-book number of "fulfilled" quota, usually with decimal points. That number was then compared to the quota to determine the deficit for which a province was required to make up in the future. In 1741, in addition to the annual quota of timber, Jiangxi delivered the accumulated timber due from the previous terms of 1735, 1738, and 1739, which totaled 14.56 mast logs and 206.42 proper fir.[40]

The practice of discounting the number of logs by their quality in effect encouraged Jiangsu and Jiangxi to deliver smaller logs in larger numbers, which, after being discounted by their inferior quality, would still meet the quota. For example, in 1754 all of the twenty mast logs delivered by Jiangsu were smaller than the standard; however, the problem was resolved easily as ten more such logs were submitted to make up for the deficit.[41] The increasing prevalence of this practice worried the Board of Works. In a memorial of 1765 the ministry's secretariat complained that although it was permitted to "compensate for quality by number" (*zhesuan tianbu*), increasing reliance on this practice would result inevitably in a serious shortage of large logs for imperial use in the future. In response, a new regulation was issued by an imperial edict that mast logs must conform to the standard, and the practice of "compensating for quality by number" could be applied to no more than a handful of logs. While the standard for mast logs was reinforced, the requirements for the other classes were relaxed in recognition of the difficulties faced by the provinces. The quotas for each of the remaining three classes of logs were divided equally into three subclasses, the first of which followed the same standard as the original specification, while the second and third subclasses were downgraded slightly.[42]

To meet the challenge of supplying large timber, Jiangxi and Jiangsu contracted their procurement to timber merchants increasingly often. These merchant delegates of Jiangxi and Jiangsu, just like the Hunan timber tribute officials, frequented the Miao territories along the Hunan-Guizhou border.[43] When these delegates from Hunan, Jiangxi, and Jiangsu went to the Miao areas, they still made purchases at existing local markets. Unlike the practices during the Ming and the initial years of the Qing, they did not organize the labor force directly to go deep into the mountains and undertake the cutting and transporting from the ground up. Ying'an, in his capacity as the subprefect of Changsha, was appointed to purchase and transport Hunan's timber tribute in 1777 and 1781. He recorded his activities and correspondence during these two assignments in a manuscript, *Documents of Imperial Timber Procurement* (Caiyun huangmu andu), which provides detailed insight into the practices of tribute timber procurement in Hunan.[44] On the matter of purchasing large timber from the market relative to cutting directly from the forests, Ying'an remarked: "It is difficult to find 'proper fir' [from the market], the price also fluctuates greatly from time to time. Sometimes, it is just ten-some taels [per log]; other times, it could be twenty or more than thirty, forty, even fifty taels. Despite the high price, we should take it whenever it is available. It would cost much more if we were to 'cut from the mountains' [*kan qingshan*]. Upon calculation, it is often more economical to 'purchase at the rivers' [*mai pingshui*] than to cut from the mountains."[45] This complete reliance on the market was made possible by the increasing commercialization of timber trade even in these remote areas.

INSUFFICIENT OFFICIAL FUNDING

The fixed amount of formal funding was far from sufficient to cover the cost. Not only were transportation costs not accounted for, the official purchase prices were only a fraction of market prices. To get a rough idea of the extent to which official prices of tribute timber deviated from market prices, a useful source is *Regulations and Precedents on the Prices of Materials* (Wuliao jiazhi zeli) issued by the Board of Works, a 1769 compilation of the market prices for building materials, transport costs, and labor wages down to the county level to serve as the reference to estimate the cost of public constructions. As part of a larger state effort to enforce the regulation that provincial and local governments should procure necessary materials and hire labor at market prices, the compilation project was initiated in 1761 to have market prices investigated and submitted to the ministry in statistical lists.[46] Among the six counties in Hunan for which market prices of timber were reported, the lowest prices observed in Yizhang county of Jingzhou prefecture are shown in table 1.2. A timber-exporting county in the Yuan River basin, Yizhang represented the lower-bound market prices in the areas where tribute timber was requisitioned. Even these lower-bound market prices were much higher than the fixed official prices for tribute timber procurement.

For the ordinary "scaffold logs" and "slim fir," Hunan tribute timber officials imposed a compulsory requisition at the low official prices from commercial rafts passing through Changde. The rate varied between one to two logs out of one hundred. Such official requisitions were a de facto transit tax levied on commercial timber. For large timber, however, the discrepancy between official and market prices presented greater challenges to the tribute officials as they could not be obtained by requisitioning from regular commercial rafts. Market prices for "mast logs" and "proper fir" reported in 1729 by Wang Rou, the Chen-Yuan-Jing circuit intendant, which he had obtained from the expense books of the Hunan timber tribute officials, were several times higher than the official prices (see table 1.2).[47] In the

TABLE 1.2 Official and market prices of tribute timber, taels per log

[1]	[2]	[3]	[4]	[5]	[6]	[7]	[8]
				OFFICIAL PRICE			
CLASS	SUBGRADE	LENGTH (FEET)	CIRCUMFERENCE (FEET)	1687	1759*	1798*	MARKET PRICE
"mast logs"		60	4.5	24.0	21.45	21.45	40–170[a]
"proper fir"		**30**	**3.9**	**10.8**	**8.99**		**26[a]**
	Grade 1	30	4.1			8.99	
	Grade 2	30	3.8			8.29	
	Grade 3	30	3.5			7.57	>10[a]
"scaffold logs"		**30**	**1.5**	**0.24**	**0.23**		**0.39**
	Grade 1	30	1.6			0.24	0.41[b]
	Grade 2	29	1.4			0.21	0.35
	Grade 3	28	1.3			0.18	0.31
"slim fir"		**25**	**1.3**	**0.16**	**0.15**		**0.28**
	Grade 1	25	1.4			0.16	0.30[b]
	Grade 2	24	1.3			0.14	0.27
	Grade 3	23	1.1			0.12	0.22

Source: Unless noted below, information is from GX_HDSL, *juan* 875, 877.

Notes: The bolded rows for each class are before the subgrades were introduced in the 1760s, so the 1687 and 1759 standards and prices apply to the whole class.

* Average level across provinces. In general, official prices in Hunan and Jiangxi were lower than those in Jiangsu and Zhejiang.

[a] Market prices in Changde in western Hunan in 1729 as reported in the memorial by Chen-Yuan-Jing Circuit Intendent Wang Rou, GZD 4020009317.

[b] Market prices for "scaffold logs" and "slim fir" are calculated by the inferred unit price for fir logs in Yizhang county of Jingzhou prefecture in western Hunan as reported in *Hunan sheng wuliao jiazhi zeli* (ca. 1769). The source lists prices for fir logs of six different sizes in each county. Those sizes are close to the range of "scaffold logs" and "slim fir" but do not exactly correspond to the classes and grades in this table. However, the pricing does seem to follow a uniform unit price in each county, which is explicitly stated as the pricing principle in the *Wuliao jiazhi zeli* for Yunnan prefecture. The unit in question was not volume, but radius multiplied by length, measured in square feet. It can be inferred that the unit price for fir logs was 0.027 taels per square feet in Yizhang, which was much lower than the prices in five other counties in Hunan for which this information is available. *Source*: *Wuliao jiazhi zeli Databases*.

1770s a good mast wood cost more than 50 taels even in Guizhou, while the official price remained only 20 taels.[48]

The officials in charge of timber tribute purchases were occasionally tempted to invoke the authority of local magistrates to force the sale of high-quality "mast logs" at lower prices. Delegates of the different provinces and other timber merchants all competed for the rare large timber. Consequently, in this sellers' market, coercion had little effect—the final price might be just a few taels lower than the initial charge, still much higher than the official price.[49] More often than not, the timber tribute officials settled for the high market prices of large timber, fearing that if missed, there might not be enough to fulfill the quota. As Ying'an instructed his fellow, who was dispatched to Jingzhou:

> Although the prices for these "mast logs" [in Jingzhou] seem higher than the prices in the Miao regions, so long as they are of good quality, [just buy them so that] we don't need to worry about fulfilling the official quota anymore. If you see any "mast logs" there, purchase them all, don't hesitate. Only, the actual [higher] price you pay in Jingzhou—never let it slip to the ears of Tuokou merchants. I worry that if they learned about the higher price that we have settled for in Jingzhou, it will become more difficult to make purchases here in Tuokou in the future.[50]

Apparently, Ying'an was so desperate to fulfill the official quota that he was willing to pay the higher market price even when it was beyond the capacity of official funding (how he made his ends meet and even made profits out of this is discussed in the next section). From Ying'an's instruction we can also appreciate a tribute timber official's acute awareness of price differences in different markets and his sharp business sense to restrict the spread of commercial intelligence. The procurement of tribute timber should be understood as a part of the tribute timber official's overall business enterprise, whose ultimate purpose was profit-making.

BUREAUCRATIC ENTREPRENEURSHIP OF TIMBER TRIBUTE OFFICIALS

The four provinces developed different arrangements to deal with the lack of official funding. Jiangxi drew extra funds from the "nourishing virtue silver" (*yanglian yin*) of the local officials. With the increased funding, the procurement of timber tribute was then contracted to private merchants.[51]

Jiangsu entrusted the limited official fund to the major timber trade associations in Nanjing, which became accountable for assembling the full quota and transporting it to the imperial storage at whatever extra cost. These timber trade associations, in turn, stipulated how many logs of various qualities should be extracted from their member merchants' rafts and the amount of monetary contribution, usually at a progressive rate by the size of the members' businesses. Hunan, however, allowed the appointed officials to conduct private timber trade alongside the official assignment, making the task appealing despite limited official funding.[52] This section mainly examines the practices of Hunan tribute timber officials.

In Hunan the personnel who were involved in the purchase and transportation of the timber tribute—including officials, sub-bureaucrats, and hired crews for transportation—were all allowed to bring their private timber alongside the official rafts.[53] The officially stated legitimization was that these privately owned rafts, called "logs for protection" (*humu*), would be floating on the four sides of the timber tribute rafts to protect them from potential damages when they bumped into rocks. If the timber tribute was found to be short in number or inferior in quality during the final inspection at the Imperial Timber Storage, logs could be drawn from these private possessions to make up the difference so that no deficit would be accumulated for the future. Although the timber tribute was tax-free at domestic customs, these private possessions should, in principle, be declared and taxed at normal rates.[54]

In practice, the tribute timber officials handled their official assignment and private business not separately but as indistinguishable parts of a whole operation. The official assignment and the associated opportunity to attend to one's private enterprise were considered as a combined bundle. Although the potential for promotion upon prompt delivery of timber tribute and the strict punishment for delays incentivized against lingering too long along the route trying to engage in more private transactions, the daily considerations of tribute timber officials focused on maximizing the total profit from the assignment, with the quota of timber tribute regarded as a fixed cost.[55]

Ying'an's missions illustrated this profit-oriented business approach. Ying'an and several of his private retainers spread out strategically to make purchases in different localities. Ying'an and one assistant stayed in the large timber market in Changde requisitioning ordinary timber logs from passing commercial rafts. Another assistant stationed himself in Tuokou, a timber market upstream on the Yuan River, drawing ordinary logs as well as trying to purchase some "proper fir." Yet another assistant went farther to the timber market in Jinping county, located in the Qingshui riverine in Guizhou, purchasing "mast logs" and "proper fir" from Miao sellers through local bilingual brokers. Others might visit Jingzhou, Chenzhou, or other timber-exporting localities responding to market intelligence about the availability of large timber. The previously quoted passage from Ying'an's letter, for example, was an instruction sent to his retainer stationed in Jingzhou.[56] In addition to assisting in Ying'an's business, these assistants also made their own investments. Although Ying'an and his retainers shared information and advised each other on business decisions, their capital remained separate, rather than being pooled into a partnership. Hired transportation crews also brought their private timber for sale along the way. Moreover, Ying'an himself operated on a personal loan at an interest rate of 3 percent per month, signifying the essentially private nature of his enterprise overall.[57]

Beyond the required quota, purchases were made with an acute awareness of the changing conditions in the downriver markets. In particular, market conditions in Nanjing were keenly monitored. One retainer was specifically tasked with obtaining and reporting Nanjing prices in a timely manner so that Ying'an could "deliberate over the comprehensive situation."[58] He evaluated prospective deals based on expected prices in Nanjing: "Among the 'mast logs' available for sale, there is one with a length of 7 feet and a circumference of 5 feet (diameter at breast height 1.6 feet). Referencing to the table of Longquan *ma*, its size corresponds to 16.03 Longquan *liang*. Say the market price in Nanjing is 10 taels of silver per Longquan *liang* for timber of this class, this log will be worth more than 160 silver taels in Nanjing. Given this calculation, [the price charged by the seller] is not too expensive."[59]

Despite the potential for such a handsome profit margin on "mast logs," the demand and price for such high-end timber were not as predictable as for the more ordinary varieties. Therefore Ying'an instructed his assistants that except for taking advantage of good bargains, no exceptional efforts should be made to purchase "mast logs" beyond the official quota, for they were "unique goods with rare demands [*yijia huo*]. After all, the price is too high. It is difficult to resell them."[60] Their private businesses centered on regular-sized logs destined for the mass market. By the time of Ying'an, Hankou had become an emergent timber market on the Yangzi River.[61] Ying'an and associates planned to sell some timber when they reached Hankou to reduce the taxes payable to the downriver customs stations in Jiujiang, Wuhu, and Nanjing.[62] They also fostered good relations with Huizhou and Jiangxi merchants who were purchasing timber in Guizhou, in the hope of relying on these experts for market information and connections once they arrived in Nanjing. In particular, Ying'an forged a good relationship with a Huizhou merchant named Hu Tingkui, who "had a lot to teach me about the benefits and malpractices of timber brokerages and could be relied on as our eyes and ears for all the businesses once we get to Nanjing."[63] Moreover, Ying'an operated a sideline business in which he delivered other merchants' timber to Nanjing. In return for a contracted payment, he would take care of all the matters along the way, including declaring and paying taxes at the three customs sites, as well as providing for and paying wages to the hired crew. This arrangement was mutually beneficial, because merchants' rafts, while acting as a shield of protection, would enjoy faster passage through customs stations floating alongside the timber tribute; Ying'an, of course, also profited personally from this business.[64]

The procurement of timber tribute was market-dependent and more like a private business on the part of appointed officials. The state chose not to interfere as long as the profit-seeking activities of these agents did not disturb the normal market order or inhibit the punctual arrival of the timber tribute. However, by the mid-eighteenth century such disturbances increasingly came to the attention of provincial officials, who called out several forms of malpractice that had arisen from the timber tribute officials' profit-seeking practices, including instances of forced sales at reduced prices for their personal gain as well as prolonged lingering in Nanjing trying to sell their private timber, "sometimes spending more than a year on the way before making it to the capital."[65] Despite successive admonitions and disciplining measures, tensions between the court's demand for timely delivery, tribute timber officials' eyeing for private gains, and the begrudging merchants who had to surrender their logs at low prices continued to play out in various forms and demanded constant negotiations and readjustments.

NEGOTIATIONS BETWEEN MERCHANTS AND OFFICIALS

Officials acknowledged that the purchase of timber tribute from commercial rafts at official prices was a burden on timber merchants. Merchants often engaged in negotiations with the officials in charge to decide how to allocate the quota among traders in different marketplaces or from different native places. Such negotiations centered on the rhetoric of "fairness" and "capability": the more heavily burdened groups would attempt to enlist other groups to share the responsibility, those so called upon would attempt to dodge the task by pleading helplessness, and the officials struggled to strike a balance.[66]

A dispute in Hunan that made its way to Beijing in 1814 was illustrative of the various tensions involved in timber tribute officials' purchases in the market.[67] The dispute originated from the different rates of requisition from the rafts owned by local and long-distance timber merchants. Since 1774, the Hunan Provincial Administration Commissioner had stipulated that, in the timber market of Changde, timber tribute officials could procure two logs per one hundred logs from Hunanese merchants at official prices, and one log per one hundred logs from Huizhou and Linjiang timber merchants, the two major itinerant timber merchant groups throughout the eighteenth century. It was likely that the distinction between local and nonlocal groups was established initially because at that time the local timber merchants only traded along the Yuan River and had not entered the long-distance trade along the Yangzi River.[68] The more favorable rate for Huizhou and Linjiang merchants was probably offered in consideration of the many other tax points they had to pass through later. For the same reason, in 1808 a group of timber merchants from Susong, Anhui, was also granted the lower rate in accordance with the nonlocal precedent set for Huizhou and Linjiang merchants.

By 1812, as increasing numbers of timber merchants from Hunan joined the long-distance trade, they felt their disadvantage compared to the nonlocal groups more acutely.[69] Inspired by the success of the Susong group, Li Daoyuan, an employee of a local timber merchant, solicited monetary contributions from a group of other Hunan timber merchants to launch a united appeal to the provincial governor's office requesting equal rates. Li personally promised lower rates to all the merchants who contributed money for the lawsuit regardless of the result. The request was initially granted by the provincial governor and administration commissioner, only to be revoked immediately after the timber tribute official claimed that he would not be unable to fulfill the quota at the reduced rate. Four timber merchants, reassured by Li's promise and emboldened by the provincial governor's initial consent, attempted to refuse the 2 percent rate when stopped by the timber tribute official's runners at the market of Changde. Eventually, however, they were intimidated by the runners into paying a bribe in addition to accepting the 2 percent official requisition.

The enraged merchants then entrusted their appeal to Jian Yuanji, who volunteered to *use his own name* to sue the timber tribute official and his runners at the Board of Works in Beijing. Jian accused the timber tribute official of a series of malfeasance: "setting up illegal tax stops, drawing merchants' timber without compensation, reselling the collected timber immediately to make a profit, carrying private timber with the tribute, evading taxes at customs stations, and demanding bribes."[70] Upon receiving Jian's petition, the ministry referred the case to Hunan governor Guang Hou, who made the final judgment. Li Daoyuan and Jian Yuanji, the two persons who initiated the litigations, were convicted of contracting litigation (*baogao*), fabricating evidence, and "deceiving the authorities for profit" (*zhaqi guansi qucai*). Li was punished with ninety whippings with bamboo strips, and Jian received one hundred whippings and three years of banishment. The runners who demanded bribes were also punished accordingly. The other timber merchants were judged to have been duped by Li and Jian, and therefore pardoned. The 2-percentage requisition from Hunan locals remained intact.

This case illustrates some general issues. The stipulation of the rate of requisition in itself showed the state's recognition that official purchases were in effect taxation. Timber merchants' bitter attitudes toward the timber tribute official resulted directly from the latter's mingling of his private gains and the official mission. The official tried to procure as much timber as possible at the low official price. Ying'an's account shows clearly that the same official mark—"for imperial use"—was carved on all of the timber he purchased, including what he purchased privately. This lack of distinction meant that his private timber would not necessarily be taxed at the domestic customs as required by protocol.[71]

Governor Guang Hou, in his verdict, recognized this central contention but defended the indispensability of the tribute official's private timber as "logs for protection." In addition to providing a cushion around the imperial timber, the "logs for protection" generated profits that were necessary to make up for the deficiency of official funding for the expensive large timber and high transportation costs. It was impossible for the provincial government to determine and enforce what might be a reasonable amount of "logs for protection" and what would be considered as excessive pursuit of private profit. In the niche market for large timber in the Miao areas, for example, it was relatively easy for the sellers to track the number of large logs that had been purchased by the official and refuse to forgo the higher prices offered by other competing merchants when they knew that the quota was already fulfilled.[72] By contrast, timber merchants passing through Changde would not be able to do the same. Meanwhile, the universal imposition of the requisition ratio (albeit differentiated by local and nonlocal), regardless of whether the required tribute quota was already reached, in itself provided a sense of fairness among competing timber merchants—one's competitors could not evade the burden simply by delaying passage until after the quota was filled.

The long-term acceptance of the different requisition percentages for local and nonlocal merchants was predicated upon the fact that they operated in totally separate markets, thus not competing directly with each other, and could be identified easily by the size and style of their rafts. Huizhou and Linjiang merchants had to transport their timber over long distances and pass through several domestic customs stations along the way, so they "always trimmed the ends of the timber logs and tied the rafts very tightly—all in order to cut down the payment of transit taxes at domestic customs," where taxes were assessed roughly by the size of the rafts instead of the exact number of logs. Local timber merchants, by contrast, "never bothered to trim the logs; nor did they care so much about the differences between big and small, straight and curved, when making purchases." Given these visible differences between the practices of long-distance and local merchants, "it was easy to curb the malpractice of local merchants pretending to be Hui-Lin merchants [in an attempt to avoid higher requisition rates]."[73] However, once the locally originated merchants started to expand their business toward the downstream markets in the middle and lower Yangzi areas, the established differentiation in local and interregional tax rates as well as the method of detection were disturbed. Disputes began to emerge when the sense of fairness broke down as Hunan merchants not only competed among themselves but also began to compete with the nonlocal groups in long-distance trade.

The case also sheds light on the nature of merchants' collective litigations against government officials and clerks. The practice of "outsourcing litigation," although outlawed by the state, seemed to be quite common when civilians brought suits against government officials and clerks. In both instances of litigations, most of the timber merchants pooled their funds but concealed their names during the legal proceedings. They would benefit universally if the appeal were granted, while anonymity would protect them from any punishment if failed. Although the two who came forward had some experience in the timber trade, they were not big merchants. Li Daoyuan was an employee of a timber merchant, and Jian Yuanji was a former *yamen* runner who only conducted some timber retailing after being dismissed.

There are two possible interpretations of this. It could indeed be the case as the Hunan governor's report described, that Li and Jian were the initiating parties and the merchants simply took the opportunity to speculate. The outsourcing agreement was consensual between two unrelated, voluntary parties. An alternative scenario, one not directly acknowledged in the sources but nonetheless plausible, was that the merchants actually initiated the matter. They could have developed the strategy, pooled the money, and appointed an employee or hired a delegate to carry out the litigation to shield themselves from nonmonetary risks, with the knowledge that the punishment for "outsourcing litigation" would fall on the hired agent. I cannot determine which scenario was more likely in this case. In fact, for outsourced litigations in general, either could have taken place. Either way, it provided the merchants with the option to engage in risky legal adventures, especially against powerful state personnel.

SIDELINE TIMBER TRADE IN THE GRAIN TRIBUTE SYSTEM

To put into context the private businesses conducted by timber tribute officials alongside their formal assignments, let us consider a similar phenomenon in the grain tribute (*caoyun*) system, which occupied a far more important position in the Qing fiscal system than timber tribute. State personnel and employed sailors routinely engaged in sideline businesses of conveyance and private trade along the routes of tribute grain transportation. As one of the many kinds of commodities involved in such sideline enterprises, timber, because of its bulkiness, sometimes managed to upset the high court for its obstruction of Canal traffic and the timely arrival of tribute grains.

The grain tribute system—namely the state transportation of taxed grains to imperial capitals and sometimes to military forces stationed at borders—had a history as long as the imperial period. During the Qing, approximately 150,000 to 200,000 tons of tribute grain was collected annually from eight provinces (Anhui, Henan, Hubei, Hunan, Jiangsu, Jiangxi, Shandong, and Zhejiang). The tribute grain was transported along waterways, in particular the Grand Canal and the Yangzi River, to the capital.[74] Like the Ming, the Qing state relied on a system of tribute grain transportation that was entirely under government control and operated by government personnel, rather than depending on the agency of private merchants. The total number of boatmen employed in the transport of tribute grain varied from 70,000 to 120,000, most of whom were drawn from a class of hereditary imperial tenants who held land in the form of military tenure (*tuntian*). The crew of grain junks received a meager salary and grain allowance for their service, which was barely enough to cover their traveling expenses, let alone support their families.[75]

To make up for the modest official stipend, the boatmen were permitted to carry a certain amount of private merchandise when making trips in government service.[76] Officers and boatmen on the tribute fleets were able to make multiple transactions at the markets along the route and became an important force in facilitating the economic exchange between the north and the south. Moreover, because of tribute junks' priority in passing through the dikes and locks along the Grand Canal and the tax-exempt status of the allowed quota, a kind of conveyance business developed as some brokers became specialized in arranging for merchants to load their commodities on the tribute grain junks.[77]

Here, the rationale of the state's policies and the problems it encountered were very similar to those in the tribute timber system. The upper cap of the allowed amount of private merchandise had been repeatedly elevated, which reflected the state's recognition of the insufficient official compensation and was a compromised policy to relieve the boatmen's hardship and prevent them from stealing from the grain tribute. In essence, the state chose to forgo some transit taxation and allow the boatmen some access to its transportation facility for private gains, rather than raising formal taxes to increase the boatmen's wages. However, these sideline businesses sometimes caused concerns as they messed with the elaborate timetable for the junks to progress up the Grand Canal, either because the boatmen lingered at big markets to make sales or because the junks could not make it through the treacherous northern section of the watercourse as they were overloaded with private merchandise.

Timber was especially problematic because, unlike other commodities that were loaded on the junks, timber logs were tied into rafts and attached to the sides of the junks. While the attached rafts were not a problem on the broad Yangzi River, even offering a good protection of the grain junks against stormy waves, they could easily block the traffic along the much narrower Grand Canal. In 1737 the director general of grain transport, Buxi, laid out the various considerations given to the problem that too much timber was attached to the Jiangxi grain tribute fleets. His multifaceted reasoning deserves quotation at length:

> We have found that the Jiangxi tribute junks carry a large amount of timber in addition to their quota of planks. Upon inquiry, we learn that this has been the case for a long time. The tribute grain junks of Jiangxi are larger and longer than those of other provinces and carry much more rice, so they incur double expenses in hiring trackers to drag the junks through dikes and

> locks. All these expenses along this long journey could only be covered thanks to the extra profit they make from timber. This is why such practice has been carried on for so long.
>
> If all of these junks are allowed to pass through, [it would be problematic because] the Grand Canal is different from the Yangzi River. The Yangzi water is very turbulent; the grain junks can be protected by the timber logs on the sides. Along the Grand Canal, by contrast, grain junks have to pass through dikes and locks. If overloaded with timber, it is inevitable that their passage would be much delayed.
>
> However, if we demand that all the timber should be unloaded [upon entering the Grand Canal, it would also be inappropriate because] this timber has already been taxed at the Wuhu Customs Station; if the poor boatmen have to dispose of their timber in midway, they will lose all their capital investment. That would certainly cause dispute and entanglement along the way, or even lead to malpractices like stealing and selling from tribute grain. The progress of grain fleets will be delayed. These possible situations have to be contemplated and prepared for in advance. Moreover, Shandong and northern Zhili have always relied on the timber carried by the tribute grain junks from Jiangxi, Huguang, and Anqing to manufacture the appliances used by officials and commoners. Now if all the supply was blocked, it would be rather inconvenient.[78]

Apparently, Buxi was concerned with the delayed arrival of grain tribute caused by the difficulty of dragging timber along the Grand Canal, for which he was ultimately held accountable in his capacity as the director general of grain transport. Nevertheless, he still highlighted the necessity of allowing the Jiangxi boatmen to take on extra timber along the tribute fleets to compensate for their high transportation cost. He was also worried about the impracticality of forcibly ordering the boatmen to dispose of their private timber before the fleets turned into the Grand Canal, as they had an invested interest and were already assessed for transit taxes at Wuhu. The possible fierce resistance to such an unreasonable policy might delay the schedule of tribute grain even more. Moreover, the logs carried by the grain tribute junks were an important source of timber supply for the northern provinces.

Based on these considerations, Buxi argued against completely prohibiting tribute junks from taking along the timber. He proposed a lenient policy allowing a small amount of timber loaded onto the tribute junks, with the rest detached from the junks and tied into small rafts upon entering the Grand Canal. The rafts were allowed to follow the tribute fleets, and the boatmen might freely make sales along the route. After this particular instance reported by Buxi, similar complaints that overloaded private merchandise obstructed the timely progress of grain tribute time and again caught the emperors' attention over the years. Apart from restating the allowed quota and demanding any amount beyond the quota be assessed for transit taxes as normal merchant goods, the state largely condoned such practices.[79] It was the state's reluctance to raise the formal compensation to the boatmen, which would further increase the already high cost of maintaining the grain tribute system, that ultimately led to the tolerant attitude toward the private sideline businesses conducted by the boatmen.

Hence, in both the timber and grain tribute systems, insufficient official funding was remedied by the profit made from the private sideline business conducted by officials and government employees, who largely followed the business norms in the private sectors when pursuing profits. Their activities were both enabled and constrained by market principles. In both cases, the state tolerated, even formally approved, government personnel attending to private gains while on official trips. This was in recognition of the inadequacies of the formal channels to fulfill the funding needs of these tasks. If we use the modern standard of fiscal rationality, it is tempting to label these arrangements as lacking clear distinctions between public and private enterprises. One might wonder, why not provide enough official funding and forbid these private activities altogether?

Although there is no explicit treatise on this alternative from Qing sources, it is not difficult to appreciate some of the important considerations. First, the state would have to expand its tax revenue, either by elevating the overall tax rate or by levying the extra cost on a particular sector of the society based on location, occupation, or status. Such a move would challenge some of the foundational ideals of good governance that committed the Ming-Qing state to low taxes wherever possible.[80] This is not to say that ideals could not be compromised in reality—which happened often in different guises, but that in the minds of Qing statesmen the minor issue of tribute management might not be worth the trouble of entering into such a fundamental debate. Second, it would require a much closer match between the amount of official funding and the actual cost. Fixed "official prices" simply would not do. Any attempt on the state's part to estimate in advance the would-be cost of these missions would be difficult given market fluctuations and the information cost in obtaining reliable price estimates in all the disparate parts of the empire. Should a reimbursement system be adopted, there would be a further problem of field officials reporting more expenses than actually incurred. Moreover, the volatility of market prices would introduce annual variations to the national account, which was built on the principles of budgeting and predictability. All this is not to say that the Qing way of doing things was the only way or the best way, but it is important to understand the rationale behind this system before dismissing it as outright irrational. "Weak institutions" as they might be, as a form of bureaucratic entrepreneurship, such practices offer a way that works well with certain conditions and constraints and have resonances in both distant and very recent histories of China.[81]

CONCLUSION

Since the medieval economic revolution, a sizable timber market had developed to link the commercial centers in the lower Yangzi Valley to areas of timber supply. As natural forests in the nearby hinterland became exhausted, demand for a reliable supply of construction materials motivated specialized tree plantations in some mountainous areas and also gradually pushed the extension of the timber market to tap resources from farther-away forests. During the late imperial period, the development of interregional trade, the state's shift to market purchases to obtain timber, and the expansionist empire in the southwest were interconnected, mutually reinforcing processes. State expansion paved the road for the commercial capital, which in turn spurred the expansion of the interregional timber trade network. As the matured timber market could provide reliable supplies of tribute timber to the state, it freed the latter from having to manage direct loggings from the forests. The Qing state's complete reliance on market purchases to obtain tribute timber also meant that its options were conditioned by market principles and the discrepancies between market cost and official funding had to be resolved with flexible arrangements. The state's acquiescence to tribute officials' private businesses was a result of such compromises, which reveals the state's priority in securing strategic supplies (whether timber or grain) without shaking the foundation of its austere fiscal system.

The difference between the state's procurement of imperial timber and the private trade of ordinary timber for mass consumption is an important distinction, which has not been given due attention in existing discussions on timber consumption and deforestation.[82] The imperial demand for timber features predominately in the scholarship on the late imperial state's involvement with forests.[83] Such attention is understandable given the visual impact of the magnificent imperial palaces and mausoleums as well as lengthy treatises in official memorials and local gazetteers on the hardships endured by corvee laborers who were conscripted into imperial logging commissions. However, existing literature has not provided a clear sense of the relative scale of imperial timber procurement and the mass timber market. This negligence is especially problematic for the broad areas in southern China, where the Qing state's presence was much more limited compared to its more interventionist forest management beyond the Great Wall. What resulted is an imagination of imperial consumption that is out of proportion and, consequently, incorrect evaluation of the extent to which the state could have dominated or manipulated the timber market—or if the state were to restrain itself, how much forest could have been saved in southern China.

While ordinary-sized timber constituted much of the state's regular demand and could easily be satisfied by the market's supply from plantation forestry, the central court also needed extraordinarily large timber for grand constructions. Historical accounts about the increasing difficulty to find certain types of timber for the imperial court, though valuable for many other purposes, could be a misleading indicator about a locality's level of involvement in the timber market and its forest coverage. Official reports of the increasing difficulty in locating large timber surely indicated the disappearance of old-growth forests in places with good water access, but they could not account for managed forests and plantations that were cut and regenerated with plans. Even with the most conservative estimation of the mass-market timber trade along the Yangzi River and tributaries, the amount of timber purchased by the imperial state from this system was minimal compared to the estimated volume of market trade, which was supplied in no small part by plantation forestry. The Qing state's procurement was in a market, not in replacement of it. Imperial logging was only sporadically carried out in the deeper old growths of Sichuan and Guizhou to obtain what the market could not reasonably provide. This should be the basis of our imagination of the dynamics in the timber market of southern China.

CHAPTER TWO

The Interregional Timber Market

THE market structure of the Yangzi River timber trade system matured in the eighteenth and nineteenth centuries. Estimates of timber tax revenues and tax rates put the annual volume of interregional timber flow to the lower Yangzi area at a scale of five million logs, which far surpassed the few thousands of logs procured by the imperial timber tribute system. Half a dozen customs stations dotted the major waterways and levied transit taxes on passing timber rafts, which provided the statistical basis for the reconstruction of this trade system. Notably, this statistical reconstruction has to be premised on a careful analysis of the policies governing the bureaucracy of domestic customs stations, as changes in the required revenue quotas and the way in which surplus customs revenues were appropriated and rewarded had a great influence on how the revenue was collected and how much revenue was reported. Customs revenue data was not an unbiased reflection of commercial development, but a product of the constant contention between the central court and its local agencies. This understanding applies not only to the timber trade but to the whole system of commercial taxation. Taking into account the possible direction and magnitude of the data's potential biases in different periods allows us to examine the time-series of transit taxes to detect the trends in timber consumption and supply.

Two trends stand out. First, markets continued to expand in size and sophistication. The volume of timber consumed in Jiangnan experienced substantial growth during the eighteenth century, which sustained the level of per capita consumptions in the face of continuous population growth. Some fluctuations were experienced in the nineteenth century, resulting from sluggish demand, transportation blockages, or supply-side difficulties. Second, timber exported from Hunan and Guizhou made up ever-increasing market shares, rivaling established networks of supply in Jiangxi and the lower Yangzi highlands. Managed plantations gradually replaced natural forests as the main source of such supplies. Merchants traveled west to replenish their inventories, and customs stations were opened up in western regions to tap such commercial activities. The growing importance of southwestern timber contributed to the rise of Hankou as the central hub of timber trade in the middle Yangzi region, second only to Nanjing in its influence and prosperity. The high level of integration of the interregional trade along the Yangzi River was testified by the uniform adoption of the Longquan *ma* system of timber measurement and pricing, an early seventeenth-century invention in Longquan County that set the basic vocabulary and algorithm for the practitioners to negotiate quality and price.

MING-QING TIMBER-TAXING CUSTOMS

During the Ming dynasty, customs stations that taxed domestic long-distance trade along main river systems became an important contributor to the central state's commercial tax income.[1] The number and locations of the main customs stations, managed by the Board of Revenue, underwent frequent adjustments before they became relatively stable after the 1510s, primarily featuring the six stations along the Grand Canal and one on the Yangzi River, Jiujiang Guan.[2] While transit duties were originally paid in paper money, by the mid-1430s they were increasingly commuted to silver.[3] Besides these Board of Revenue stations, the Board of Works managed a dozen timber-extracting stations (*choufen ju*), which specialized in collecting duties on timber and bamboo. Among the larger ones were the stations in Hangzhou, Jingzhou (Hubei), Nanjing, and Wuhu. At these Board of Works stations, in-kind taxes of timber were increasingly commuted into silver payments as well since at least the late fifteenth century.[4]

Two years after its conquest, the Qing state reinstituted the Ming customs system. The Board of Revenue and the Board of Works largely inherited their respective customs stations from the Ming.[5] Moreover, taxation on timber and bamboo was fully commuted to monetary payments. A few localities, including Hangzhou, Nanjing, and Wuhu, saw the coexistence of two customs stations, under the jurisdiction of the Board of Revenue and the Board of Works respectively. In Nanjing, for example, Longjiang Guan was a Board of Works station specializing in timber and bamboo taxes, while Xixin Guan was a Board of Revenue station taxing all the other major commodities. The singling out of timber and bamboo taxes, even after the payment had long been converted into silver just like for other commodities, still made sense largely because it served to divert the traffic of rafts away from congesting the main customs stations for junks to pass through. The two stations in the same city kept separate accounts but were managed by the same superintendent and both remitted their revenues to the Board of Revenue; the difference in jurisdiction only affected which board carried out the annual auditing of the customs' account.[6]

In addition to the Board of Works stations in Hangzhou, Jingzhou, Nanjing, and Wuhu, timber taxes constituted a significant portion of the customs revenues at the Board of Revenue stations in Jiujiang and Ganzhou, both in Jiangxi. Furthermore, by the late Kangxi era, two local timber-taxing stations—Yu Guan in Chongqing, Sichuan, and Chen Guan in Chenzhou, western Hunan—were formalized as central-level Board of Works stations, reflecting the central state's recognition of the developing timber trade in the southwest.[7] Some other customs stations included timber as a taxable item, such as Yangzhou Guan, Linqing Guan, and Huai'an Guan, but timber taxes constituted only a small portion of their revenues. Besides, a number of much smaller timber-taxing stations were set up in Manchuria and northern Shanxi and Zhili.[8] Map I.1 shows the eight major timber-taxing customs in the Yangzi River trade network during the Qing, including six Board of Works customs (Longjiang Guan, Wuhu Gong Guan, Nanxin Guan in Hangzhou, Jing Guan, Yu Guan, and Chen Guan) and two Board of Revenue customs (Jiujiang Guan and Gan Guan).

Table 2.1 shows the basic information for these customs stations. The formal tax quotas of these stations underwent some adjustments during the Kangxi reign and became fixed from the early eighteenth century. The table shows the formal tax quotas as in 1753 (reported in the 1764 edition of *Collected Statutes*), which were later increased by the imperially formulated "surplus quotas" (*qinding yingyu*) in 1799.[9] The proportion of revenue taken up by timber taxes varied among these customs stations and was not regularly disclosed in either *Collected Statutes* or the annual revenue reports to the emperor. Tax rates for different varieties of timber also differed. Per their specialization, the Board of Works stations derived most of their revenues from timber, while the Board of Revenue stations had a much broader tax base. More important, actual customs revenues often deviated from the quotas. Column 5 in the table shows the average annual revenue of each customs stations between 1725 and 1850 based on available data. In most cases the average revenue was

TABLE 2.1 Eight main timber-taxing customs stations

[1] CUSTOMS STATIONS	[2] LOCATION	[3] 1753 QUOTA (TAELS)	[4] 1799 QUOTA (TAELS)	[5] AVERAGE REVENUE 1725–1850 (TAELS)	[6] MAIN TAXABLE ITEMS	[7] TIMBER TAX RATE
Jiujiang Guan (R)	Jiangxi	172,281	520,081[a]	518,309	timber, salt, tea, junks levies	size
Longjiang Guan (W)	Jiangsu	57,607	112,607	123,737	timber, junks levies	size
Wuhu Gong Guan (W)	Jiangxi	70,146	117,146	114,704	timber, junks levies	size
Gan Guan (R)	Jiangxi	90,682	128,682	99,466	multiple commodities	
Jing Guan (W)	Hubei	17,019	30,019[b]	39,780	timber, junks levies	3%
Nanxin Guan (W)	Zhejiang	30,247	30,247	29,210	timber	10%
Chen Guan (W)	Hunan	12,500	16,300[c]	18,496	timber, salt	3%
Yu Guan (W)	Sichuan	5,000	5,000	5,630	timber	3%

Source: QL_HDZL, *juan* 47 and 136; QSG, *juan* 125; and GX_HDSL, *juan* 235 and 941.
Notes: Column [1]: "R" stands for the Board of Revenue; "W" stands for the Board of Works. Column [3]: 1753 quota includes both "formal quota" and "copper transportation cost," if applicable. Column [4]: 1799 quota includes "formal quote," "copper transportation cost," and the "imperially formulated surplus quota." Column [5]: average revenue is calculated based on annual revenue data compiled from memorials from GZD and FHA. Column [7]: "size" means taxation by the dimensions of timber rafts as measured in specific ways; the percentage tax rate, if specified, is per valorem based on estimated value.
[a] The quota of Jiujiang Guan was increased to 539,281 taels in 1804.
[b] The quota of Jing Guan was decreased to 24,819 taels in 1863.
[c] The quota of Chen Guan was increased to 27,711 taels in 1801 and further to 29,692 taels in 1807.

far greater than the 1753 quota. The adjustment in 1799 brought the quota closer to the actual revenue. It is important to notice that the tax quotas, though roughly informative about the overall sizes of these customs stations, should not be taken directly as accurate reflections of customs revenues nor the volume of timber passing through.

In assessing the value and volume of timber trade based on the data of customs revenues from the eighteenth and nineteenth centuries, one must keep in mind that the way in which the Qing state managed customs revenues in different periods introduced certain biases to the reported revenue data. In the early years of the Qing, tax quotas for domestic customs were established roughly following the Ming levels in 1630. With the recovery of the economy from the tumultuous years of the Ming-Qing transition, initial deficits turned into consistent surpluses. Accordingly, the quotas were adjusted up on several occasions during the Shunzhi and early Kangxi reigns. Eventually, the quotas set in 1681 became generally fixed, referred to as the "formal quotas" (*zheng'e*) in later government documents, including *Collected Statutes*. For those customs stations newly founded during the Qing, their quotas were also established and adjusted during the Kangxi and Yongzheng eras.

By the early eighteenth century, most of the quotas had become stable. The "formal quota," despite its name, was not necessarily all that was expected by the center. In 1706 the state set up quotas for the customs stations' contributions to the transportation cost of copper, used for minting bronze coins, from the southwest to the capital. This item, called "copper transportation cost" (*tongjin shuijiao*), became a required quota besides the "formal quotas" for applicable stations.[10] Comparing the section on domestic customs in the 1764 and 1899 editions of *Collected Statutes*, "formal quotas" and "copper transportation costs" for the eight main timber-taxing customs stations remained unchanged from 1753. They are combined and reported as the "1753 quota" in table 2.1.[11]

Surplus revenue beyond the quota (*yingyu*) became common after the 1680s. The assessment and appropriation of surplus revenues presented a principal-agency dilemma for the central government, and the related policies went back and forth between the two extremes of fixation and centralization on the one hand and laissez-faire decentralization on the other. In the first decades of the dynasty, especially during major military campaigns such as the Revolt of the Three Feudatories, to ease the financial difficulties of the central state, reported surplus revenue was rewarded with the promotion of the superintendent's grade (*jiaji*). Accumulated grades, although not an outright promotion of one's substantive post or rank, was an important factor in personnel evaluations and would give the official considerable advantage when being considered as a candidate for promotion.[12] Rewarding surplus revenue with the promotion of grade provided strong incentives for the superintendents to collect revenues diligently and report truthfully to the center. However, these practices might also result in excessive exactions on commerce, which concerned the Kangxi emperor and led to the abolition of the promotion policy after the war in 1686. Thereafter, the central state, while encouraging full declaration and submission of surplus revenues, forfeited any effective command of the intelligence about the actual amount of surpluses.[13]

Accompanying a series of fiscal reforms initiated by the Yongzheng emperor, reformist provincial officials conducted a full investigation on customs revenues for the first time in decades. Reported surpluses increased steadily during the 1720s and 1730s, reflecting both the prosperity of commerce as well as previously concealed revenues in the late Kangxi era. Because of the consistent increase in surpluses during the Yongzheng reign, a new administrative *norm* developed in the bureaucracy. Meeting the formal quota was only a minimum requirement. By default, customs revenues were expected to increase on an annual basis. If the reported surplus was less than that of the previous year, the Board of Revenue would impeach the official in charge. Therefore the revenue collected in the previous year became the de facto quota for the next year.

However, once the problem of concealed revenues was redressed and the reported revenue reflected more truthfully the actual volume of commerce, fluctuations in customs revenues were all but natural. The expectation of an ever-increasing surplus turned out to be impractical. In 1741 the Qianlong emperor issued an imperial edict to address this issue. He expressed the concern that the customs superintendents would excessively burden the merchants in order to avoid the board's impeachment, and such procyclical tendencies would make things worse in years when commerce was already depressed. Emperor Qianlong's new policy was that only when the amount of surplus was severely less than that of the previous year should the board order a full investigation by the supervising provincial officials. So long as no malpractices such as embezzlement were detected, the decreased revenue was accepted as a reflection of market fluctuations and the superintendent should not be blamed.[14]

In 1749 the Board of Revenue, concerned about the implications of the emperor's lenient policy for revenue stability, made the counterproposal that the superintendent should be held responsible when the surplus decreased for more than 10 percent compared with the previous year, and punishment in the form of grade demotion should be linked to the percentage of surplus decrease. In response, an imperial edict stipulated that instead of the surplus of the previous year, surplus accrued in the year of

1735—the last year of the Yongzheng reign—should be set as the benchmark thereafter. Since the midcentury customs revenues were generally higher than the 1735 level, the edict was meant as a gesture of imperial benevolence while elevating the formalized expectation for customs revenues.[15]

With sustained revenue increases in the 1750s and 1760s, surpassing the 1735 level was not a problem. Customs superintendents still cited the surplus of the previous year as the benchmark for comparison in their memorials, a practice insisted on by the Board of Revenue and acquiesced to by the emperor.[16] By the late 1770s, however, customs revenues, especially those from stations on the Grand Canal, decreased steadily and even fell below the levels of the 1750s—a trend manifesting the secular decline of the north-south trade along the Grand Canal. In view of this the emperor adjusted the policy in 1777 so that surpluses should be compared not only with that of the previous year, but the previous three years: only when the surplus reached a four-year low would the superintendent be blamed and charged with the deficit.[17]

Continued revenue declines in the 1790s eventually resulted in the "imperially formulated surplus quotas" (*qinding yingyu*) by the Jiaqing emperor in 1799 at levels considerably lower than the peak level of actual revenues in the eighteenth century. This fact is often overlooked by only comparing the formalized quotas between 1753 and 1799, which leads to the false conclusion that the Jiaqing emperor was trying to extract more revenues from the customs when he was actually adjusting the expectation down.[18] Table 2.1 reports the resulted total quota of 1799 as the sum of "formal quota," "copper transportation cost" if applicable, and the new "imperially formulated surplus quota." Another major adjustment happened in 1804, which did not involve the customs stations under consideration here except for Jiujiang Guan, whose surplus quota was increased by another 19,200 taels, resulting in a total quota of 539,281 taels. The "imperially formulated surplus quotas" finally completed the conversion of floating surpluses into fixed quotas. Further surplus beyond the "surplus quota" was now called "extra surplus" (*e'wai yingyu*). After the 1820s, however, declining customs revenues became increasingly widespread and frequent, in particular for previously prosperous Grand Canal stations such as Hushu and Huai'an, whose "surplus quotas" were further adjusted down in 1831. Recessions of customs revenues in the first half of the nineteenth century, especially after the 1820s, seemed to signal a general economic depression and regional disintegration.[19] In the 1850s several major customs stations were closed off during the Taiping Rebellion (1851–1864) and were never reopened; moreover, with the opening of treaty ports and the spread of the Lijin tax, revenues from domestic customs never recovered to the eighteenth-century levels.[20]

This brief review of the Qing management of customs revenues offers important insights on the central state's perspective, particularly its considerations regarding the trade-off between claiming more revenues on the one hand and restraining corruption and excessive burdens on commerce on the other. The domestic customs institution, like other branches of the Qing fiscal system, was faced with the irresolvable problem of information asymmetry and conflicts of interest between the central state vis-à-vis individual customs superintendents as well as local governments that benefited from concealing revenues from the center. The formal quotas and the changing terms under which surpluses were managed could be understood within a framework of a generalized tax-farming model, in which an assigned superintendent was held responsible for meeting a minimum requirement (either by formal formulations or informal administrative norms), and any shortage must be made up from his private purse. Moreover, although it was against officially stated principles, the superintendent could in practice retain any income beyond the requirement without any substantive risk. These aspects of Qing public finance would certainly merit a full-scale investigation elsewhere.

For our purpose here, the main takeaway is how changing policies of revenue management might have affected the reliability of the reported revenue data and how our interpretation should be adjusted to account for the potential biases. At the turn of the eighteenth century, the expansion of trade had already rendered the "formal quotas" set in the early years of the dynasty obsolete. However, surpluses beyond the formal quotas were not fully revealed in the reported customs revenues, not the least because of the central state's deliberate negligence in order to weaken the incentives for officials to overtax commerce. In the 1720s and 1730s, with the Yongzheng emperor's efforts at consolidating customs revenues, reported revenues reflected more truthfully the extent of market expansion. Meanwhile, steady increases in customs revenues during these years built up an administrative norm that guided the board's evaluations for the rest of the century, with the expectation that stable, if not ever-increasing, revenues should be reported each year.

Therefore, from the 1730s through the 1790s, while decreases of *any* amount and increases of *significant* amount in customs revenues more likely reflected actual market fluctuations, single-digit steady annual increases over many years should be interpreted as reflecting only the lower boundary of the actual trade volume, as they were most plausibly the result of the superintendents' guise to pass the board's audit and embezzle as much to their own purse as possible. Similarly, after the fixation of surplus quotas in 1799, significant deviations from the quota would indicate market movements, whereas continuous reporting of a few taels higher than the quota would more likely indicate only the lower boundary. In sum, variations seen from the reported customs revenues must be lower than actual market variations. The effect is likely to be asymmetrical: while decreases in trade volumes would be reflected more directly in the data of customs revenues, increases tended to be underrepresented.

Bearing these qualifications in mind, customs data can still be informative about changes in market conditions. Since detailed breakdowns of customs revenues were not included in the annual memorials, the data of timber taxes shown in the remaining sections are based on estimations. For the Board of Works stations of Wuhu Gong Guan, Nanxin Guan (Hangzhou), Jing Guan, and Yu Guan (Chongqing), timber taxes constituted the vast majority of their revenues and were often given as the primary reason to explain revenue fluctuations, so the trend of their total revenues can approximately represent the trend of timber taxes. In addition, the estimation for Chen Guan is detailed in this chapter, and estimation methods for Longjiang Guan (Nanjing) and Jiujiang Guan are detailed in appendixes A and B. Unfortunately, Gan Guan, which was a Board of Revenue station in Ganzhou, Jiangxi, is omitted here. Although Gan Guan taxed a major source of timber in southern Jiangxi, it also taxed a wide variety of commodities along the only overland trade route to Guangzhou. Taxes from silk and tea, instead of timber, contributed the most to its revenues, and I have found no available information on the percentage of revenue from timber.[21]

TIMBER CONSUMPTION IN JIANGNAN

Nanjing was the axis of the whole timber market connected by the Yangzi River and its tributaries. Prices generated in Nanjing served as the ultimate market signal for all the upriver timber trade. It was the final stop for merchants who brought timber downriver from regions to the west. Wholesale merchants from cities and market towns in Jiangnan and Jiangbei came here to make bulk purchases. The timber market was located in the town of Shangxin He in the western suburb of Nanjing, which was named after a canal first constructed during the Hongwu reign of the Ming dynasty to connect the Qinhuai River to the Yangzi River. During the early Ming the riverbank of the Shangxin Canal became known as the "imperial timber sawmill" and the "riverbank of treasure boats," for it was used to stock timber logs for the construction of imperial palaces and the famous treasure boats used in Admiral Zheng He's voyages (1405–33). One of the first timber-extracting stations of the Ming was established here in 1393, the predecessor of Longjiang Guan.[22]

Merchants initially gathered here to supply timber for government projects. By the mid-Ming this location had already developed into a large timber market, where the three merchant groups (*bang*) of Hui, Lin, and Xi began their history as the most influential players in the timber trade until the mid-nineteenth century. Hui *bang* merchants were from the Huizhou prefecture in southern Anhui, mostly the county of Wuyuan. Lin *bang* merchants were from the Linjiang prefecture in Jiangxi, mostly the county of Qingjiang (the current city of Zhangshu). And Xi *bang* included Jiangxi merchants in general other than those from Linjiang, and among them the group from the provincial capital Nanchang was biggest in number.[23] These three merchant groups not only traded timber from their native places but were also pioneers in expanding the timber trade further to the southwest. They traveled upriver to make purchases and started bringing Hunan timber in volume to the Nanjing market since the late Ming. Timber merchants with abundant capital also engaged in money lending to finance the business of fellow merchants in the southwest.[24]

From the nineteenth century, timber merchants from Hunan and Hubei rose to challenge the dominance of Huizhou and Jiangxi merchants. They began to take advantage of their geographical closeness to southwestern timber and increasingly traveled downriver to make sales. Merchant groups from different regions of Hunan and Hubei gradually joined the traditional three *bangs* in the market of Nanjing.[25] By the late Qing each of the major groups occupied separate sections along the bank of the Shangxin Canal and established their own trade association (*gongsuo*). From the west to the east along the canal, there erected the association halls for the *bangs* of Nanchang, Ganzhou, Hubei, Hunan, Linqing, and Huizhou. The boundaries between the zones occupied by different *bangs* were often contested and redrawn in response to the rise and decline of each *bang*'s power.[26]

A small portion of the timber that arrived at Nanjing was consumed locally. Besides the suburban Shangxin He timber market that mainly served interregional trade, there were two smaller-scale timber markets located at the West Water Gate and the Hanzhong Gate of the Nanjing city. Timber merchants in these two markets made purchases from Shangxin He and retailed to local customers within the city wall, mainly carpentry workshops and construction contractors.[27] Apart from the timber consumed locally in Nanjing, the majority was retied into smaller rafts and transported along the Grand Canal to cities in Jiangnan and the Huai River valley. Timber rafts heading for Jiangnan entered the Grand Canal at Zhenjiang and reached Changzhou, Wuxi, Suzhou, and Shanghai. Those heading north would enter the Grand Canal at Yangzhou and be distributed to Taixing, Nantong, and Yancheng.

The revenues of Longjiang Guan and Wuhu Gong Guan relied most heavily on timber taxes (*yi zhumu paiba wei dazong*).[28] The two customs stations shared a similar revenue base in upriver timber rafts. Wuhu Gong Guan taxed the timber that floated down the Yangzi River from Jiujiang as well as a small amount of timber that was produced in southern Anhui and transported up for the Nanjing market. Local consumption in Wuhu was minimal compared to the volume of passing timber, most of which was taxed again at Longjiang Guan upon arrival at Nanjing. Not only was timber the biggest taxable item at both stations, but it also accounted for most of the variations in their revenues. Therefore we could approximately appreciate the changes in timber volume from the trends of their total revenues. As shown in figure 2.1, the revenues of Longjiang Guan demonstrated a fair amount of annual variations, while Wuhu Gong Guan seemed a typical case of underreporting increases (partly because in accounting its surplus was often used to offset the deficit in the same-city Board of Revenue station). Not surprisingly, given their similar revenue bases, the instances of revenue decreases did coincide between Longjiang Guan and Wuhu Gong Guan. The overall trend shows substantial growth for most of the eighteenth century, big fluctuations from 1785 to 1795, moderate recoveries in the first three decades of the nineteenth century, and after that a downturn till midcentury.

A very conservative estimation of the share of timber taxes in Longjiang Guan's total revenues and approximations based on its taxation methods places the average annual volume of timber reaching Nanjing at about five million logs between 1725 and 1850 (see appendix A). At the high levels of the 1760s to the early 1780s, the estimated annual timber volume could reach six million to seven million logs. This estimation is almost certainly a lower bound. For reference, the Maritime Customs Service estimated that from 1882 through 1891, more than eighteen million poles from Hunan, Guizhou, and Jiangxi passed through the Inland Custom House of Wuhu annually.[29] Recall from chapter 1 that the central state annually demanded seventy-four hundred regular-sized timber logs, which were negligible compared with this market capacity.

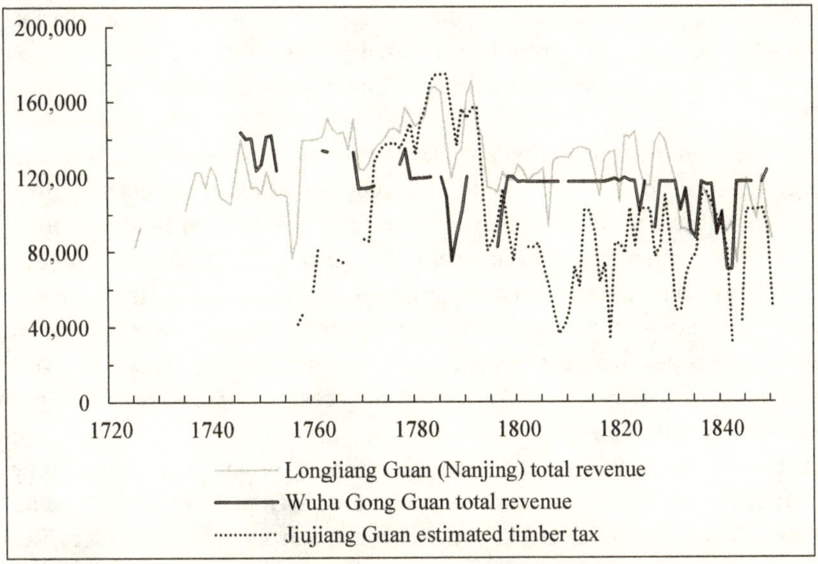

FIGURE 2.1 Revenue collected at Longjiang Guan, Wuhu Gong Guan, and Jiujiang Guan, 1720–1850, taels of silver. *Source*: Liao Shengfeng, *Qingdai changguan yu quyu jingji yanjiu*, 119, 371–75, 381–88; Ni Yuping, *Qingchao Jia Dao guanshui yanjiu*, appendix tables 10, 12, 13, 15, and 16; and memorials from FHA and GZD.

Besides timber that reached Nanjing through the Yangzi River, timber from southern Anhui and western Zhejiang was transported to Hangzhou and redistributed from there. So the combined amount of timber at Longjiang Guan in Nanjing and Nanxin Guan in Hangzhou could roughly represent the amount of timber distributed in the core areas of Jiangnan and Jiangbei. The volume of logs at Nanxin Guan is estimated based on its 10 percent tax rate per valorem, assuming a price of 0.5 taels per log.[30] Per capita consumption can be estimated by dividing the estimated number of logs that reached Longjiang Guan and Nanxin Guan by the combined populations of Jiangsu and Zhejiang.[31] This method might overestimate per capita consumption because it does not take into account the population along the Grand Canal in the North China provinces (Anhui, Shandong, and Zhili) that were served by the timber transported up from Nanjing; it might also underestimate per capita consumption because it does not take into account the supply of timber transported by sea from Fujian to Zhejiang. Despite such flaws, the long-term trend it reveals should be valid.

Juxtaposing the estimated number of logs with the trend of population growth, the substantial growth in the total volume of timber from the 1720s to the 1780s largely kept up with a 30 percent population growth during this period, sustaining the level of per capita consumption at around ninety logs per thousand population per year. A recession in timber trade began in the 1790s and continued through the first decade of the nineteenth century. Although there was some recovery with fluctuations from 1800 to 1830, it never again attained the peak level of the early 1780s. With a continuous population increase, timber consumption at the per capita level consistently dropped in the first half of the nineteenth century, hovering around seventy logs per thousand population in the first three decades. The 1830s and 1840s experienced another round of recession, around fifty logs per thousand population.

I have found fifty-seven memorials that have included explanatory remarks to account for forty-five instances of revenue decreases at Jiujiang Guan, Wuhu Gong Guan, and Longjiang Guan from 1725 to 1852. Tax shortages occurred rarely before 1780 and were mostly attributed to disruptions to river transportations due to either flood or drought. Revenue decreases occurred more often after the 1780s and about half the time were ascribed to sluggish demands in the lower Yangzi area, confirming a general economic depression, especially during the Daoguang era. During the nineteenth century, problems encountered in river transportation due to flood or silting were also reported more frequently, suggesting that long-term issues in water management and lake reclamation were starting to impact the nation's most important transportation infrastructure.[32] By this point contemporary observers came to be aware of a systematic environmental vulnerability, as the delicate balance between population, hydraulics, forests, and agriculture was reaching its extreme.[33] Despite effective plantation management to supply the market with timber, commercial tree planting could only deal with one cause of deforestation and environmental degradation. Population growth and land reclamations presented bigger threats to existing forest coverage and natural water systems, leading to erosion, silting, and more frequent floods, which compromised the ecological underpinning of the expansive commercial network.

The reconstruction of Jiangnan after its devastation during the Taiping Rebellion led to a demand-induced boom in the timber trade from the 1860s. Many accounts of the Nanjing timber market in the Republican period traced its origin to the post-Taiping reconstruction. Although such accounts surely neglected the long-term development of Nanjing's timber market throughout the late imperial period, they signified the extent of the post-Taiping boom.[34] With half the population lost during the war, per capita timber volume in Jiangnan should have risen. However, since its closure in 1853 because of the war, Longjiang Guan was never reinstituted.[35] The new timber-taxing institution in Nanjing after the Taiping Rebellion, Timber Lijin Bureau (Mu Li Ju), was beyond the direct control and audit of the central state. Without regular reports of the bureau's revenues, it is impossible to have similar estimations of timber volume and per capita consumption after 1850.

SOURCES OF TIMBER SUPPLY

Jiujiang Guan was the location where the two most important sources of timber flows first merged: southwestern timber that had continued to float down the Yangzi River from Hankou and Jiangxi timber that had been transported north along the Gan River. The main station of Jiujiang Guan sat over the Yangzi River, while a Gutang branch station was set up at the connection of the Poyang Lake to the Yangzi River, targeting the Jiangxi exports. The methods used for estimating the timber taxes at Jiujiang Guan are detailed in appendix B. The estimated timber tax revenues collected at Jiujiang Guan exhibited similar trends to those in Wuhu and Nanjing (see figure 2.1), with substantial increases from 1755 to 1785, sharp declines in the next two decades back to the level of the 1750s, followed by moderate recoveries until the mid-nineteenth century.

Much evidence suggests that Jiangxi remained the largest source of timber in the eighteenth century. In 1744, at Wuhu Gong Guan, taxes from Jiangxi timber amounted to 95,601 taels (78 percent), while taxes from the Huguang timber were 26,376 taels (22 percent).[36] In another example, for the term of 1780 (from the fourth month of 1779 to the fourth month of 1780), the total timber tax at Jiujiang Guan was 131,489 taels by my estimation. According to a memorial by Jiangxi governor Hao Shuo, 82,364 taels (or 62 percent of that estimated total) were collected in the Gutang branch station that specialized in taxing Jiangxi timber—and this amount of tax from Jiangxi timber was considered unusually low. In fact, Hao Shuo mentioned that in the fifth and sixth months of 1780 alone, timber taxes collected at Gutang had already reached 95,223 taels, surpassing the total amount collected at this branch station in the previous annual term. In just these two months, timber from Jiangxi had already contributed 64 percent of the estimated 149,201 taels of timber tax for the term of 1781 (from the fourth month of 1780 to the fourth month of 1781).[37] With the steady expansion of timber supply from Hunan, the proportion of timber supplied by

Jiangxi decreased in the nineteenth century. Jiangxi timber was typically smaller than the timber from western Hunan and was priced lower accordingly. Presumably this is because most of the natural sites in Jiangxi had been logged out sooner and plantation timber was cut younger, while the western Hunan forests still contained more mature stands. Nevertheless, Jiangxi continued to be an important timber source alongside Hunan throughout the Republican period.[38]

Since the Yuan dynasty, Jiangxi had begun to export timber at some scale to the lower Yangzi delta. By the late imperial period it had become the most important timber exporter. Timber was cultivated in plantation forestry all over the province in the river valleys of Gan Jiang and its tributaries (map 2.1). Timber produced in the southern prefectures of Ji'an and Ganzhou were of better quality and bigger sizes thanks to the longer rotation in planting (thirty-five to forty years) and constituted the bulk of Jiangxi's export.[39] The 1752 gazetteer of the Longnan County in Ganzhou stated: "Fir is the only major export of the county. Its plantation became increasingly widespread in recent decades. Annual timber output can reach hundreds of thousands of logs. The locals sell them to Jiangnan and make big profits. . . . Longnan makes 70 percent of its profit from agricultural lands and 30 percent from the mountains."[40]

According to a 1930 investigation conducted by the Republican Ministry of Finance, southern Jiangxi (including the Qing prefectures of Ganzhou, Ji'an, Nan'an, and Ningdu) had an annual timber output of eleven million to thirteen million logs; another five million to six million logs were produced in the Fuhe and Xiushui river valleys in the north and the border area with Anhui.[41] However, compared to Hunan timber, Jiangxi exports were smaller in size, mostly ranging from 1 to 1.5 feet in circumference (*fen ma* in the Longquan *ma* category).[42] The best Jiangxi timber came from "Above Gan Guan" (somewhat counterintuitively, Guan *shang*, areas to the *south* of the customs station are "above" it when viewed from the north), especially those from around Ruijin and Longnan in Ganzhou. The next class was timber produced "Below Gan Guan" (Guan *xia*, areas to the *north* of the customs station) from Longquan and Wan'an counties in southern Ji'an. Further down the ladder was timber from western Ji'an.[43]

Although timber for interregional export was mostly produced in southern Jiangxi, big merchants in the timber trade came from the northern part of the province, mostly Linjiang and Nanchang (Lin *bang* and Xi *bang*). These merchants operated long-distance businesses that connected purchasing offices in Ganzhou and sales offices in the lower Yangzi markets of Nanjing and Changzhou. Backed by the capital from native banks, they

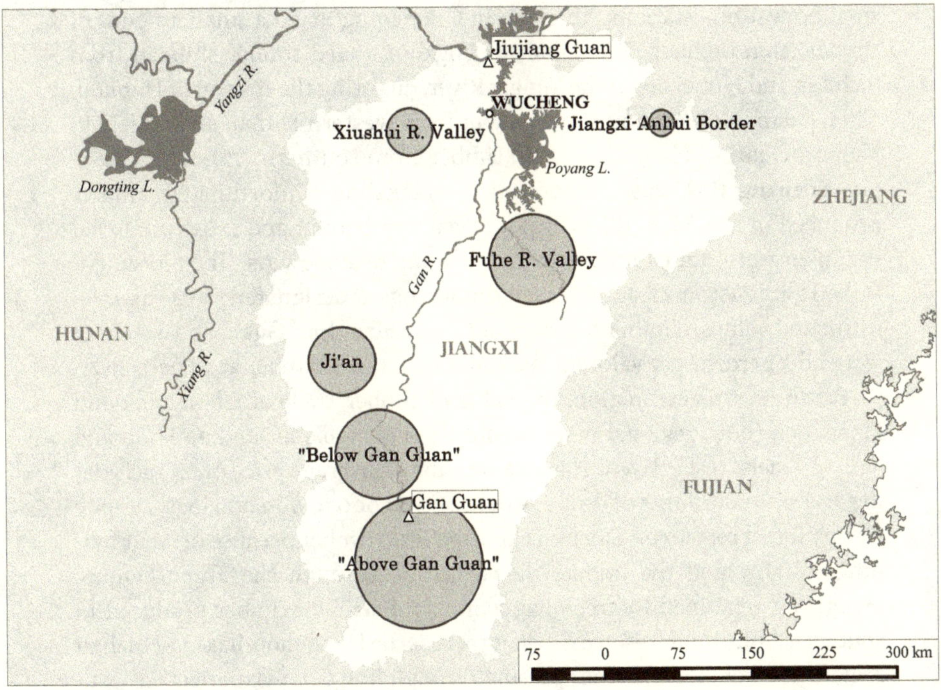

MAP 2.1 Timber-producing regions in Jiangxi.

collaborated with the timber brokerages in Ganzhou to make purchases from smaller merchants who logged directly from the forests, often with interest-bearing advance loans. They also relied on the brokerages to hire the porters to transport the timber rafts.[44] While medium-sized rafts were used for distributions within the province, those meant for export were combined into big rafts at Wucheng upon entering the Poyang Lake.[45] In the Nanjing market, Lin *bang* was the most prosperous merchant group. At its prime, twenty to thirty Linqing firms shipped timber to Nanjing every summer, often congesting the storage spaces on the southern bank. There were fewer firms in Xi *bang*, but each operated at a much larger scale, some with working capital of several hundred thousand taels. Over time, some Ganzhou natives extended their businesses beyond brokerages and tapped into the long-distance trade as well. By the late Qing, the Ganzhou *bang* had become a formidable force and held permanent establishments in Nanjing and Changzhou.[46]

Apart from the timber from Jiangxi, patterns of timber supply from other locations can be glimpsed from the timber tax revenues at four smaller customs stations. Yu Guan in Chongqing taxed a small amount of timber from Sichuan. Jing Guan in Jingzhou taxed timber shipped from Sichuan and Hubei down the Yangzi River, targeting the market of Hankou. Chen Guan in Chenzhou taxed timber from western Hunan and Guizhou. Nanxin Guan in Hangzhou taxed timber from southern Anhui and western Zhejiang that was transported to Hangzhou. Unfortunately, timber produced in the Xiang River valley in eastern Hunan and those produced in Fujian were not captured by the customs revenue data. The aforementioned four customs stations taxed timber logs at designated rates based on estimated values. Timber tax rates at Chen Guan, Jing Guan, and Yu Guan were all 3 percent per valorem. Nanxin Guan taxed timber at 10 percent.[47]

Based on this estimation, the value of timber trade at Chongqing and Hangzhou (both regional markets) stayed very stable around 200,000 and 300,000 taels, respectively. Again, assuming an average price of 0.5 taels per log, the annual volume of timber would be 400,000 to 600,000 logs. Despite its rich forest resources, Sichuan exported little timber because of its forbidding terrains and the impossible navigation through the Three Gorges. Hangzhou remained the regional center to distribute timber produced in southern Anhui and western Zhejiang across the Hangzhou-Jiaxing-Huzhou region. The volume of timber passing through Jing Guan experienced secular declines except for some mild growths between the 1760s and 1780s. By contrast, the volume of timber passing through Chen Guan underwent substantial growth (detailed in the next section). The contrasting trends of Jing Guan and Chen Guan suggest the decline of Hubei and the rising importance of western Hunan and Guizhou as sources of timber supply. Notice that Jing Guan accounted for almost all the Sichuan and Hubei timber that would reach Hankou, while Chen Guan only taxed timber from the western end of Hunan—timber from the Xiang River valley in eastern Hunan was not reflected in Chen Guan's revenue. Timber from Hunan, Guizhou, Hubei, and Sichuan converged at Hankou. The rise of the Parrot Island timber market in Hankou in the early nineteenth century was closely associated with increasing timber supplies from Hunan and the dominance of Hunan timber merchants over the local Hubeinese.[48]

Merchants from Huizhou and Jiangxi had traded timber in Hankou since the late Ming. The local gazetteers of the Wuyuan County in Huizhou recorded many Ming-Qing timber merchants who conducted their trade back and forth between Nanjing and Hankou. This particular trade route was described with a specific term: "Nanjing as head and Hankou as tail" (*wutou chuwei*).[49] According to the local tales, the timber market in Hankou first developed because of the expanding sales of Jiangnan's cotton cloth in the upper and middle Yangzi areas. As the marketing of cotton cloth reached the Miao regions in southwestern Hunan, the interregional timber-for-cloth exchange gradually developed, with Hankou as a central entrepôt.[50] Although it was typical to purchase timber in Hankou and transport it to Nanjing directly, timber could also change hands at several timber markets along the way—in particular Jiujiang and Wuhu, where rafts had to be stopped in any case to declare taxes at the customs stations. In Wuhu the riverbank for timber storage was called the "Hui-Lin band," for the timber merchants were mostly from Huizhou and Linjiang.[51]

Only in the early nineteenth century did Hankou become a major center for the trade of timber and bamboo, which benefited from two concurrent processes: the silting up of Parrot Island and the rise of Hunan merchants, who started to compete with the Jiangxi and Huizhou outsiders to export timber from their home province. The original timber market was located in Hankou proper, accessible through the Han River from the Yangzi River. Parrot Island first appeared in 1769 off the shore of the Hanyang city in the middle of the Yangzi River, then gradually silted up to form a long sand band, providing a more convenient site for mooring and unloading timber rafts. When the Hunanese timber merchants began coming to Hankou in the early nineteenth century, the old timber band in Hankou proper was already fully occupied by the Huizhou and Jiangxi pioneers, so the Hunanese started to use the growing Parrot Island. By the time the island's merit as a harborage had become clear, the Hunanese had already established a monopoly over the most advantageous locations on the island: the long beachhead and the straits that separated it from the Hanyang shore. When the Jiangxi merchants relocated to the Parrot Island, they found themselves left with high lands far from the river, where customers were reluctant to visit except when in search of some rare varieties of timber.[52]

By the 1840s the timber market on Parrot Island had eclipsed the one in Hankou proper, and the Hunan merchants had become the dominant group. In the post-Taiping era, with surging demand for reconstruction in the ravaged middle and lower Yangzi areas and a series of state-sponsored military and industrial modernization reforms centered in Wuhan, the Parrot Island timber market experienced a great period of growth.[53] Known collectively as the Nan *bang*, the Hunan merchants were divided by their places of origin into eight prefecture-level groups and eighteen subgroups. These groups federated into two big alliances for the trade of "eastern Hunan timber" from the prefectures of Baoqing, Changsha, and Hengzhou, and "western Hunan timber" from the prefectures of Changde, Chenzhou, Jingzhou, Yongzhou, and Yuanzhou (map 2.2). More than twenty trade

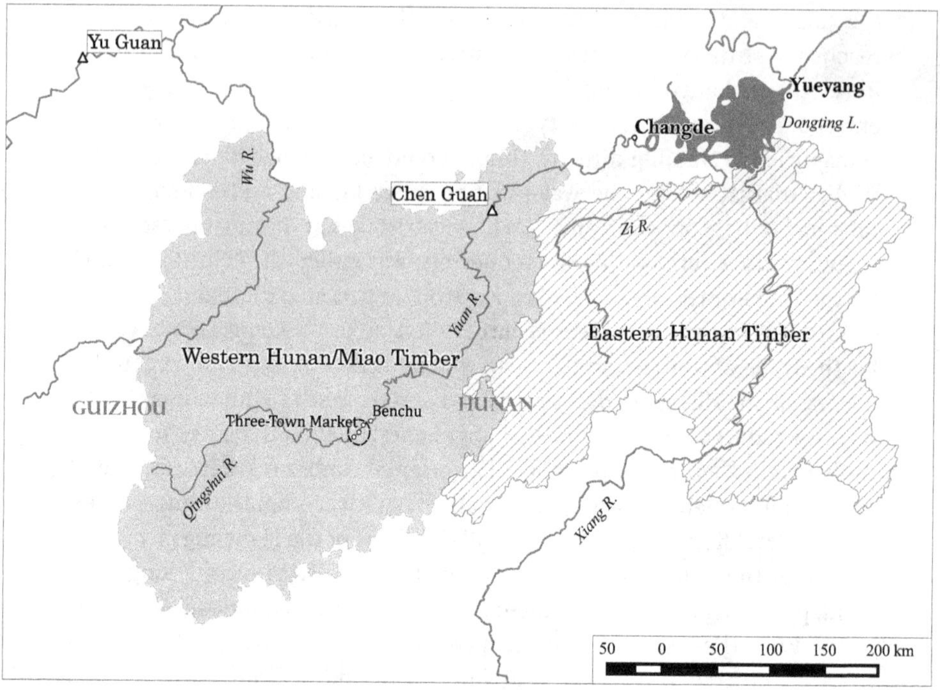

MAP 2.2 Timber-producing regions in Hunan and Eastern Guizhou.

associations constructed their halls on the island, representing alliances at all these different levels.

Around 1865 an overarching Lianghu Huiguan was established by the entire community, uniting the eastern and western Hunan groups. The locals referred to Parrot Island as "little Hunan" and spoke of the "five prefectures and eighteen *bangs*" united under the multiplex association of Lianghu Huiguan. The phrase "five prefectures" is not exact, as there were in fact eight prefecture-level groups. When the western Hunan and eastern Hunan groups united to form the Lianghu Huiguan, there was the issue of how to allocate fees between the two. Instead of dividing the fees equally among the eight prefectural groups, it was agreed that the three eastern groups should be responsible for 60 percent, while the five western groups should be responsible for 40 percent. So in name the five western prefectures were represented as only "Changde" and "Chenzhou" in the Lianghu Huiguan to match the percentage allocation of financial responsibility, although the responsibility was in fact shared by all five western prefectural groups. The phrase "five prefectures and eighteen *bangs*" reflected the internal financial arrangement of the Lianghu Huiguan, with two prefectures representing all the western groups and three prefectures from eastern Hunan.[54] The fee allocation scheme likely reflected the relative value of timber traded from eastern and western Hunan, confirming the importance of eastern Hunan timber despite the lack of tax data.

Another major group in the Parrot Island market was the local Hubei merchants. Known as the Han *bang* or Bei *bang*, these Hubeinese initially served as the local agents for the Jiangxi, Huizhou, and Huangzhou merchants and later entered into the long-distance trade. As the timber market continued to expand in the second half of the nineteenth century, they sought to claim a share of the mooring space on the island. They appealed to the local magistrate, accused the Hunan merchants of monopolization and barring the locals from entering the timber trade, and questioned the legality of the Hunanese's claims on the land properties on Parrot Island. After some back and forth in the legal proceedings and even outbreaks of physical conflicts, an agreement was reached that the Hunan merchants could continue to occupy the moorage and import timber to Hankou without obstructions, but the sale of timber had to be conducted through the intermediation of licensed brokerages, the eligibility to which was now limited to Hubei locals. After this settlement the Hubei merchants began to apply for the licenses and set up brokerage firms on the island.[55]

An interesting interlude during these lawsuits concerned the Lianghu Huiguan. The Hubei merchants included as one of their accusations that the "Hunan merchants seized the co-owned meeting hall, the Lianghu Huiguan, as their own." Here, the Hubeinese twisted the meaning of the term "Lianghu" as referring to "Hunan and Hubei," while it actually referred to "western and eastern Hunan." That this accusation was groundless became apparent instantly in the legal proceedings, when the founding documents from the association were submitted as evidence. Still, because of such ambiguity of "Lianghu," the Hunan merchants changed the name of their association to "Hunan Huiguan" to avoid future troubles.[56] Because the Jing Guan station missed all the timber that came through the Dongting Lake from Hunan, it was not well positioned to tap revenues from the flourishing Hankou timber trade. The superintendents of Jing Guan consistently reported revenue shortages from 1806 to 1823.[57] In 1857 a new timber-taxing custom station, named Xin Guan, was set up in Wuhan to capture all the timber flows into Hankou, with a quota of 27,700 taels. By the 1890s, Xin Guan generated a surplus of 12,295 taels beyond the quota, to which Human timber contributed greatly. This was an impressive accomplishment considering the general decline of domestic customs revenues in the second half of the nineteenth century.[58]

CHEN GUAN IN WESTERN HUNAN

Given the rising importance of western Hunan as a source of timber supply, this section closely examines the Chen Guan customs station. Its institutional history and revenue trend illustrate the aforementioned nuances of the customs revenue data and demonstrate the substantial development of timber trade in the Yuan River basin in western Hunan and eastern Guizhou during the eighteenth century. The exact time of Chen Guan's establishment is unclear. The earliest extant mentioning of this station dates to 1686, but it was not included as one of the regular Board of Works customs stations until after the 1730s.[59] The station was directly managed by the prefect of Chenzhou.

Chen Guan's position in the structure of timber trade needs to be clarified. Map 2.2 shows the main timber-producing regions in Hunan and eastern Guizhou. Fir produced in Hunan and parts of Guizhou and Guangxi was known as Guang *mu*. The character *guang* was used because Hunan and Hubei used to be parts of the same province of Huguang before 1664 and the name continued to be used colloquially thereafter. The quality of Guang *mu* was generally considered better than that of Xi *mu* (timber from Jiangxi). Guang *mu* was further divided into two kinds by places of production. Timber produced in the drainage basins of the Xiang and Zi Rivers in the eastern part of Hunan was known as "eastern Hunan timber" (*dong*-Hu *mu*), while timber produced in the Yuan River basin of western Hunan and eastern Guizhou was known as "western Hunan timber" (*xi*-Hu *mu*). Of the two, western Hunan timber was the preferred variety.[60] Chen Guan was well positioned to tax all the western Hunan timber closest to its source. However, Chenzhou itself was not a site for much market exchange. The first major market for western Hunan timber was located farther down the Yuan River in Changde, where timber merchants gathered to trade in the town of Deshan (where Hunan tribute timber officials frequented to procure regular timber as well). The Yuan, Li, Zi, and Xiang Rivers converged into the Dongting Lake and entered the Yangzi River at Yueyang, where timber was refastened into larger rafts to survive the Yangzi currents.[61]

Chen Guan only taxed timber and salt. In 1726 the Hunan governor Bulantai began to scrutinize the revenues of Chen Guan. In the Kangxi era the quota of Chen Guan was only 2,400 taels, of which 1,375 taels were for salt and 1,030 taels were for timber. Bulantai's investigation reported that by the 1720s the surplus had reached more than 6,000 taels, two-thirds of which were attributed to the growing volume of timber passing down the Yuan River. Given the central government's loose control over the customs during the Kangxi reign, this surplus had been concealed from the Board and retained in the prefecture, or, according to Bulantai, more often than not embezzled by the prefects. Bulantai proposed to assign a special official to sort out the revenues of Chen Guan and reset the formal quota.[62] After Bulantai's initiative, Wang Rou, the Chen-Yuan-Jing circuit intendent, supervised the taxation at Chen Guan from 1728 to 1730. Based on the revenues of these years, the formal quota for Chen Guan was increased to 12,500 taels in normal years and 13,400 taels in years with intercalary months, effective from 1732.[63]

The reported revenues of Chen Guan for the rest of the eighteenth century showed very interesting patterns that clearly indicated underreported revenues (figure 2.2). The first noticeable feature in the revenue series is the serrated shape that corresponds to different quotas in normal years and leap years. The tax revenues collected by Wang Rou in 1728, 1729, and 1730 were 9,370, 12,452, and 13,417 taels, respectively. When setting the formal quota based on the revenues of these three years, local officials reasoned that since 1730 was a leap year (in traditional Chinese calendars, seven leap months are inserted to every nineteen years), the higher revenue of that year represented the extra taxes collected in the intercalary month

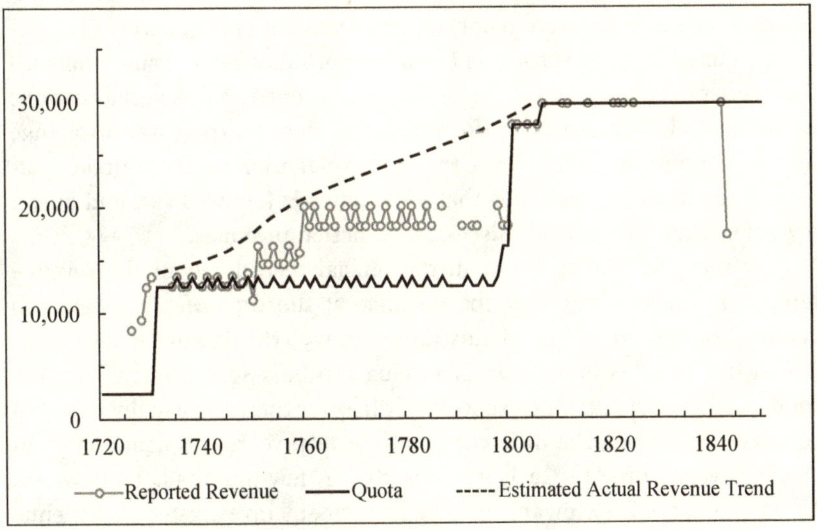

FIGURE 2.2 Customs revenue and quota of Chen Guan, 1720–1850, taels of silver. *Source*: memorials from FHA and GZD.

and should not be set as the quota. In the end, the middle level of 12,500 taels was set as the quota for normal years and 13,400 taels as the quota for leap years.[64] In fact, however, considering the revenues in 1725 were about 8,400 taels, as mentioned in Bulantai's memorial, the steady increase of revenues in these years most probably reflected the significant growth of timber trade thanks to the dredging of the Qingshui River around this time, which opened up merchants' access to the timber supply in the Miao areas.[65] The rise of timber taxes over these few years were likely a prelude to the secular trend of the trade boom fostered by improved transportation and the conclusion of military campaigns in the region. The mere fact that 1730 was a leap year does not explain the trend from 1725 to 1730. More important, the timber trade was a seasonal business, an extra month in different seasons was unlikely to increase tax revenues uniformly.

Therefore the serrated shape of the revenue series was more likely than not the result of intentional revenue concealment. During the Yongzheng and Qianlong eras, customs surpluses should be compared with those of the previous years. In the case of Chen Guan, revenues of normal years were compared with those of the previous normal years, likewise for leap years. If we separate the normal-year revenue series and the leap-year series, the two series remained extremely stable over the years, except for a few jumps, indicating that most officials just reported the previous comparable year's revenue, adding an extra couple of taels. The staircase fashion of revenue increases also supports this inference. In 1751 and 1760 substantial revenue increases were reported, up 18 percent and 23 percent respectively. Interestingly, in subsequent years, reported revenues caught up with the higher levels and then immediately flattened. Market fluctuations would not follow such neat, uniform patterns. Because there was no change in taxable items or specific rates, the only explanation for the staircase pattern of reported revenues was that most officials followed suit and only a few reform-minded officials disclosed the actual revenues.

Few remarks can be found in the official records about the revenue jumps in 1751 and 1760, but the instance at the turn of the nineteenth century could serve as a good illustration. In 1799 the Jiaqing emperor stipulated the "surplus quota" for Chen Guan to be 3,800 taels, making the total quota of 16,300 taels close to, but still lower than, the usually reported revenues. Moreover, the different quota for leap years was abandoned. In 1800 a revenue of 18,215 taels was reported. A few months later, however, Hunan governor Zu Zhiwang, who had personally investigated the revenue of Chen Guan, sent a memorial to the emperor that the actual amount of revenue accrued in 1800 was 27,711 taels.[66] This exact amount was reported for the following few years until 1807, when Hunan governor Jing An incorporated into reported revenues as an income item that had previously been retained in the customs—that is, the residual of the 10 percent meltage fee (*huohao*) after covering the customs' expenses. This move rendered the de facto quota to 29,692 taels—exactly the same amount that was reported for the next few decades.[67]

Customs data became scattered after the 1840s, but the midcentury depression and the later recovery in the 1870s and 1880s are noticeable. For reasons that are unclear, there is a steep drop in the early 1900s. However, with the general trend of the encroachment of domestic customs by Lijin tax stations in the second half of the nineteenth century, the revenue data after the 1850s would not be directly comparable to the eighteenth-century series. If we can agree that the spikes in the reported revenues represented true disclosures and link these points together, the dash line in figure 2.2 should give us an approximate idea of the trend of market expansion during the eighteenth century. The monetary value of timber passing through Chen Guan can be estimated at these time spots. After subtracting 3,600 taels of estimated salt taxes from the customs revenues in the eighteenth century, the remaining amount should be the approximate taxes from timber.[68] Based on Chen Guan's 3 percent tax rate, I estimate the value of timber passing through Chen Guan to be about 300,000 taels in 1730, 400,000 taels by 1750, and 800,000 taels by 1800. Since the taxes were assessed with a more or less prefixed "price" at the customs stations, this increase reflected mostly a growth in volume. With a rough price estimation, the Yuan River basin was contributing 15 to 30 percent to the overall Yangzi River timber trade by 1800.

All the pieces of information from the customs data now fall into place. Timber consumption in the lower Yangzi areas experienced substantial growth during the eighteenth century. The trend of growth slowed down at the turn of the nineteenth century, but the annual volume of timber that arrived at Nanjing still maintained at more than four million logs by conservative estimations. This level of consumption was sustained by continued supplies from Jiangxi, which by this point practiced plantation forestry extensively, as well as by expanding supplies from Hunan and Guizhou. Commercialized forestry also became entrenched in the southwest by the nineteenth century. The changing landscape of timber supply was intertwined with the reshuffling competition among different merchant groups and the emergence of new timber markets in the western regions. Despite its vast spread and diverse participants, the interregional timber trade system exhibited a high level of integration, which can be appreciated from the seasonal movement of people and goods, the pivotal signaling effect of

Nanjing and Hankou for the whole chain of supply, and the universal adoption of an industry-specific system of jargon and algorithms.

JARGON, MEASUREMENT, AND PRICING: LONGQUAN *MA*

The most distinctive cultural feature of the timber business, which was also prohibitively difficult for outsiders, was vocabulary associated with a peculiar system of timber measurement and pricing, known as Longquan *ma*, which was invented in the early seventeenth century. The geographic scope of its widespread use, covering the southern provinces of Zhejiang, Fujian, Jiangsu, Anhui, Jiangxi, Hunan, Hubei, Yunnan, Guizhou, and Guangxi, corresponded exactly to the span of the Yangzi system of timber trade. Longquan *ma* had been so entrenched into every aspect of the timber trade that the Republican government's measurement reform in 1930 met the strongest resistance from the timber business. It was not replaced by the metric system until 1954.[69]

Measurement and pricing are the basis for any commodity exchange. The everyday pricing of commodities such as grains and textiles has long been expressed in a linear function of a specific amount of money per unit-volume of goods—a certain amount of silver per *dan* of rice, or a certain number of coins per *pi* of cloth, and so forth—an expression that we tend to take for granted. Timber was somewhat different. The inventor of Longquan *ma* perceived the value of a timber log as not a linear but a convex function of its volume, meaning that its value grows at a faster speed as the volume grows. The intuition is that a big integral trunk is worth much more than two smaller ones that together make up the same volume. As the production of timber increasingly took the form of commercialized plantations instead of cutting old-growth forests, this transformation of production mode further enhanced people's perception of this convexity, since the trunk's growth in volume was now directly linked to incremental investments of waiting time and the associated time value of money. The appreciation of the nonlinear relationship between a timber log's value and its volume and, by extension, the appreciation of the monetary value of time is directly represented in the design of the Longquan *ma* system.

As the legend has it, the system was devised by Guo Mingzhu, the elder daughter of a Ming loyalist *jinshi* scholar and official Guo Weijing. The Guo family was native of the Longquan county (renamed Suichuan after 1914) in Jiangxi, an area famous for its fir planting and export. Miss Guo devised a set of tables that had nine categories of *ma* to represent different stages of timber growth. Each timber log can be assigned a *ma* by an algorithm based on its circumference at eye level and length.[70] This system came to be widely used during the Ming-Qing transition years. In the early Qianlong era two Huizhou timber merchants further fine-tuned the Longquan *ma* system to better suit practical needs.[71]

The idea is quite straightforward. The Longquan *ma* system introduced a measure that was a convex function of a trunk's circumference measured at eye level. The circumference of a log was measured at a 0.05-foot interval from 0.95 to 7 feet. Each of these 122 grades corresponded to a value called *liang*, an abstractive unit that shared the same character as "tael," the monetary unit for silver. To avoid confusion, hereafter, it will be referred to as Longquan *liang* (LQ *liang*) for clarity. The correspondence between each grade of circumference and its Longquan *liang* value was usually listed in a complete table for the timber merchants' reference, which, if expressed as a mathematical formula of Longquan *liang* as a function of circumference, looks like the equation below. A log with a circumference of 1.5 feet (dbh 0.48 foot), for example, would be 0.09 LQ *liang*; while a 2-foot log (dbh 0.64 foot) would be 0.28 LQ *liang*. Plotted in figure 2.3, the function looks very much exponential. Although the circumference goes up to 7 feet in the algorithm, in practice logs larger than 5 feet in circumference ("mast logs" by tribute timber categories) were so rare that their prices were usually negotiated individually in transactions.[72]

Longquan *liang* as a function of circumference

$$LQ\ liang = f(c) = \begin{cases} 0.02, c \le 0.95 \\ 0.03 + (c-1.0)\times 0.1, c \in [1.00, 1.40] \\ 0.07 + (c-1.4)\times 0.2, c \in [1.45, 1.50] \\ 0.09 + (c-1.5)\times 0.3, c \in [1.55, 1.80] \\ 0.18 + (c-1.8)\times 0.5, c \in [1.85, 2.50] \\ 0.53 + (c-2.5)\times 1.0, c \in [2.55, 3.00] \\ 1.03 + (c-3.0)\times 2.0, c \in [3.05, 3.50] \\ 2.03 + (c-3.5)\times 4.0, c \in [3.55, 4.00] \\ 4.03 + (c-4.0)\times 8.0, c \in [4.05, 4.50] \\ 8.03 + (c-4.5)\times 16.0, c \in [4.55, 5.00] \\ 17.63 + (c-5.0)\times 32.0, c \in [5.05, 5.50] \\ 32.03 + (c-5.5)\times 64.0, c \in [5.55, 6.00] \\ 64.03 + (c-6.0)\times 128.0, c \in [6.05, 6.50] \\ 128.03 + (c-6.5)\times 256.0, c \in [6.55, 7.00] \end{cases}$$

Where *c* is the circumference of a log measured at eye level by an interval of 0.05 foot.

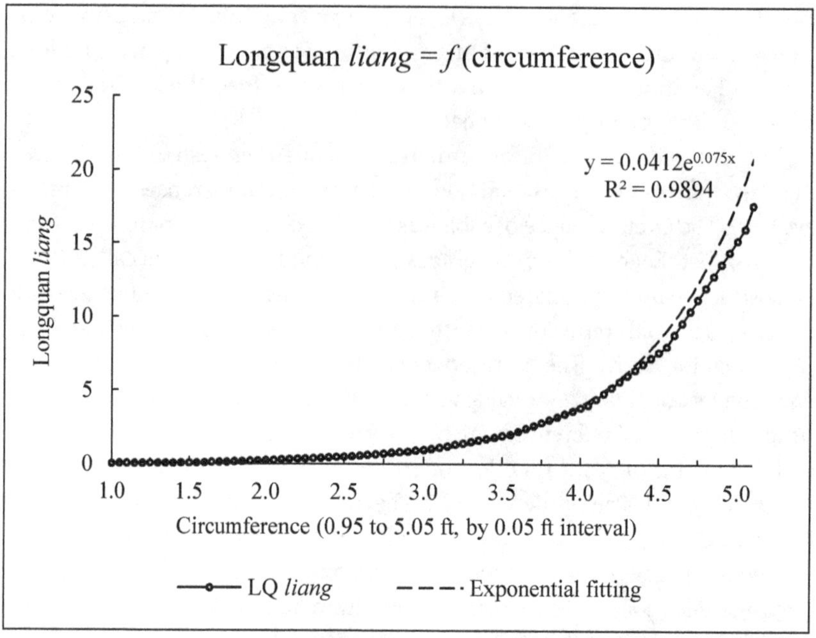

FIGURE 2.3 Longquan *liang* as a function of log circumference. *Source*: Tang Bingnan, "Hankou ce mucai zhi fa"; Wu Chuanjun, "Nanjing Shangxin He de mushi," note 14; and Wang Boxin, "Nanjing shi mucai maoyi jijia fangfa gaiyao," tables 1 and 2.

Once a log's circumference measurement is translated into a number in Longquan *liang*, it can be put into one of nine classes of *ma* (table 2.2). Each *ma* category is clearly named after the corresponding Longquan *liang* range. In the use of *liang* as either a substantive or an abstractive unit, 1 *qian* is 0.1 *liang*, and 1 *fen* is 0.1 *qian*. For example, 0.03 to 0.1 LQ *liang* (i.e., 3 to 10 *fen*) falls into the *fen ma* category, while 0.1 to 0.2 LQ *liang* (i.e., 1 to 2 *qian*) falls into *xiaoqian ma* ("small *qian*"). Similarly, *zhongqian ma* ("medium *qian*"), *daqian ma* ("big *qian*"), *qibajiu ma* ("seven-eight-nine *qian*"), *danliang ma* ("single *liang*"), and *shuangliang ma* ("double *liang*") are all intuitively named in such ways.

In timber transactions, the unit price for each class of *ma* differed. The market price was expressed as taels of silver per LQ *liang*. For example, consider a pole with a circumference of 2 feet (dbh 0.64 foot) and a length of 42 feet. These measures render it 0.28 LQ *liang*, which puts it in the category of *zhongqian ma*. If the current market price for *zhongqian ma* is 13 taels of silver per LQ *liang*, this log is worth 3.64 taels of silver (13 × 0.28).

TABLE 2.2 Categories of Longquan *ma*

[1] CATEGORIES OF *MA*	[2] LONGQUAN *LIANG*	[3] MINIMUM LENGTH (FEET)	[4] CIRCUMFERENCE (FEET)	[5] DIAMETER AT BREAST HEIGHT (FEET)	[6] AGE (YEARS)
zimu	0.02		≤ 0.95	≤ 0.3	≤ 15
fen ma	[0.03, 0.1)	32	1.00–1.50	0.3–0.5	15–35
xiaoqian ma	[0.1, 0.2)	36	1.55–1.80	0.5–0.6	35–45
zhongqian ma	[0.2, 0.4)	40	1.85–2.20	0.6–0.7	45–60
daqian ma	[0.4, 0.7)	46	2.25–2.65	0.7–0.85	60–80
qibajiu ma	[0.7, 1)	52	2.70–2.95	0.85–0.95	
danliang ma	[1, 2)	60	3.00–3.45	0.95–1.1	
shuangliang ma	[2, 4)	60	3.50–4.00	1.1–1.3	
fei ma	[4, 256]	60	4.05–7.00	1.3–2.3	

Source: Tang Bingnan, "Hankou ce mucai zhi fa"; Wu Chuanjun, "Nanjing Shangxin He de mushi," note 14; and Wang Boxin, "Nanjing shi mucai maoyi jijia fangfa gaiyao."
Notes: Column [1] shows the nine categories of Longquan *ma.* A log is put in one of the nine Longquan *ma* categories based on its Longquan *liang* (column [2]), which is computed from its circumference. Each *ma* category also comes with a required minimum length (column [3]). Column [4] shows the corresponding range of circumference for each *ma* category. Column [5] shows the corresponding diameter at breast height (dbh). Column [6] shows the age range of China fir for each *ma* category.

Each class of *ma* had a required minimum length. There were specific rules to discount Longquan *liang* to account for a shortage in length. Longquan *liang* could also be discounted if a log was slender toward the top, bent or irregularly shaped in other ways, with holes, scarred, or rot. Buyers and sellers bargained over these imperfections to adjust the amount of Longquan *liang* for the inventory in question. That is to say, in each transaction, price negotiations between the two parties centered on two fronts: the amount of Longquan *liang* and the unit price as expressed in taels of silver per LQ *liang.* While the bargaining on the unit price revolved around the prevailing market price, negotiations on Longquan *liang* largely relied on the neutral judgment and mediation of timber brokerages or other market intermediaries. The use of the Longquan *ma* system was an important reason that these intermediaries enjoyed their long-lasting prestige and wealth in this trade because their role as the neutral arbiter in the calculation and adjustment of Longquan *liang* could not be as easily bypassed.

The first section of a 1900 billing document between Wang Yisheng, a seller from Huizhou, and the Tong Fu Xing Timber Brokerage in Hangzhou illustrated the use of the Longquan *ma* system in pricing (table 2.3).[73] Wang Yisheng was selling 917 timber logs in total, of which 533 belonged to the category of *fen ma*, 11 *zhongqian ma*, and 373 *zi mu*. For each of the three *ma* categories, the total Longquan *liang* was reported in the bill, accompanied by information about any discount due to defects. For example, the 533 *fen ma* logs are in total 23.78 LQ *liang* (on average 0.04 LQ *liang* per pole), which was then subtracted by a discount of 0.09, leaving a total of 23.59 LQ *liang*. The market price for *fen ma* was 11.7 silver *yuan* per LQ *liang*, so the amount payable for this category was 276 *yuan* (23.59 × 11.7). Following this method, all the timber for sale was worth a total of 338.7 *yuan*. From this amount were subtracted the rent for the warehouse, the wages for hired porters, the "contributions" to commercial and charitable organizations and the local state as well as the cost of the Wang's accommodation. Moreover, the broker had previously extended an advance loan to Wang, which was paid out of the sales revenue as the "amount already paid to the seller previously" (129.4 *yuan*). In the end, Wang received 200.3 *yuan* of cash out of this transaction.

This bill exemplified how the Longquan *ma* system enabled a dramatic process of simplification. All the individual sizes and features of hundreds or even thousands of timber logs were rendered legible in a few *ma* categories, each measured by a single number in Longquan *liang*. Meanwhile, unlike a lump-sum volume measure like cubic meter, the *ma-liang* couplets preserved the convex relation between value and volume and enabled gradient pricing in recognition of the higher unit value of bigger trunks. This system defined the nomenclature and customs of the timber trade. Practitioners of this business rarely referred to the actual size and number of timber logs, instead of "100 logs of 1.6-foot-circumference fir," they would say "12 LQ *liang* of *xiaoqian ma* logs." In a typical discussion of market conditions for different kinds of timber, one merchant remarked: "*Fen ma* had the biggest market share . . . the timber wholesalers in Nanjing usually stocked *fen ma* for the bulk of their inventory, plus 30 percent *xiaoqian ma* and maybe 10 to 20 percent *zhongqian ma*. Lately, the demands for *fen ma* and *xiaoqian ma* are strong, but not so good for *zhongqian ma*. Every store has some *zhongqian ma* left after selling out the rest."[74]

TABLE 2.3 The billing of Tong Fu Xing Timber Brokerage to Wang Yisheng, 1900

[1]	[2]	[3]	[4]	[5]	[6]	[7]
CATEGORY	QUANTITY	TOTAL LONGQUAN *LIANG*	AVERAGE LONGQUAN *LIANG*	DISCOUNT	PRICE (*YUAN*/ LONGQUAN *LIANG*)	VALUE (*YUAN*)
Income						
fen ma	533	23.7825	0.04	0.1903	11.7	276.02
zhongqian ma	11	2.28	0.21	0.02	13	29.38
zi mu	373	3.73	0.01	0.03	9	33.3
					Total Income	**338.7**
Expense						
rent of dock and warehouse						−0.12
wages paid to laborers who measured the timber						−1.92
wages paid to laborers who tied the raft						−0.14
wages paid to laborers who transported the raft						−3.05
living expense of the seller						−1
contribution to the local militia						−0.07
contribution to the Association of Huizhou Timber Merchants						−2.2
contribution to Weishan Charity Hall						−0.51
contribution to Tongshan Charity Hall						−0.34
					Total Expense	**−9.35**
Amount already paid to the seller previously						−129.4
Amount received from the seller for living expense						0.35
					Total amount paid to the seller today	**200.3**

Source: Liu Boshan, *Huizhou wenshu di san ji*, vol. 7, p. 245.

Notes: Except for column [4], which is added by the author and equals column [3]/column [2], the information in all the other columns are included in the original document. Decimal points follow the original document. The monetary unit was silver *yuan*. It can be verified that column [7] = (column [3] − column [5]) × column [6].

When talking about the business scale of a firm, the power of a merchant group, or the size of a timber market, they often used Longquan *liang* as the measure of capacity, rather than the number of logs or the amount of monetary capital. The following comparison between the Jiangxi *bang* and the Linjiang *bang* illustrates this: "Jiangxi *bang*, even at its prime, only had twelve firms. But every firm sends rafts to Nanjing three to four times a year, each time amassing two to three thousand Longquan *liang*. . . . Linjiang *bang*'s rafts are only six hundred to seven hundred to a thousand-some Longquan *liang*, and even the bigger ones are not over two thousand Longquan *liang*. The individual scales of their firms are smaller than the Jiangxi *bang* firms, but they had many more firms, so their group is still more powerful than Jiangxi *bang*."[75] Without ample training and experience in this business, a newbie would have a hard time understanding even basic conversations among established merchants. No wonder when a licentiate-degree scholar switched to commerce and began to participate in the family business of timber brokerage, the first thing he needed to tackle was to memorize the Longquan *ma* tables.[76]

There was also a practice of discount closer to regions of supply in calculating Longquan *liang*. The benchmark unit prices for each category of *ma* were determined in large markets such as Hankou and Nanjing, while transportation cost along the river was partially reflected in a series of upriver markets by the discount of Longquan *liang*. For example, in the mountains of production, when measuring the circumference of a trunk, 1.1 feet was taken as 1 foot, and the circumference should be measured at 9 feet above the "water hole" (*shuiyan*), which were the holes drilled on the thick end of logs to tie them into rafts. The total Longquan *liang* so measured was then discounted by taking 8 percent off. Once the timber was transported to Jinping, a local Miao market town, 1.07 feet was taken as 1 foot, the circumference was measured at 8 feet above the water hole, and the overall 8 percent discount stayed the same. By Changde, 1 foot was 1 foot, the circumference was measured at 5 feet above the water hole, and the overall discount decreased to 5 percent. Further down the river, the measurement methods would stay the same as in Changde, while the rate of discount continued to decrease, until it was only 1 percent in Hankou and 0.5 percent in Nanjing.[77]

This discount system signifies the high level of integration of the timber market along the Yangzi River and the extent to which southwestern timber was oriented toward the lower Yangzi markets. The real price differences along the supply chain, which reflected the cost of transportation among other things, were realized through the two factors: different unit prices as well as the discounts of Longquan *liang* toward sources of production. Economic historians have to recognize that observed differences in the quotes of unit market prices per se could not reflect the full extent of real price differences without considering the discounts of Longquan *liang*.

CONCLUSION

Overall timber consumption in the lower Yangzi area and, to a lesser extent, per capita consumption, experienced significant growth during the eighteenth century. Although the impetus of market demand slackened in the first half of the nineteenth century, the incorporation of frontier forests into the mass timber market remained steady. In the second half of the eighteenth century, Hunan and Jiangxi had become the two most important sources of timber for Jiangnan, with the relative importance of Hunan continuing to grow throughout the nineteenth century. It is clear that the historical developments of marketplaces and merchant groups correlated with the general changes in the sources of timber supply. During the seventeenth and eighteenth centuries, successful timber merchants based in Nanjing, particularly the Huizhou and Jiangxi groups, marched upstream the Yangzi River toward the southwest in search of new supplies of timber. With the increasing incorporation of Hunan and Guizhou into the interregional timber trade, Hankou rose to be the largest timber market in the middle Yangzi area in the nineteenth century.

Accompanying this process, merchant groups from Hunan and Hubei first established their foothold in the timber trade as the local agents of the eastern *bangs* and gradually succeeded in expanding their influence eastward, eventually becoming powerful players in the lower Yangzi markets. Following the traveling merchants, the Longquan *ma* system of measurement and pricing, which was first adopted in Jiangxi, spread to broader regions in southern China and set the standard lingo for this interregional business. The capacity of the Yangzi timber trade system developed to an unprecedented level by the 1780s, pumping more than six million poles to Nanjing annually. How this level of consumption was sustained by forestry practices is the subject of the next chapter.

CHAPTER THREE

Sustaining the Resources

WHAT factors allowed forest management in China to take place historically despite general conditions of deforestation?[1] Even before large numbers of local genealogies and contractual documents were available for researchers, scattered evidence pointed to a set of plausible conditions necessary for durable plantation. At the center of these necessary, though not sufficient, conditions are market demand for forest products and the capacity to enforce boundaries on access to the resources.[2] Although excessive demand for forest resources has always been blamed as a major factor leading to the exhaustion of natural forests, in China and elsewhere, the market's demand for an increasingly scarce resource could also translate into considerable profit to be made from managed forests. This in turn could motivate long-term investment.[3] Historically in the United States, for example, big timber companies have found profits from replanting clear-cuts since around the 1920s, after indiscriminate cutting had prevailed throughout the late nineteenth century. In China, as early as the twelfth century, the development of plantation forests in the Southern Song dynasty was interlinked with the growing urban markets, which left a market-oriented legacy for forest management in southern China.[4] During Ming-Qing times, in the mountainous areas connected to Jingdezhen, wealthy lineages and entrepreneurs cultivated fuelwood to supply the imperial kilns.[5] Planting of fir and camphor was practiced in Fujian to supply the well-established timber marketing structure in the Min River system.[6]

While market demands and regulated access were motivating forest management, a big obstacle frustrated the long-term practicality of private endeavors at tree cultivation. Even when lured by the potential profit from a thriving market, small households could be easily put off by several risks involved in this endeavor. Setting aside potential risks of fire, theft, and harvest failures, the time required for tree growth was a severe challenge.[7] Requiring at least thirty years before maturing enough as useful timber, "the profit from fir is thick but very delayed."[8] Timber cultivation could not have become so widely practiced if the liquidity problem associated with the long-term nature of tree growth was not solved. Even in China's recently acclaimed Returning Farmland to Forest program, which was initiated by the State Council in 1999 and has since received substantial government subsidies, the waiting period before timber harvest remains a central issue of concern among the local households that demands careful calibrations in policy to get people to plant trees.[9] What sorts of institutional solutions, either formal or customary, were in place in the private, rural, and small household–based economy of the Qing period to make long-term tree cultivation plausible, profitable, and sustainable? This was a classical economic problem of financing long-term investments under capital constraint.

The answer lies in the ownership and tenancy structures of mountain lands. The development of active transactions around entitlements to mountain landholdings and tenancy rights, which were increasingly divided into shareholdings that were independently tradable before the standing crop of trees was harvested, enabled investors to deal with the inherent risk in the timber crop's long duration of growth and to transform expected future proceeds into cash flows to match a household's consumption pattern. A common set of shareholding and tenure practices existed in southern China forestry despite varying local conditions: private (instead of state) ownership of mountain lands; rotational planting of timber trees for sale in the market; claims of profits from timberlands based on shares; construction of divisible and tradable shares based on landownership and labor input; and transfers of shares using written contracts. These similarities, especially the remarkable resemblance in the specific terms used in the written contracts, point to possible transfers of silvicultural and managerial know-how associated with the massive westward migration during the late imperial period. However, additional studies are required to pin down the mechanisms of such transfers.[10]

The broader implications of these findings can be appreciated from two perspectives. The first is how private entrepreneurs in early modern societies financed long-term investments. Tree planting had the dual characteristics of agricultural cultivation and commercial enterprise. As a cultivation industry relying largely on the two factors of labor and land input, it drew comfortably from the set of rhetoric, concepts, and contractual instruments developed from grain production: land tenure, specification of boundaries, witness of mediators, and contract templates for the transfer of various kinds of rights defined on the land.[11] However, these similarities disguised some important differences in their economic nature—namely, the efficient scale and term of production. Take, for example, wet-field rice cultivation, from which the most complex contractual land-tenure system arose. Cultivators could expect at least one, or even two or three, harvests per year. The efficient unit of production was small. In the late imperial period the high productivity of rice production was achieved precisely through labor-intensive cultivation on finely divided rice paddies.[12]

Tree cultivation was different. Not only was harvest a couple of decades in the future, but it also required a certain level of scale. Physical division of tree plantations could not go too far, making it difficult and counterproductive for small cultivators to hold multiple tiny plots of different-aged trees. In these aspects, tree cultivation shared a closer resemblance to commercial enterprises: investment was long-term, and shareholding was invented to enable flexible adjustment of ownership and avoid physical divisions. Instead of seeing agriculture and commerce as separate spheres of expertise, we need to view the tree-planting industry through a set of contractual shareholding practices that were adapted to deal with different kinds of long-term investments requiring a certain level of economy of scale. This perspective helps us understand how the Chinese met investment demands through institutions of their own design.

Another question is how reforestation practices in southern China compared with those in other regions of the world. From the existing literature, one gets the impression that to the extent that purposeful and effective forest management existed in the premodern period, the state played an important role. To deal with the perceived threats of timber shortages and fuel crises between the fourteenth and eighteenth centuries, for example, the Venetian Republic acquired mainland forest holdings and developed specialized bureaucracies to manage the most useful forests as state assets.[13] In early modern East Asia the overwhelmingly privatized forestland in China ran contrary to the experience of both Japan and Korea, where the state exerted much heavier control over the access to forests.[14] In response to the severe timber shortage that occurred as a result of nationwide population growth and a building boom from 1570 to 1670, the Tokugawa government issued and enforced a series of edicts to regulate the management, distribution, and consumption of timber. Eighteenth-century Japan saw the development of plantation forestry, where the state played a direct role either by organizing the labor force in government afforestation projects or rewarding (or compelling) entrepreneurial endeavors.[15]

By contrast, the general trend in late imperial Chinese forestry was privatization. It seems that the greatest state interventions into direct forest management occurred during the last decades of the Northern Song at the turn of the twelfth century. Even then, the state's presence was limited and abortive. By the mid-1400s, state forest programs were virtually nonexistent and registration of private forests was far from complete. The state's retreat from direct forest management paralleled its increasing laissez-faire management of the private trade of timber logs. The privatization of forestlands and the privatization of timber distribution went hand in hand. In the Old South, for instance, lineages gradually took hold of extensive forestlands and invested heavily in plantation forestry by the fifteenth and sixteenth centuries.[16] In the southwest, similar practices of private plantation forestry developed during the eighteenth and nineteenth centuries despite the lack of high-order lineages. Although the Qing dynasty maintained reserves of forests under direct state control in Manchuria for both strategic and symbolic reasons, privately managed forests and, to a lesser extent, community commons were the dominant forms in much of China proper.[17] Knowledge of effective forest management carried out in a private context enriches our understanding of the repertoire of successful early modern practices and challenges us to go beyond the abstract debate on the merits of state versus private ownership to examine the specific incentives provided by a particular property rights framework.

FOREST PROPERTY IN LATE IMPERIAL CHINA

A variety of property right regimes on forestlands existed in late imperial China. While the taxonomy of property rights in modern economics differentiates between private, communal, public (state-owned), and open-access as different kinds of rights, directly applying such concepts to the study of forestlands in late imperial China is both challenging and problematic. Some past scholarship has equated certain Chinese terms to modern economic concepts without much empirical basis (except for what the literary meanings of the words might suggest). It is of paramount importance to clarify the corresponding relationships between several Chinese designations of forestland ownership commonly seen in late imperial documents and Western property right concepts that are widely used by social scientists. Particular fallacies are the often-assumed equivalence between the late imperial *gongshan* ("public" mountains) and the modern concept of common property, and between the late imperial *guanshan* ("state" mountains) and the modern concept of state property. Establishing a set of consistent conceptualizations is the basis for making meaningful comparisons between studies of different regions and periods.

According to classical philosophical texts, the emperor owned All Under Heaven, including all the lands and the people residing upon them. In practice, however, this "ownership" was more a claim of universal sovereignty than a claim of property in the economic sense. The state's control over land allocations had already evaporated by the Tang-Song transition, and landownership had become thoroughly privatized.[18] In late imperial China, when people established suitable enterprises and made the land productive, the ownership was transferred to the people as private properties that were enforceable by the state—hence the term "civilian land" (*mindi*). Often this creation of private property was made explicit through the action of registering the land for taxation.

But even without tax registration, land property was recognized and protected by the state, which could be proved with a wide variety of evidence. Of course, the state might intervene by promoting land claiming in some areas with favorable policies and forbidding it in other places. Once private ownership had been established through labor and capital investment on the land, the properties could be utilized, transferred, mortgaged, and inherited pretty much in the same way that modern private property works, often evidenced by written contracts. For forested mountains, for example, when people—whether individual households, lineages, or village communities—imposed boundaries of access, regulated the use of the resources, or planted vegetations, their ownership was automatically established, unless it was in an area where private claims had been explicitly forbidden. With respect to the state, a village common and a privately held forest are both "civilian lands" per the Chinese nomenclature, but these are two systems with different incentives for cutting and planting.

Meanwhile, all the lands that had not been explicitly and exclusively claimed by specific groups of people were by default "owned" by the state. The term *guanshan* signified that the state held the right to dispose of the mountain however it saw fit, whether the decision was to exert active ownership, encourage privatization, or keep it an open-access resource that anyone could exploit. "Active" state ownership here refers to cases where the state expressly marked certain regions as off-limits to any private or public use (*fengjin*); directly managed the types, amounts, and methods of resource extraction; or regulated access to the forests through a licensing system. The most representative examples of active state management during the Qing were the forests surrounding the imperial mausoleums in Zhili, the Imperial Reserve for the emperors' autumn hunts around Chengde, and the restricted foraging in Manchurian forests.[19] In addition, some bandit hideouts in southern China were marked as forbidden for entry.[20] There were also sporadic cases where the state attempted to regulate or license logging activities in *guanshan* in southern China.[21] In some *guanshan*, entry was forbidden to protect the local geomancy.[22] There were even cases where officials and local gentry used their personal funds to purchase mountain tracts that were considered important for the locale's geomancy out of private hands and donated the mountain to be designated as enclosed *guanshan*.[23]

In all these cases, *guanshan* could be interpreted as equivalent to the modern conception of "state-owned forests"—that is, the state *acted* as the owner of the forests. This is not to say that the state's attempts of enclosure and management were always successful, however. Illegal reclamation and logging often haunted such sites, but the state's intention differentiated these cases from others. The second type of *guanshan* was those in the process of being privatized, regardless of how long or short the process might be. Although no private party currently claimed the land, the state ultimately saw its status of *guanshan* as provisional and awaited, often encouraged, private reclamation.[24] This was particularly applicable in the little-settled peripheries. The least fertile land that had no easy access to irrigation was often left unclaimed, thus remaining *guan* properties.[25]

In official documents such *guanshan* was often emphasized for its dual characteristics of being *huangdi* (wasteland; uncultivated land) and "without owners"—sometimes with the additional note that no agricultural taxes were being collected there.[26] The specific designation of these lands as *guanshan* denoted that there was no existing private ownership—none that was legitimately recognized by the state anyway—thus clearing the way for potential settlers. In Heping County of eastern Guangdong, for example, the magistrate employed this connotation of *guanshan*. The proclamation of these mountains as *guanshan* delegitimized any customary claims as illegal and cleared the ground for new owners:

> There are plenty of arable areas in the mountains, which have been scarcely cultivated to date. The old customs of this county were such that the owners of the agricultural lowlands extended control to the mountains nearby. Even when someone else was interested in cultivating the mountains, the residents nearby either claimed that the mountains had belonged to their ancestors or demanded tribute from the potential settlers. The poor people were afraid of causing disputes, and nobody dared to

> make a move. Having examined the tax and corvee registers, I know that these are all *guanshan*. Therefore it should be broadly proclaimed to the people that nobody should obstruct reclamation. Able cultivators are free to make profits from growing taros, beans, pine, fir, tea, and tung. Poor people can rely on them for a living.[27]

The third and most common situation seemed to be cases where the state intentionally kept *guanshan* open to public access and forbade any private party's attempt at reclamation and privatization.[28] "Trees growing on *guanshan*, if not explicitly banned by the local officials, are by default open to logging by anyone."[29] Aside from being an open source for firewood, timber, mushrooms, and other mountain products, such *guanshan* also served the important function of providing burial grounds for the poor.[30] Local philanthropic organizations, when providing burial services to the homeless, could also use *guanshan*.[31] In these cases translating *guanshan* into "state-owned forests" would be a misleading rendition. Rather, it is more appropriate to understand such *guanshan* as "open-access forests." Open-access is, in essence, nonproperty: it does not refer to any form of property but to its absence. Open-access is an appropriate method for resource management only when we need not manage resources at all—that is, when demand is too low to make the effort worthwhile. As demands intensify, open-access resources are often overexploited, leading to "the tragedy of the commons."[32]

Overexploitation was indeed an acute problem for such open-access *guanshan*. For example, Funing prefect Li Ba discussed the problem of unrestricted logging in open-access *guanshan* in Fujian in the 1760s. He suggested privatization as a solution:

> Because many mountains in Fujian are *guanshan*, there are no restrictions of logging. Whenever some branches and twigs grow out, they are immediately cut off. Even the roots are sometimes dug out as firewood for cooking. Without proper regeneration, the mountains become barren. As for privately owned mountains, industrious owners all plant pine, fir, bamboo, tung, and other trees, making a big profit. Slothful owners, only seeing the present and making no long-term plans, cannot wait to use their axes whenever some small trees appear on their mountains; as a result, good timber do not grow, only weeds flourish. Sometimes, on the same mountain, one area is lovely forested, while another

> area is lamentably wasted. Such are the divergent results of diligence and laziness, the mountains did not become bleak themselves. I propose banning premature cutting and developing profits from the barren mountains. Allow people to reclaim *guanshan* as private lands, collecting firewood on their own will and planting trees and bamboos. Direct mountain landowners to widely plant trees and ban excessive cutting. This way, regeneration will prosper, and trees will grow into forests in some years. Timber will be inexhaustible. This is a way to provide for the people.[33]

While open-access *guanshan* were overcut to bleakness, industrious private owners planted trees on their lands to make a profit from timber and other products. A 1757 memorial of Wu Pengnan, also a native of Fujian, made similar observations that *guanshan* were more susceptible to overexploitation and tree planting was only taking place on private properties.[34] This situation was not Fujian-specific but was generally true in southern China. To the extent plantation forestry was practiced, it was almost exclusively on privately owned mountains.

Private property, in the broad sense of being the counterpart of state ownership, could take several different forms. The most straightforward form was when a household owned the whole property of a forested land, with the head of the household having the ultimate authority to make dispositions of the property and all the other family members under a "common budget" system to benefit economically from this property.[35] This was the prototype and building block of other more complex private-ownership regimes. Tenancy would add a little complexity to this simplest form as arrangements would be made between the landowner and the tenant planter about how to divide the products. Furthermore, the tenant's right to use the land or his claim to the products might be formalized as a form of transferrable rights through contracts. In those situations the whole property of the land could be tranched into ownership of the legal title and ownership of usufruct right.

The discussion above pertains to a single household owning a piece of clearly bounded land, at least the legal title of it. A variation to this single-owner system was that, instead of a household, the owner could be a corporate-like entity, such as a religious temple, a lineage trust, an investment trust (*hui*), a school, a philanthropic organization, a merchant association, and so forth.[36] Although there was no formal concept of a "legal person" in China's law code, it is useful to understand these entities as something of the sort in this context. Indeed, examinations of land disputes in court have revealed that Qing magistrates regarded partnerships and other collective entities that made property claims as a single entity rather than discrete individuals.[37] While the entity itself might consist of multiple shareholders, investors, or beneficiaries, it was the corporate-like whole that was the singular owner of the mountain land. And whatever decision-making mechanism existed for the entity—whether a trusted manager, a management board, or a voting system—would have the authority to make dispositions of the property.

Apart from a single-owner regime, there could be multiple owners on one piece of forestland. "One piece" here refers to the smallest spatial unit that could not be further divided *physically* based on its ownership structure. In other words, the owners were not partitioned to mutually exclusive subunits of the land. Multi-ownership could take two different forms. The first possibility was co-ownership based on shareholding. This was still within the realm of "private ownership" as the term is usually understood today, because each owner's entitlement to the benefit generated by this property was clearly defined by the percentage of his shareholding. Although the land could not be divided physically among the owners, its profit was divided virtually by shares. One's shares could be held, divided, inherited, mortgaged, and transferred as a private financial asset.

The second possibility of multi-owner regimes was collectivized ownership, which was beyond the realm of "private" ownership and more akin to how we understand "commons" or common-property regimes. The collectivized ownership could not be divided into any independently transferrable entitlements to property, products, or profits, whether in physical forms or shares. Take a village's common forest, for example. All the users, in this case the residents of the village, shared the rights and responsibilities to the communal forests, but this right of access could not be transferred to an outsider for profit. Outsiders were by default denied access, although it could be granted on a case-to-case basis or through some sort of application process. Some communities established an organization for collective decision-making on how to use the forest resources, which could be an independent institution or embedded under existing village institutions. In such cases, the users' behaviors were governed by written community regulations that stipulated the rules of rational utilization and instituted fines or other forms of punishments on offenders to maintain a sustainable level of yield for the community.[38] Such communal management endeavors are an issue of interest in the general literature on "collective action" in the management of common-pool resources.[39] When the regulations of the commons were weak or nonexistent, they became more like open-access forests.

The Chinese term *gongshan* could refer to either community commons or to private shareholding co-ownerships when the number of stakeholders was large, which is not surprising since the line between the two in practice can be fuzzy. The equation of *gongshan* to forest commons has often been assumed in the literature—after all, *gong* literally means "public." The neglect of its divergent meanings is understandable because when the term appeared in legal documents, memorials, or local gazetteers, it was often used to convey a loose sense that *many people had a stake*, while its exact denotation was usually left unspecified. It is only through a close examination of the term's usage in timberland contracts as well as in village and lineage regulations that the different meanings of *gongshan* can be revealed.

The same is true for another thorny term, *zushan* (族山, lit. "lineage mountains"; or 祖山, lit. "ancestral mountains"), which could refer to three different situations. First, the term could refer to a lineage "common" where only the members of the lineage could log, forage, or bury their dead. Lineage commons and village commons were alike—indeed, many villages in southern China were single-lineage villages. There might be a lineage-instituted regulation governing the time of access, the prohibited areas (usually for geomancy concerns), the kinds of products available for free foraging, maybe a quota system for some products, and other restrictions.[40] Second, the term *zushan* could refer to a mountain owned by an incorporated lineage trust, the profit generated from which was not to be divided among the kinsmen but retained in the lineage trust for reinvestment or to fund collective enterprises such as ancestral sacrifices, philanthropic schools, widow support, and so forth. These incorporated lineage estates might also use lineage regulations to forbid kinsmen from trespassing and stealing. There was indeed some ambiguity between a lineage common and an incorporated lineage property. For example, a lineage trust might own all the timber trees growing on a mountain but allow members of the lineage to gather small branches for firewood, forage for mushrooms and herbs, and so forth.

Third, the term *zushan* could refer to a mountain whose co-owning shareholders were exclusively (or mostly) members of the same lineage, who divided the profit according to each household's holding of shares. The monopoly or predominance of a single surname in the shareholding structure might be a result of coincidence—for instance, maybe this lineage dominated the local population. It could also be a result of intentional restrictions, such as a clause that kinsmen should have a first right of purchase or prohibitions against selling the shares to another surname. In these cases, although the right of alienating the property was not absolute, it was still much more appropriate to think of the property as privately owned through shareholdings than as a lineage-owned property. Although it was well understood among the shareholders that the mountain was not the lineage's property, but private properties defined by shareholding, the term *zushan* was often used toward outsiders who infringed upon the property—usually members of another competing lineage, especially in lawsuits.

It is not surprising that sometimes the same piece of forested mountain property was labeled as both *guanshan* and *gongshan*, or as both *gongshan* and *zushan*, since the Chinese terms overlap in meaning (table 3.1). In legal documents, the terms *guanshan* and *gongshan* could both be used to emphasize the non-exclusive nature of a forest, which all the disputing parties in a lawsuit were entitled to use. For example, in 1832 two single-surname villages, the Fengs and the Luos, disputed over a forest located in between their villages. Although the forest had always been open to the residents of both villages, the Fengs attempted to claim it as an ancestral land to keep the Luos out, leading to a violent dispute involving manslaughter. While the details of the manslaughter case are not of interest here, the forest in question was referred to as both a *guanshan* and a *gongshan* in

TABLE 3.1 Categories of forested mountains

CHINESE TERMS	APPLICABLE SITUATIONS
guanshan (lit. "state mountains")	state-owned mountains unclaimed land available for privatization open-access forests
gongshan (lit. "public mountains")	community commons open-access forests private shareholding structures with many shareholders
zushan (lit. "ancestral/ lineage mountains")	lineage commons property owned by an incorporated lineage trust private shareholding structures when all or most of the shareholders were members of the same lineage

Source: Author's compilation.

different passages of the Ministry of Justice's critique with the same connotation that both surnames should have equal access.[41]

Similarly, the terms *gongshan* and *zushan* overlap in their meanings as forest commons as well as private shareholding co-ownerships. Such expressions as "the *gongshan* of the Chen surname" (*Chen xing gongshan*) could refer to a forest common that was open only to the members of the Chen lineage for firewood gathering and burials.[42] In addition, a forested mountain co-owned by many members of the same lineage based on private shareholdings could be called a *gongshan*, emphasizing the large number of shareholders; it could also be called a *zushan*, emphasizing the common surname of the shareholders. However, I do not interpret such overlaps in meaning as ambiguity in property rights, although they do defy the absoluteness of private property in the idealized Lockean sense, which was not borne out even in the early modern English reality and I do not think should be the single golden standard for property. When read in context, invokers of this nomenclature usually conveyed very clearly the specific rights they were trying to claim. These categories are illustrated with substantive examples below.

THE LOWER QINGSHUI VALLEY IN SOUTHEASTERN GUIZHOU

Timber produced in southwestern China, especially in Guizhou and Hunan, became increasingly important in meeting the burgeoning demand in the lower Yangzi region since the eighteenth century. The prosperous timber trade gradually exhausted the natural forests. By the second quarter of the nineteenth century, virgin forests had disappeared in the easily accessible areas of the Yuan River basin.[43] But deforestation was not the whole story. Potential profits from timber trade motivated market-oriented tree plantations after the natural vegetation was depleted. The Hunan-Guizhou border area, particularly the valleys of the Qingshui River, continues to be an important source of timber even today thanks to the widely practiced tree planting.[44] A 1942 investigation of the plantation forestry in this area reported that the annual output of small-sized timber (between 1 to 2.2 feet in circumference; diameter at breast height 0.3–0.7 foot) was up to 300,000 poles, out of a total stock of 20 million; the annual output of timber bigger than that size was about 120,000 poles, out of a total stock of 6.4 million.[45]

The main sources examined hereafter come from the Qingshui River valley in southeastern Guizhou (part of the Yuan River basin), where tree planting and the tenancy of mountain land came into common practice by the mid-eighteenth century. The local custom of tree planting and the use of Chinese-style contracts to transact property rights over timberlands can be seen in a large number of documents that have been preserved in the lower Qingshui valley communities. Known collectively as the "Qingshui River documents" (*Qingshui Jiang wenshu*), they have become increasingly accessible in recent years thanks to several extensive compilation and publication projects. The documents included in my sample center on the two villages of Wendou and Ping'ao at the county border of Jinping and Tianzhu. Dating from the mid-eighteenth to the early twentieth century, these documents feature mostly contracts of timberland transactions, tenancy contracts, and agreements on the divisions of shares and profits. Other materials include household division agreements, copies of court cases, village compacts, records of the resolution of disputes, and so forth.[46]

The lower Qingshui area was mostly inhabited by the Miao people. Based on local steles, the elite among them seemed to have become quite familiar with the Chinese administration by the seventeenth century. For the purposes of this study, the most important transformation in the local society was the adoption of Chinese-style contracts in the tree-planting industry. A Qing-era genealogy traced the practice of fir planting to the late Ming.[47] Tree planting had already become commonly practiced in the lower Qingshui area by the mid-eighteenth century. This activity seems to have spread from the lower Qingshui communities to the middle and upper ranges of the river valley. By the late eighteenth century, the "Black Miao" residents in the subprefecture of Qingjiang, which was among the least acculturated regions in the southeastern Guizhou frontier, had begun to emulate the lower Qingshui communities' investment in tree planting for sale in the market.[48]

A Qianlong-era gazetteer of Qingjiang stated: "Previously, the Miao people did not make profit from pine and fir. The trees in the mountains were left to grow on their own, even their names were not known. Nowadays pine and fir are being widely planted, the lands look lush and prosperous. The area is close to river transportation. Every year, timber is cut down and rafted to flow down the river to be sold in Hongjiang, Changde, and other places. People's livelihood improves increasingly."[49] Some officials actively promoted the planting of timber and fruit trees among the Miao.[50] As for the use of Chinese-style contracts, observations in the 1750s stated that even the more acculturated Miao seldom used written contracts.[51] By the late eighteenth century, contracts had become routinely produced by the Miao people in the lower Qingshui communities with concepts and styles similar to those found in other parts of China. The first half of the nineteenth century saw the rapid development of contracted transactions of ownership and tenancy rights on timberlands.

TREE PLANTING AND ITS CHALLENGES

The silvicultural technologies used in the cultivation of China fir had become quite mature by the late imperial period. People practiced intercropping during the first few years of the trees' growth to generate additional annual or perennial income. After the tree canopy closed up, however, intercropping was no longer a viable option. Therefore, despite these and other silvicultural innovations that improved efficiency, the unfavorable temporal structure of the payoff from tree cultivation remained a serious challenge that could not be resolved by cultivation technology alone but called for institutional innovations.

The technology of fir planting was quite flexible. China fir sprouts readily from its stump after cutting or a fire, which makes propagation relatively easy. It could be established from seed propagation, coppicing, and sprouts cut from the stump.[52] According to sporadic evidence from agricultural handbooks published at different times, the method of planting a cutting using offshoots seemed to be the mainstream practice in China from the thirteenth to the sixteenth centuries; thereafter, sprouts cut from the stumps seemed to have replaced offshoots because of their faster growth and higher success rates.[53] The seventeenth-century encyclopedia of agronomy *The Complete Book of Agricultural Administration* explains in detail the procedure of planting fir from sprouts cut from stumps as seen in southern Anhui. The handbook instructs readers to first plough the land and plant sesame for a year or more to prepare the site. Then, at the beginning of the second month, cut fresh spouts from the stumps one foot and one or two inches in length, plant them to half their lengths, and firmly press the soil down. Weed and hoe every year; or conduct intercropping by planting millet in the summer and wheat in the winter.[54] Another method used in the Qingshui River area was seed propagation. Seeds are collected in September from thriving trees and planted in a seedbed. The next June, when the seedlings have reached about one meter, they should be transplanted in rows. Compared to planting a cutting, the seed-propagation method is more labor-consuming, but the resulting trees are of higher quality and produce better sprouts after cutting. In practice, the two methods were often rotated.[55]

During the early years, crops with differing tolerance to shade were interplanted to suit the changing levels of light as the tree canopy gradually closed overhead. Annual crops included wheat, millet, maize, sweet potatoes, and cassava. Sometimes annual crops were followed by perennials, commonly oil-bearing trees such as tung tree (*Aleurites fordii* Hemsl. and *Aleurites montana* Wils.) and tea tree (*Camellia oleosa*), which could be harvested for several years. The tree canopy closes after three to five years, preventing further agricultural use; the land would then be used solely for the timber crop until the cycle was repeated following the timber harvest.[56] This kind of successional intercropping system of forest management, known as "Taungya" farming and previously thought to have originated in Burma during the British colonial period, has been used for at least three centuries in China by the Han population and other ethnic minorities.[57] The traditional practice of intercropping is still promoted as an economically productive and ecologically viable system in the modern silviculture of China fir.[58]

Despite the annual products generated by the intercropping system in the first few years, once the canopy closed up, there was a long wait of decades with hardly any income from the land before the timber crop could be harvested for sale. Compared to other timber trees, China fir is very fast-growing, which contributes to its overwhelming popularity among cultivators. But it still requires a minimum of thirty years to attain the size of general-purpose timber. As recent studies in forestry science have shown, a rotation period of more than thirty years in fir plantations could improve soil properties (especially enzyme activities and microbial community diversity), while shortening rotation periods threaten to reduce soil fertility and yield.[59] Maintaining the customary thirty-year rotation was one essential factor in sustaining long-term yields. However, in the premodern household-based rural economy, the long duration of growth meant serious difficulty in transforming expected future profits into ready cash to meet spikes in a household's consumption needs. If the planting of a few trees was meant to be a source of supplementary income or insurance in addition to a household's regular income from agriculture, the timing could be carefully planned in anticipation of significant expenses for marriages and funerals. For example, records from as early as the thirteenth century speak of the practice in southern Anhui where people would plant a few fir trees upon the birth of a child, so that the revenue could be realized in time to pay for his or her marriage expenses.[60] However, if tree planting was to be the mainstay of the household economy, as was the case in the lower Qingshui area, the challenge of its long rotation period had to be solved effectively.

To deal with the unfavorable temporal structure of the payoff from tree cultivation, an individual timberland owner could plant mixed-age stands of trees on his own plot to secure a more regular and reliable income. This way, the scale of production has to be small. Another option would be if there was an active market to trade one's claims on the future revenue at any time during the growth of the tree crop. Individuals could diversify their holdings by acquiring shares on a number of plots planted with different-aged trees and easily cash out by selling off their shares. Diversified investment in securitized shares of timberlands was indeed the mainstream strategy adopted in the lower Qingshui valley. This system, resembling a prototype of a forward-contract market, provided more flexibility and enabled an economy of scale in the production of timber, especially at the moment of felling.

CATEGORIES OF MOUNTAIN LAND TRANSACTIONS

The creation, division, and transfer of shares on growing forests were through written contracts. The style and clauses of the timberland contracts used in the lower Qingshui area are examined here. These contracts contain the familiar format, language, clauses, and special provisions that were commonly used in transactions of agricultural land all over China, which had been developed over many centuries.[61] These familiar components, however, were innovatively assembled to fit the economic rationale of timber planting and enabled the definition and transfer of timber shares.

Contracts concerning the forested mountains can be roughly put into three categories: (1) formation of tenancy relations between landowners and planters; (2) sales of rights connected to a mountain plot property; and (3) agreements among co-owners. Each category can be further divided into subcategories (table 3.2). Although the subcategories of tenancy contracts and co-owner's agreements corresponded with the titles of the documents, the further division of the sale contracts required breaking down the very general terms used in the contracts' titles such as "sale of mountain land" (*mai shanchang*), "sale of timber trees" (*mai mu*), and "sale of mountain land and fir trees" (*mai shanchang shanmu*) with the more detailed information specified in the body part of the contracts. This provides a clearer appreciation of the variety of rights being transacted. See appendix C for a detailed description of the methodology

TABLE 3.2 Categories of timberland contracts

CATEGORIES		DESCRIPTION	NUMBER OF DOCUMENTS	
[1] Tenancy relations				
T	Tenancy contract	• Establish tenancy relations between landowners and planters, usually specify each party's share in the future income from sales, which is to be reconfirmed with (D).	142	
D	Confirmation of the future profit division between landowners and planters	• Confirmation of the percentage division of future income between landowners and planters, usually in the fifth year of the tenancy tenure.	36	
[2] Sales of rights over timberlands			844	100%
W	Whole property	• Sale of the whole property of a plot.	158	18.7%
S	Shares of whole property	• Sale of some shares of the whole property.	270	32.0%
U & US	Usufruct right (U) or some portions of it (US)	• Sale of the standing trees on a plot, land should be returned to the seller after felling.	U: 20 US: 10	3.6%
Landowners' and Planters' Shares:			386	45.7%
L & LS	Landowners' share (L) or some portions of it (LS)	• Sale of landowners' share of future income, as defined in (T) and (D).	L: 36 LS: 127	
P & PS	Planters' share (P) or some portions of it (PS)	• Sale of planters' share of future income, as defined in (T) and (D).	P: 119 PS: 50	
LPS	Portions of both landowners' and planters' shares (LPS)	• Sale of some landowners' shares AND some planters' shares.	54	
[3] Agreement among co-owners (A)		• Clarification of shareholdings. • Final division of profit. • Household division documents that specify shares to be inherited by each offspring.	124	
		Total sample	1,146	

Source: Author's tabulation.

underlying my organization of the data that informs this chapter, including the design of appropriate variables based on timberland contracts themselves rather than on preconceived economic concepts. The trees being traded in these contracts invariably still required years of growth before they were ready for the market. Few sale contracts are for trees that were ready to be felled, probably because such transactions featured on-the-spot payment and did not require contracts or long-term holding of the contracts.[62] The sale of mature trees is usually known to us from the profit division contracts among co-owners.

Sales of whole property right (W) over a mountain plot become increasingly rare over time (figure 3.1). The practice of two-tiered landownership similar to the structure in rice paddies, whereby the landowner sells the usufruct rights while retaining the legal ownership of a plot, was well established. Sale of usufruct rights (U & US) was for the tenure of one crop of trees. "Usufruct right" refers to the ownership over the standing trees on the plot in question. When the trees became mature, the usufruct owner harvested the trees and returned the land to the original owner, who could not share the profit from the trees. In those cases where the usufruct right of a barren plot was sold, the buyer had the right to plant trees by himself

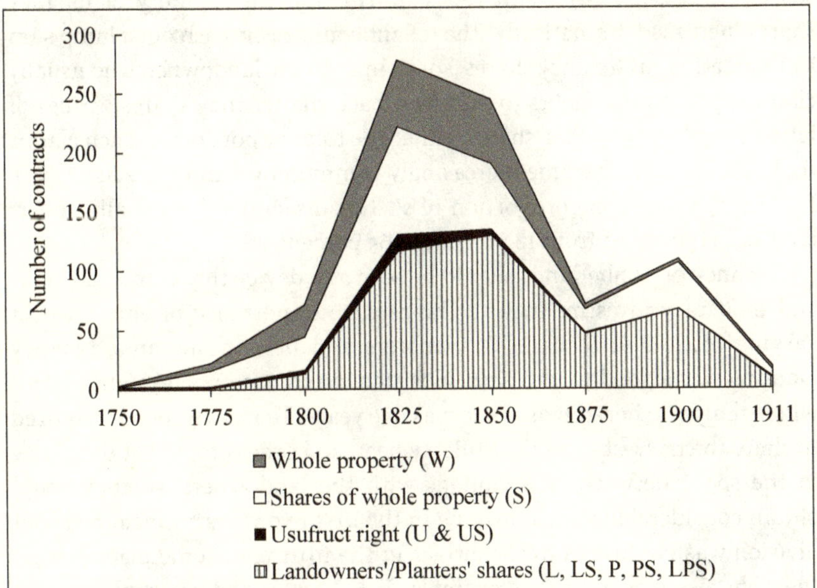

FIGURE 3.1 Types of timberland transactions by year, 1750–1911.
Source: Timberland contracts from GZM and JYZ.

and then return the land after the felling of that stand of trees. In such cases, buyers of usufruct rights might also sublease the land to tenant planters, with whom he would divide the profits.

CREATION OF LANDOWNERS' AND PLANTERS' SHARES

Planters entered into tenancy contracts (T) with the landowners (i.e., holders of the whole property rights) or, on occasion, with holders of usufruct rights (see table 3.2). The tenant planter's share of the timber crop was usually 40 percent or, less often, 50 percent. The average planter's share from 493 tenancy contracts was 42 percent.[63] The planting of trees and other crops was concentrated in the first five years; the required work thereafter was minimal, mainly looking out for theft and preventing fire. So at the end of the fifth year, the tenant would invite the landowner over to inspect how his mountain plot had been thickly planted—that is, it had "turned into a young forest" (*chenglin*). At that moment a contract that confirmed the profit division between the landowner and the tenant planter was signed; this contract was called *fencheng hetong* (D).

The signing of this contract completed the separation of the usufruct rights of the timberland into landowners' shares (L, *dizhu gu*) and planters' shares (P, *zaishou gu*). With this confirmation the liquidity of tenancy shares increased dramatically. The tenant could easily cash out a lump sum by liquidating his tenancy shares, sometimes to the landowner, who usually claimed preemptive rights to purchase back the tenancy shares.[64] Sales of landowners' and planters' shares, either the total or portions of such claims (L, LS, P, PS, LPS), became increasingly common over time (see figure 3.1). From 1775 to 1875 the proportion of such transactions among all timberland sales increased from 18 percent to 65 percent.

Tenancy on timberlands should be seen as a device that combined labor and monetary investment, with the relative importance of either aspect varying from case to case. For laborers and new in-migrants, tenancy planting was a good way to earn subsistence and accumulate some wealth with a temporal horizon of as short as five years. Tenants were not required to share the harvest from the millet, wheat, and other crops that they grew in the space between tree saplings with the landowners, so they could obtain considerable annual income in the first five years.[65] Once the profit division was confirmed by a contract in the fifth year, some planters sold their shares right away. For example, Fan Yutang and his nephews sold their tenancy shares in 1819 to Jiang Yinghui for 76 taels of silver just a month after a contract confirming their share of 40 percent was signed with the landowners (also of the Fan clan). This is a case where the landowners did not exercise their preemptive rights and the planters' shares were sold to someone of a different surname.[66]

Many planters would move on to another tenancy tenure every five years, while choosing to hold or sell the earned planters' shares depending on their own financial situations. Tenant planters who stayed with a crop from start to finish were rare. The few tenants who did see to the maturity of the crop would likely be one of the biggest beneficiaries from the sale of trees, especially when the landowners' shares had become divided into numerous small portions as they always did through transactions and partible inheritance. The final realization of a planter's profit should be understood as a combination of the return to his initial labor input and the accumulated time value of his waiting.

Confirmed planters' shares were viewed as a purely monetary investment by people with capital. It was very common for the same party to hold portions of both the landowners' and the planters' shares on various plots.[67] Sporadic evidence indicates that merchants from other provinces, particularly Hunan and Jiangxi, also invested in timberland shares, which worked as forwards to secure their timber supply at a future time.[68] The relative profit and power that one could derive from a tree stand depended not on the kind but the number of his shares, blurring the sharp distinctions once thought to obtain between the labels of "landlords" and "tenants."[69] In some contracts, when someone holding a mixture of both kinds of shares was transferring his holdings, he might just state the total number of shares he owned, bypassing the usual section where one should explain the division of ownership and tenancy shares and his holding of each kind.[70] Of the 223 contracts that featured sales of planters' shares, 76 did not specify any details about the origins of the shares, while 147 contracts (66 percent) did, whether earned by labor or previously purchased from someone else. There were 129 contracts where the sellers of the shares personally planted the trees (*qinzi dianzai*). Among these, 65 (50 percent) contracts showed that the planters sold their shares back to the landowners, sometimes one or more persons among all the co-owners of the land. And 18 contracts stated explicitly that the planters' shares being sold were previously purchased from someone else.

Since the necessity to disclose details could very well vary for different kinds of sales, the percentages drawn from these 147 contracts should be taken only as rough indicators instead of confident estimations. For one thing, it is probable that tenant planters, when selling their shares, tended to use the established phrase of "personally planted the trees" more than someone who was selling previously purchased shares. If this was indeed the case, by an educated guess, it was likely that a larger portion of the remaining 76 contracts where detailed information was lacking featured the reselling of previously acquired planters' shares. Take the extreme case, where all 76 contracts were resales. This would mean that, roughly speaking, among all the planters' shares that tenants had sold out, 73 percent of them were sold for a second time. At the other less likely extreme, suppose all 76 contracts were sales initiated by the planters. This means that 91 percent of the people who purchased planters' shares from the tenants had kept the shares and only 9 percent resold them. The actual case would be somewhere in between and more complicated, not the least because planters' shares could be transacted multiple times before the harvest of the crop.[71]

Sales of ownership shares entailed the landowner's share of only the current crop of trees, which was separated from the legal ownership of the subsoil. Some sales contracts of landowners' shares made this explicit by adding the phrase "after the trees are cut in the future, the land should be returned to the original owner."[72] When the landowner was selling both his share of the crop and the legal title of the land, both would be specified in the contract.[73] The separation of ownership and tenancy shares became so popular that even when selling property rights over a whole mountain site, some might choose to be explicit that "tenancy shares, ownership shares, and the land are all for sale" instead of the commonly used ambiguous phrase of the "sale of mountain and trees"; those selling usufruct rights might specify that "tenancy shares and ownership shares are all for sale."[74]

Part of the reason for this specification was that the current landowner might have acquired the whole property by purchasing ownership and tenancy shares successively, including the situation where the landowner had redeemed tenancy shares from the planter and was now selling the whole property or usufruct rights.[75] But even in cases where the seller had always possessed the whole property outright and the trees were planted by himself, such a phrase might still be used in the contract for clarification.[76] Such practices testified to the deep perception that rights over mountain land could be separated into that of the subsoil and that of the standing trees, the latter of which was further divided into landowners' shares and planters' shares when a tenancy relation was involved.

DIVISION AND SECURITIZATION OF TIMBERLANDS

Shares, once created, were divided and transacted based on an individual household's needs. This could involve partitioning household property among heirs, adjusting the household's investment portfolio, or disposing of its shareholdings to meet spikes in consumption expenses. Securitization—that is, the division of rights over a property into independently tradable shares—featured all kinds of rights claimed over a mountain plot (witness S, US, LS, PS, and LPS in table 3.2).[77] Unless otherwise noted, the term "share" refers to the right over a portion of the monetary proceeds to be accrued from the sale of the trees, rather than a part of the physical divisions of a specific plot or a specific number of standing trees. Partible inheritance might be the initial mechanism that created shares out of a family's whole ownership of a mountain plot. While agricultural land and real estate were usually physically divided among sons, forested mountains were normally kept intact and divided into equal shares of rights to revenue from future sales. Property division documents commonly said that "the mountain land and trees are not yet divided. In the future, when the trees are felled and sold, the proceeds should be equally allocated among the sons." For example, in the family of Jiang Yinghui, mountain land was not physically divided in the household divisions for three generations (in 1819, 1859, and 1896, respectively).[78]

Indeed, to divide up a mountain site with trees in growth would present difficulties in drawing up the demarcation of the land and designating who owned which trees, especially when the family's holding of mountain land was dispersed over a number of plots. In addition to the problem of fair division, tree planting required a certain level of scale management. In this, it was very different from rice paddies, the efficient size of which was inherently small, requiring intensive cultivation, and the physical division of a family's holding of paddies usually did not require breaking up individual production units. By contrast, if a forested mountain was divided up into excessively small plots owned by different agents, it required additional risk-sharing mechanisms and coordination to avoid boundary disputes. Just imagine the potential disputes if the trees allocated to one son suffered fire or theft while those of the other son standing on the side stayed intact. In addition, over time these small plots would be planted with trees of different ages, making lump-sum selling to an outside timber merchant at the time of maturity untenable. Using shares for profit division instead of physically dividing up the land and trees provided a way to preserve the unit of management at a larger scale, reduce boundary disputes, and better spread risks.

In addition to partible inheritance, shares became more finely divided when the seller chose to alienate portions, instead of the total, of his holdings or when several parties purchased together and divided the shares among themselves. For individual investors the guiding principle was to diversify resources in different plots growing trees of different ages. Even for large mountain landowners, their holdings were shares of scattered sites. Shares transacted in sale contracts might just be one of dozens or even a hundred total shares.[79] In cases of complex parcelization, there were two ways to express the shares. The first method, which was more commonly used, specified the multi-tiered division of shares to explain the origin of one's holdings and what was being sold, usually using the expression of dividing one "big share" (*dagu*) into a number of "small shares" (*xiaogu*). For example, when Jiang Laogui was selling his shares on two plots in 1844, for the first plot he explained: "This mountain is divided into five shares, among which the landowners have three and the planters have two. Among the landowners' three shares, Laogui and his nephew Laoping collectively own one. This one share is further divided into two small shares—Laogui owns one small share. Laogui also owns one of the two planters' shares."[80] So, in total, Laogui owned one-sixth of the ownership shares and half of the tenancy shares. The benefit of this method was that the route of previous transactions was clear, and the shares of the other co-owners, which are not explicitly mentioned in the contracts, could stay intact in case of disputes.

Another case shows how shares could be further divided among multiple buyers during a transaction. The timberland in Wuqi was equally divided into two big shares, one for the landowners and one for the planters. The landowners' single share was further divided into four smaller shares, and the brothers Wenshang and Wenhan collectively owned two of them. The brothers then sold these two small shares to a group of seven buyers, who divided them in the following way: Zibin, Zixiu, and Laoxian collectively took one share; Yingxian took a half share; and Zhimo and his two brothers took the remaining half share.[81]

The second method used to express shares in cases of complex parcelization, usually used when previous transactions were too numerous to be expressed as big shares and small shares without confusion, was to attach an arbitrary number of *liang* to the whole property and list the number of *liang* owned by the party in question. *Liang* in this case did not refer to the actual monetary value of the land in terms of silver taels but was merely an arbitrary number used to denote shares. This is another example of the use of *liang* as an abstract unit of account, in addition to the Longquan *liang* discussed in chapter 2. Because the Chinese character for "share" (*gu*) was usually not used for fractions, except for half of a share, this method of using the abstract *liang* provided a convenient way to report the total percentage of a property owned by one person. For instance, Jiang Changtai was selling his 0.75 *liang* of a 5 *liang* mountain in return for 21.5 taels of silver: "This is a mountain of 5 *liang*, Jiang Danyan and Jiang Tingzhu have 2 *liang*, Yinghui has 1.5 *liang*, Jinkui has 0.75 *liang*, Changhai has 0.75 *liang*. Now I [Jiang Changtai] am selling my share of 0.75 *liang* of the mountain to Jiang Tingkui. In the presence of both parties and intermediaries, a price of 21.5 taels of silver was agreed upon, which I have received in person."[82]

The shortcoming of this method is that we cannot know if his holdings had different sources. In the previous example for big and small shares, Jiang Laogui held some portion of the landowners' shares and some portion of the tenants' shares, resulting in a total of 30 percent of the property. If Jiang Laogui had adopted the second method of using *liang*, the only information revealed would be the fact that 30 percent of the total property was being sold. Sometimes both methods were used in the same contract for complex cases. For example: "This mountain is divided into two big shares, one for the planters, and one for the landowners. The landowners' one share is further divided into two shares, one owned by Jiang Shaolü, the remaining one share is divided as a mountain of 10 *liang*: Jiang Ziwei has 2.5 *liang*, Daxiang has 1.25 *liang*, Tingchang has 1.25 *liang*. . . . Now my own share of 1.25 *liang* is sold to Uncle Jiang Shaolue. In the presence of both parties, a price of 9.2 taels of silver was agreed upon, which I have received in person."[83]

Based on transactions of portions of landowners' and planters' shares in the nineteenth century (LS, PS, LPS, US, S; N = 422), the average percentage of owners' share being sold was 26 percent, the average percentage of planters' share being sold was 51 percent. Comparing each twenty-year bracket, there is a detectable positive correlation between the frequency of timberland transactions and the extent of finer parcelization.[84] The mid-nineteenth century saw a decrease in the frequency of timberland transactions, which coincided with the local turmoil in the southwest during a Miao rebellion and the shutdown of the interregional timber trade due to the blockage of the Yangzi River during the Taiping Rebellion. This suggests a strong connection between the liquidity of timberland shares on the production sites and the conditions of local and interregional timber trade.

CO-OWNERSHIP STRUCTURES

The co-ownership structure that resulted from the complex transactions delineated earlier resembled the structure of a shareholding partnership:

an individual holder's shares might come from multiple sources of labor input, landownership, and purchases; the voice one part-owner had in determining the sale of the trees on a plot depended on the number of his shares; corporate entities of investment (*hui*) were also formed and governed by principles of shareholding and behaved like individuals in making investments in timberland shares.

Timberland contracts commonly specify the number of shares being sold and the total number of existing shares. But they only occasionally included the names of other shareholders. Although it was common practice to have one or two other shareholders as intermediaries and witnesses of transactions, usually not all of the shareholders were involved. After several such private transactions, co-owners felt the need to compose a detailed list of all shareholders and their shares, called "the agreement on mountain division" (*fenshan hetong*).[85] Such lists always included dozens of signatories, and some of them were representatives of a group, making the number of stakeholders even more numerous. Such lists might also be the result of the resolution of disputes among owners, listing the agreed-upon division of shares and announcing any previous contracts proving otherwise to be invalid thereafter.[86] These documents were intended to replace all previous purchase contracts and become the sole legal record of the land and the basis of future allocation of the proceeds from the sales of the trees. Sometimes a mountain division contract was composed right before the trees on the mountain plot in question were ready to be felled, and the new contract was supposed to be the uncontested basis for profit division.[87] Most of the time the portions designated in the lists referred to shares of future revenues, but occasionally it could actually be physical divisions of one tract of mountain land into a few plots to be separately managed, mostly because of a disagreement regarding whether to allow some potential buyers to be co-owners or the time of felling.[88]

The notion of *gongshan* sometimes came up in the documents. Here, this term denoted a mountain plot that was divided by shares into the hands of a lot of shareholders, who could trade their shares freely.[89] The character *gong* in this term conveyed a sense of "many," rather than collective ownership. The ownership structure of such *gongshan* resembled more that of a publicly listed corporation, where one's claims of control and profit corresponded to the number of independently tradable shares he held (see the example in figure 3.2 of Randugan timberland), rather than a village common to which every member of the community had inalienable equal access and responsibility.

Distinguished from such *gongshan* controlled by shareholders, there were indeed some community endeavors at regulating the access to, and utilization of, common timberlands, sometimes to protect the beneficial geomancy of the village's graveyard. These community-managed forests conform to the modern economic concept of "commons." For example, the villagers of Zhangshan had collectively contributed the initial endowments to establish a plot of geomantic timberland and prohibited any cutting.[90] In another case, Guigu village inscribed stone steles that specified the enclosed area and the penalties for illegal cutting and burial.[91] Such village management of collectively owned forests and woodlots were also found in other parts of southern China.[92] The rich documents of the lower Qingshui area show that the scale of such collective timberlands was very small compared to those claimed by private shares and sustained by contracts. This information is not often known for other regions where private, household-level documents have not been preserved as well. In fact, the nature of extant written documents from the late imperial period, such as stone steles and literary works, tends to overrepresent the community regulation of commons while underrepresenting private market-oriented plantings.

Recent field studies in the Old South provinces of Jiangxi and Fujian indicate that a village community's geomancy forests (*fengshui lin*), which were collectively preserved and banned from cutting, can be easily distinguished by age and height from their market-oriented fir planting that was household-managed and meant to be cut rotationally.[93] The lower Qingshui case and these findings from field studies invite us to reexamine the different forms of timberland ownership in China and their relative popularity, while being mindful of the potential biases from each genre of evidence.

Many villages were dominated by one or two surnames, such as the Fans in Yanwan and the Jiangs in Wendou and Ping'ao. A large tract of timberland that had been acquired by an ancestor early in the eighteenth century would, by the late nineteenth century, seemingly mimic lineage-owned land thanks to generations of partible inheritance. However, the resemblance is only superficial. Like many *gongshan*, such timberlands dominated by members of the same lineage were in fact shareholding structures, rather than incorporated lineage estates that were more popular in Lingnan and, to a lesser extent, Jiangnan.[94] In the lower Qingshui area individuals were left to their own devices to possess rights over timberlands, instead of through their lineages. They could freely alienate their shares, although the norm was that close kinsmen, including both agnates and affines, should have preemptive rights to buy them before outsiders. There was no management board, like that at the head of a lineage, that made overarching decisions regarding these properties. The final proceeds from the felling and sale of the trees would actually be divided among all the shareholders instead of being retained as lineage funds. In other words, the lineage as a corporate institution that managed a separate set of properties to generate revenues for common activities was *not* a significant phenomenon in the Qingshui valley.[95] This is a big difference between Guizhou and timber-producing areas in the Old South, such as Huizhou, where powerful lineage corporations dominated most timberlands.

The final sale of the trees was usually conducted by the landowners. Tenants were explicitly forbidden to directly chop down their portion of the crop.[96] Once the revenue from the sale was realized, landowners first apportioned the amount due to the tenancy shares and then divided the residual among holders of ownership shares. The names appeared in the contract of profit division might be deceased ancestors, whose shares were taken by one or a few representative descendants, who would then divide the amount among all legitimate inheritors.[97]

The division of the final revenue from selling the trees on the Randugan mountain, which was sometimes referred to as a *gongshan*, serves a good illustration of the kind of complex ownership structures derived from generations of partible inheritance and transactions of shares.[98] Figure 3.2 shows the division of final revenue among holders of landowners' shares after the planters' share of 40 percent had been paid off, leaving a total of 16.7 taels of silver in 1891. The division of shares roughly follows the framework of patrilineal inheritance. Each party had the right to freely alienate his shares. The dash lines in the figure indicate purchases of shares instead of inheritance. The brothers Chengzu and Gengzu, who were from a distant branch, came to invest in this timberland by purchasing shares from two sets of landowners. Existing holders also transferred shares among themselves (as in the case of Zhizheng and Zhimo acquiring shares from Qihua, and Weihong acquiring shares from Qixun), contributing to some members of the lineage eventually claiming more or less profit than his initial inheritance right entailed.

Despite the lack of a lineage-wide endowment, various kinds of private trusts (*hui*) appeared as investors in the mountain lands during the nineteenth century. Some *hui* were trusts founded by religious institutions or kinship groups to generate revenues for ritual ceremonies and ancestral sacrifices, such as the Qingming Hui (see figure 3.2). Other examples of *hui* that appeared in the collection of sources from this community included the Trust of Nanyue Palace (Nanyue Gong Hui) and the Trust for Ancestral Worship (Jisi Hui).[99] Some seemed to be purely economic associations founded by kin and nonkin members alike for rotating credit and profit-making.[100] Some might be ad hoc constructions of existing co-ownership

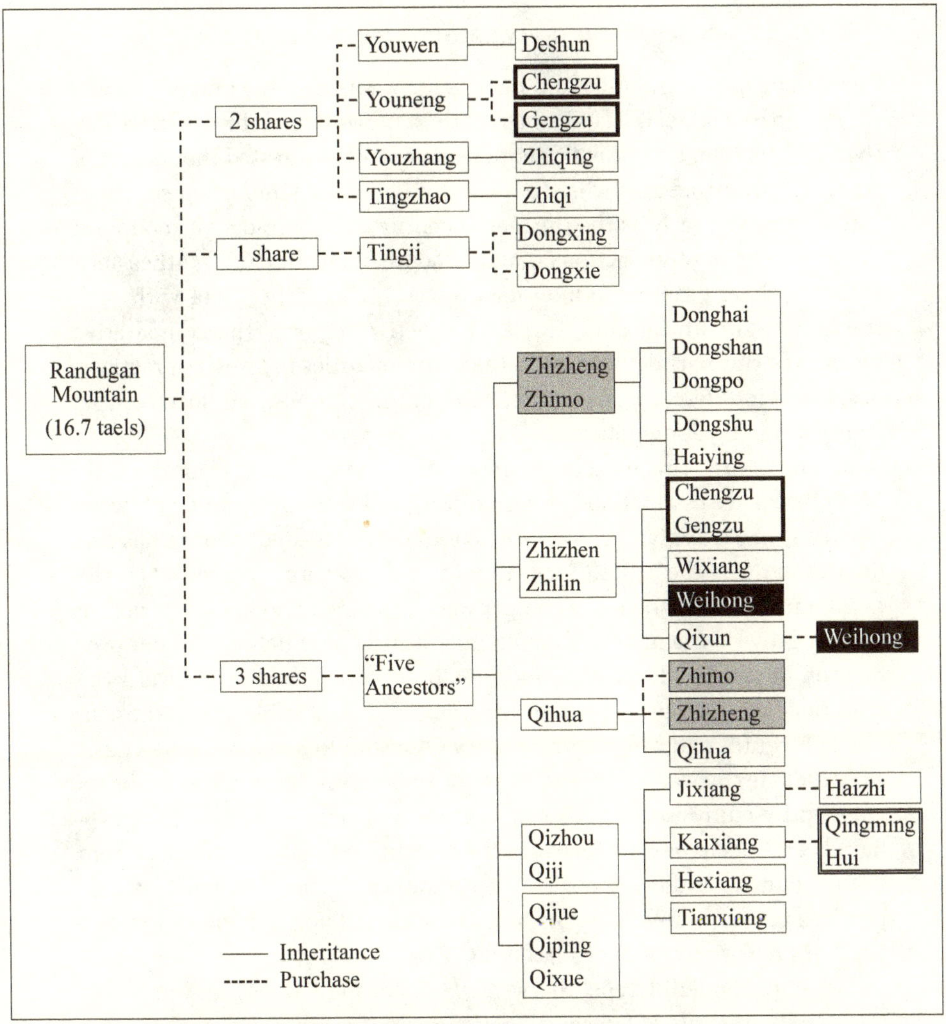

FIGURE 3.2 Profit division of Randugan Mountain, 1891. Shading indicates the same people appear more than once in the structure. *Source*: GZM E0039, E0060; and Aihara Yoshiyuki, "Shindai Chūgoku Kishū Shō Seisui Kō ryūiki," 126–27, 138.

structures. These *hui* as corporate entities engaged in purchasing mountain land, tenanting, and money-lending. Some properties of the *hui* might also come from the confiscation of collateral on unpaid loans extended to members and outsiders.[101] The *hui* itself was a shareholding structure. Members held shares, called "feet" (*jiao*), of the *hui* trust, which could be freely inherited, transferred, and collateralized.[102]

The strategies of mountain land management found in the Qingshui River valley in the eighteenth and nineteenth centuries resembled remarkably the patterns seen since the fifteenth century in the forested mountains of southern Anhui, an area where trade in timber was an important source of income from as early as the thirteenth century.[103] Contracts for mountain land tenancy and transactions found in southern Anhui and southeastern Guizhou shared more common features with each other than with contracts for agricultural land in their respective regions. The comparative analysis in this part demonstrates the commonalities in forestry practices, despite their differences in local customs, ethnic composition, social organizations, and taxation policies.

In Huizhou, terms used in the mountain land contracts from the early Ming revealed a distinction between topsoil and subsoil. Granting of "work portions"—that is, planters' shares—to tenants of forested mountain is evident as early as the 1450s. Beginning in mid-fifteenth century, when the cities and towns of the lower Yangzi were entering an extended period of secular growth, the intensive commercialization of Huizhou's timber production became widespread, which required constant efforts toward the maintenance and replacement of tree stocks.[104] Practices similar to those in the eighteenth- and nineteenth-century Qingshui River valley—the sale of shares during a stand of trees' growth, tenants' transfer of their shares entailed by cultivation rights, clarification of shares among co-owners—have been evident in Huizhou since the fifteenth century.[105] Contracts from both Huizhou's and Guizhou's forested mountains can potentially be analyzed as representative samples of a common economic logic in forestry practices in various parts of southern China.

An important difference between Huizhou and the Qingshui valley seems to be the role of lineages.[106] Existing lineage trusts in Huizhou took the opportunity of the Yuan-Ming transition in the fourteenth century to expand the trusts' landholdings and endeavored thereafter to prevent alienation of the trusts' property by their members, though with mixed rates of success. The Doushan Trust of the Chengs illustrates the agenda of Huizhou lineages. In the early fifteenth century, the Doushan Trust possessed clear and uncontested claims of full ownership over its listed properties, acquired during the extensive depopulation and destruction of land records during the Yuan-Ming transition. The trust endeavored to guard its whole property rights over mountain land by barring the members of the trust from privately purchasing work portions from the trust's tenants and thereby pocketing extra profit for themselves. The trust's 1547 pact called for the purchase back of all the tenancy shares of the trust's mountain property. By the end of the sixteenth century, the Doushan Trust's purchases and holdings leaned even more toward land and tenancy shares, eventually rendering its principle of inalienability of its holdings untenable.[107] By the end of the sixteenth century, even with the stronger presence of lineages in Huizhou, the fragmentation of mountain ownership and tenancy rights into alienable shares compromises past claims of strong lineage control of Huizhou's forested mountains, despite some lineages' rhetorical claims of extensive ownership.[108]

In the lower Qingshui valley, by contrast, lineages in the eighteenth century were never active holders of mountain land properties. As mentioned before, some primitive forms of lineage trusts existed. Small private trusts were established by groups of kinsmen engaged in mountain land holdings and money-lending, and some used the income for group sacrifices, but they by no means covered the whole lineage. Trusts established by kinsmen for ancestral sacrifice were just one kind of many private trusts founded by kin or nonkin to finance various religious activities or simply to make a profit for shareholders. When these organizational investors came into the game, securitized shares were already the norm in the Qingshui valley. So from the beginning, the holdings of private trusts took the form of parcelized shares rather than extensive whole property rights, an arrangement unlike the powerful fifteenth-century lineage trusts in Huizhou.

Other differences between the contracts in Huizhou and the Qingshui valley reflect the different extent to which state apparatus had penetrated into the local rural society.[109] In Huizhou, from the Song era if not earlier, taxation on mountain land was assessed as a distinct category.[110] In the first half of the Ming dynasty, mountain land sales increasingly drew on early Ming cadastral surveys for information on the land's location, type, identification number, and boundaries. Many of the contracts found in Huizhou were official contracts with red seals (*hongqi*), with the tax quota of the land in question specified in the context. As late-Ming fish-scale registers failed to update regularly, owners and buyers were prompted to include even more details in their deeds.[111] While land registration might have played a crucial role during the Song-Yuan-Ming transition period in turning boundless woodlands into bounded property and establishing the recognition of private ownership of planted forests, once such private ownership had become entrenched by the Qing it was secured with official support even without formal tax registration, as long as other supportive evidence, especially private contracts, was strong.[112] In the southwestern frontier, cadastral survey and land registration were never fully carried out even for agricultural reclamations, let alone forestland. In the Qingshui valley, although transfers of tax payment responsibilities were occasionally mentioned in the sale contracts of agricultural land, no reference to taxation was found in mountain land contracts.[113] There is no evidence of land identification numbers generated from cadastral surveys; "white contracts" (*baiqi*) without official seals served the basis of ownership claims.

Although timberland contracts on the scale of Huizhou and the lower Qingshui collections have not been found in other locations, similar forestry management practices in many timber-producing regions in southern China can be glimpsed from the late Qing and Republican investigations on local customs.[114] Evidence from Anhui, Fujian, Hunan, and Zhejiang suggest that claims to the legal title to the land and to the standing trees were established as separate rights and could be traded in shares independently. Planters' shares could range from 20 percent to 80 percent, depending on the conditions of the land and other arrangements, such as whether annual rent would be paid to the landowners. From the few timberland-related court disputes found in the Longquan County Archives of Zhejiang, it is apparent that the use of shares for planted forests was prevalent and that shares were also finely parcelized in this long-established fir-growing locality.[115]

In terms of lineage powers and the state's presence, it seems that the cases of Huizhou and the lower Qingshui were at two extremes. When commercialized tree planting started to take off in Huizhou, it happened within the contours of established lineage organizations and the existing taxation frameworks of the state. The lower Qingshui, however, quickly developed its timber industry in response to the opening of the market and readily adopted a set of matured contractual practices before kinship organizations, which were also a new introduction, took control over local economic resources. Other timber-producing regions in southern China seem to have been somewhere in between. In southern Jiangxi, for example, while some lineages claimed common assets through genealogies, their dominance was far less than in Huizhou and private ownership substantiated by contracts was common.[116]

CONCLUSION

The flexibility of shareholding solved the challenge of long-term investment posed by the rigid nature of tree growth. Shares attached to future proceeds from the trees enabled individuals to invest or divest with ease and avoided physical parcelization of forestlands. In late imperial China a shareholding entity might be devoted to a variety of purposes that required pooling of resources, demanded long-term engagement, or denied fine physical divisions, ranging from rural coalitions for tax payments or fishing rights to urban trading enterprises to more capital-intensive industrial entrepreneurship. In rural areas, shareholding coalitions established by contract permeated even the lowest levels of village life. Shares in both kin and nonkin shareholding entities had become dividend-bearing commodities and could be bought and sold.[117]

Shareholding partnerships, whereby each partner bore liability that was unlimited but only proportional to his share of investment, was a very common organizational form for multiple-owner trading firms during the Qing era, particularly for business partners from different lineages or native places who wanted to pool their capital.[118] Toward the more capital-intensive end, the Zigong salt mining industry featured high capital requirements, long-term commitment, and uncertain success. Vertically integrated salt enterprises developed through shareholding partnerships, which had impressive numbers of shareholding partners, flexible transfer and acquisition of shares, long duration of partnerships, and the advent of full-time managers and shareholder meetings.[119] Similarly, the smaller partnerships in the coal and iron industry in eastern Chongqing often combined capital from unrelated partners, and sometimes incorporated labor shares.[120] The remarkable resemblance of the shareholding practices evident in all these different industries in late imperial China suggest institutional spillover across agricultural, commercial, and industrial sectors and provide important insight on how indigenous practices and conceptualization of *gu* were created and adapted in response to changing demands.

In forestry the decision in the household division contract not to physically divide up the family's holding of immature trees and the consequent formation of a primitive trust denoted by shares among brothers seemed to be an important initial template that laid the groundwork for more complex shareholding structures. This was similar to cases in which a successful merchant could keep his firm intact by creating a trust and allowing his sons to inherit equal shares in an undivided pool of assets, which could likewise be divided among their heirs.[121] Once the shares were commodified and independently transferrable, ownership of a parcel of forestland increasingly became a multisurname shareholding entity. Contrary to previous literature that has blamed the absence of primogeniture as a cause for slow capital accumulation and economic backwardness, the Chinese practice of equitable inheritance was not an obstacle, but most likely a driving force for the conceptualization of *gu* and the development of perpetual shareholding entities to pool capital. Trusts established by kin and nonkin alike, although always stating as their purpose a charitable or religious cause, could be viewed as a type of shareholding partnership that behaved like individual legal persons in the marketplace and that specialized in portfolio investment. These findings from the economically less-developed part of the country further enhance the perception that trusts were the fundamental Chinese templates for the creation of shareholding corporations that pooled and protected investable assets.

The economic analysis of transactions of timberland properties also provides new perspectives on the issue of environmental sustainability. In core-periphery theory, market integration between the core and periphery led to the exploitation of natural resources in peripheral lands to benefit the center. For forest resources this could lead to "forest mining" where logging or clearance was not followed by sustainable management to renew the resources. The case of southern China shows that the general depletion of natural forests notwithstanding, in some scenarios, strong market demand could also motivate long-term labor and capital input into reforestation. High demand, low transportation cost, proximity to markets, and the unsuitability of the land for the cultivation of higher-value grain or cash crops all provided the necessary conditions for tree farming in the lower Qingshui valley. Market integration further encouraged specialization in tree cultivation in the local economy by ensuring access to other consumer goods from the market.

Another line of literature in environmental economics stresses the importance of well-defined property rights to forestlands and forest products, the lack of which leads to exploitation rather than management. In this argument the importance of a proper property rights regime to sustainable development was seen from the angle of "externalities," which occur when the negative consequence of economic activity is not fully reflected in the cost borne by the party that chooses to undertake this activity. In the case of open-access or undermanaged common resources, externalities would lead to overexploitation, even depletion, of the resource. Such tragedies of overexploitation for common-pool resources could potentially be addressed through clearly specified property rights, effective boundaries, and enforceable rules of use.[122] It could be argued that the well-defined private property created by written contracts in southern China helped restrain overexploitation of forest resources.

Still, the delineation and protection of property rights alone were not enough to foster the plantation of timber trees. Large-scale tree cultivation would not be plausible if individual cultivators had to deal with the thirty year waiting time before harvesting. This leads to an aspect of property-related environmental practice that has yet to be fully examined. The key was a property rights framework that was compatible with the long-term commitment required by tree cultivation. The liquidity problem associated with the long-term nature of tree growth was solved through the division and securitization of landownership and tenancy rights in southern China. Such practices proved successful in promoting commercialized reforestation in a rural household-based economy.

The development of state forestry in some countries during the early modern period has been praised for laying the groundwork for the smooth adoption of modern scientific state forestry. However, we should be mindful that these early modern states were motivated to take hold of forestlands less for a preservationist ideal but more for the utilitarian purpose of securing sustainable timber supply for construction and military uses, either for fear of the overexploitation of forests by local residents or for the lack of reliable market supply of good-quality timber. For example, after acquiring the forested territories in the fifteenth century, the Venetians initially relied on timber supply from the market and only started to implement direct state control over the forests when the market alone failed to guarantee stable supply.[123] If the successful establishment of state forestry contributed to the conservation of forests at an overall level, it also had the redistribution effects that prioritized state needs over those of the population. The expansion and enforcement of state claims often forced local communities to make compromises that harmed their livelihood.[124]

To a considerable extent, the private economy and market development in late imperial China eased these concerns for the Chinese state. Private replantation in southern China was motivated by its economic profit without coercion from the state, and the integration of a nationwide timber market consistently supplied the central and local states' need for regular-sized timber. The late imperial Chinese state did not develop an extensive state forestry program across the mountainous areas in the south not necessarily for the lack of capacity but more for the lack of necessity, as the domestic market was both expansive and efficient (pressure on the Qing state was further relieved as extraordinary timber could be obtained from beyond the Great Wall). The following chapters turn to the economic institutions that sustained the operation and expansion of this long-distance trade structure that spanned more than a thousand miles.

CHAPTER FOUR

Merchants, Brokers, and Market Dynamics

THE state's reliance on market purchases for imperial timber and the development of regional specializations in sustainable tree plantations were both premised on a well-functioning market system that facilitated the circulation of goods and capital to meet demands, generate profit, extend credit, and hedge risks so that all the players along the supply chain could benefit and continue their work. Just like its retreat from direct management of natural resources, the state's market regulation increasingly became laissez-faire. By the time the Qing state came to establish its rule, the late imperial market management system had already undergone a long-term transition from direct bureaucratic regulation over physically confined marketplaces to indirect control through licensed brokerages.

Despite their exclusive legal stance, however, licensed timber brokerages cohabited the intermediation space with other economic agencies with blurry legality. In addition to their informational function of matching sellers and buyers from afar, these legal and semilegal intermediaries also performed important financial functions, which facilitated the flow of credit from urban centers to rural suppliers. Regional variations in trade environment were prominent. Market dynamics in the southwestern Miao frontier were different from those in the Yangzi basin heartland, involving interplays between the state's priority of ethnic stability and different local agents' economic pursuit in the frontier setting.

TRADERS AND WORKERS ALONG THE SUPPLY CHAIN

The timber trade is a multi-tiered business, in which traders operated at varying scales and scopes. Operating closest to the site of production were the so-called mountain guests (*shanke*), usually locals who contracted with the forest owners for the right to log the mountains, a practice called "cut-and-buy" (*pinmai*) in Anhui and Zhejiang.[1] They hired the lumberjacks and porters to get the logs out of the mountains. Logging operations were labor-intensive and technologically sophisticated. It was sometimes necessary to build trestles and slipways in rough terrains to bring the logs to the water. A system of cable logging was used on exceedingly steep slopes, which consisted of a capstan device turned by oxen or dozens of men.[2] Many local peasants participated in this seasonal occupation and formed labor organizations of dozens or even more than a hundred people. The head of such groups (*gongtou*) negotiated labor contracts with the mountain guests.

Once at the nearest waterside, rafting became the primary mode of transportation. In small streams logs could only be floated one by one. As the water level rose, bamboo hawsers were used to bunch the logs to form a triangular-shaped raft. The hawsers were also passed through holes drilled at the bottom of the logs to add rigidity. The mountain guests accompanied the small rafts to preliminary distribution markets, where they sold the timber to local traders or itinerant merchants through brokers. The itinerant merchants were often known as the "river guests" (*shuike*), some operating on their own while others were hired agents. Big timber firms based in national or regional markets of sale might set up permanent branch offices in the production regions to bypass the local brokers and purchase directly from the mountain guests.

Two common problems in the floating of timber rafts were the contest over the passage of timber and the redemption of lost logs, as both issues involved bitter negotiations with the inhabitants of the river valleys. The mutual agreements derived from such negotiations were often inscribed on stone steles. In 1789 the villagers of Diya (Jinping, Guizhou) complained that the timber dealers were careless when passing through their dams and broke the irrigation system. The villagers and timber merchants reached the common agreement that the merchants had to hire porters from this village to transport the logs through a designated segment of the river; outside laborers were not allowed. If the dam was damaged in any way in the process, the timber merchants should pay for the repairs. In effect, the villagers took advantage of their location and monopolized the labor supply for this section of the river.[3] Such agreements seemed to be common in the communities along timber passage routes. Local history from Jianghua, Hunan, included similar complaints by villagers and the collection of "dam fees" on passing rafts.[4]

The other contested issue was about the redemption fees for logs that drifted away in stormy waves and got pulled up by local villagers. Some villagers concealed the logs for their own use or took the opportunity to ask for very high compensations from the merchants. In 1828 the magistrate of Jinping granted the petition of the timber merchants and erected a stele in Liangjiang village that specified redemption prices for logs of varying sizes, ranging from 0.4 to 1.5 taels per log, and recognized the brand marks carved at the base of the logs as evidence of the merchants' legal ownership.[5] A similar stele from 1880 was found in Wangzhai, the preliminary local timber market, which forbade the villagers from destroying the brand marks and set the redemption price at 1,000 *wen* of bronze coins per Longquan *liang* of timber. Timber merchants and the village *baojia* heads should together examine the brand marks and supervise the measurement of the logs. If the merchants failed to claim the logs within forty days, the villager could freely dispose of them.[6]

From the preliminary markets, itinerant merchants refastened the logs they purchased into bigger rafts to enter main rivers. The size of the rafts continued to increase as the water surface widened. In the Yuan River basin, for example, at Hongjiang, the small rafts of 40 feet long and 9 feet wide were retied into 90-feet-long rafts maneuvered by seven to eight workers. Upon entering the Dongting Lake, the rafts were reconstructed to be more than 100 feet wide, hundreds of feet long, with a draft depth of 7 feet.[7] Often after spending a winter in the lake, these larger rafts would slowly make their way down the Yangzi River to Hankou. If intended to proceed still further, they were once more reconstructed at Hankou and then drifted slowly toward the lower Yangzi region.[8] The rafts from southern Jiangxi were first retied at Ganzhou and then at Wucheng, from where it would take six weeks in the high water season to reach Nanjing. These rafts looked narrower and longer than the Hunan rafts and had a deeper draft. Shelters were built on the surfaces of the rafts for the crew of more than a hundred people to live in; the crew grew vegetables and raised pigs and chickens in these shelters. These huge rafts were tied with hundreds of feet of specially made bamboo hawsers. Manufacturers of such hawsers constituted a specialized profession in the major timber markets.[9]

Indeed, skilled labor such as the manufacturers of bamboo hawsers played an essential role in the timber trade. In the Shangxin He town of Nanjing, for example, thousands of workers employed in the timber business constituted the main population. Some were permanent residents; others were seasonal visitors who traveled with the rafts. They were specialized in twelve professions and belonged to nine groups based on native-place origins. The twelve professions could be roughly put into three categories: transportation, measurement, and raft tying. The transportation-related professions were further divided by modes of transportation and route coverage. Some laborers specialized in maneuvering the rafts in high waters, others in towing timber rafts with junk boats, and still others in transporting timber with carriages overland. Measurement and raft fastening were more skilled jobs that required years of apprenticeship, and the practitioners were less mobile than those employed in transportation. Other workers specialized in casting the timber firms' seals to the logs as an indication of ownership and brand name.[10]

Itinerant traders usually traveled with their timber. Once they arrived at the market of destination, they stayed in the lodges of local timber brokers and sold the commodities through them. Larger merchants set up permanent trading firms (*muhao*), usually within the zone of their native-place group. According to Qing regulations, these stores still had to trade through licensed brokers. Some timber firms obtained certificates of official brokerage to trade directly with customers.[11] Buyers were mainly retailers and constructors from the region, very few were average consumers. Extra-local buyers resided at the brokerage and often entrusted delivery to the broker after a deal was struck.[12] Therefore the timber brokerages were involved in brokering, accommodating, and freighting at the same time. They earned good compensations from providing these services and enjoyed a privileged position in the market place as the trusted mediator between the state and the market.

THE LICENSED BROKERAGE SYSTEM

Brokers were crucial for intermediating transactions between strangers with the expansion of interregional trade during the late imperial period. Their economic importance took on regulatory significance as the Chinese state gradually withdrew from direct commercial taxation and bureaucratic control over local marketplaces between the thirteenth century and the nineteenth century. Instead, the state developed increasing reliance on indirect market controls through officially recognized intermediaries, most notably the licensed brokerages.[13] The Great Ming Code explicitly forbade unlicensed brokers from interfering in the market and bestowed upon the licensed brokers all of the functions of facilitating exchange, registering deals, and monitoring the movement of goods and individuals.[14] As licensed brokers became official conduits of market information, official procurements of goods and labor services were increasingly delegated to these brokers.[15] The Qing state inherited and further formalized the licensed brokerages (*yahang*), which were administered through a nationwide system of licensing, auditing, and renewing. Brokers' licenses were to be examined every five years, and any attempt at illicit impostering, monopolizing market access, overcharging in the name of "taxation," or delaying payments to customers was prohibited.[16]

The eighteenth-century state understood the licensed brokerages as the pivot of market exchanges. Its central importance also meant that most of the problems in the market system could find their roots in the abuses or malfunctions of *yahang*. One abuse was the local officials' overissuance of new licenses to generate revenues. Local magistrates not only had incentives to force unregistered brokers to obtain licenses but also to introduce brokerage licenses to industries for which licenses had not been required previously, such as local petty trade. The number of brokerage licenses proliferated at the hands of fund-hungry local officials and raised the cost of market participation for small-time local traders. In view of these problems, from 1733 the Yongzheng emperor deprived county-level magistrates of the authority to issue brokerage licenses. The management of brokerage licenses was transferred to provincial governments and centered on monitoring the retirement and reissuance of existing licenses rather than issuing new ones. The number of brokerage licenses became largely fixed to spare small-time traders the extortions.[17]

Other regulatory measures were introduced to restrain local officials and privileged groups from maneuvering the brokers for profit. Local state offices were ordered to purchase goods at market prices and were prohibited from extracting supplies through licensed brokers without compensation.[18] Government employees and imperial degree holders, who might use their formal or informal privileges to bully others and interfere with fair trade, were forbidden from taking up brokerage licenses. "Those undertaking a brokerage license must have a considerable estate and commoner status" so that they could conduct business with others as equals and had enough resources to facilitate the resolution of disputes should the deal go bad.[19]

The reforms produced mixed results in the decades that followed. The regulation with the most long-lasting impact was the strict quota system on brokerage licenses. Its direct administrative objective of curtailing the local bureaucrats' extortions from overissuing licenses seemed to be effective. However, the fixation of license quota also restricted the capacity of the brokerage system to respond to changing market conditions. Between the 1730s and the end of the dynasty, there was only one occasion of widespread adjustments on license quotas, which was during the recovery years after the Taiping Rebellion in the 1860s. Imaginably, the rigid quota system could hardly keep up with a century of changes in the trade volumes of different commodities and market sizes. In declining trades, licenses could not all be issued for want of applicants. For those trades that emerged in a market after the fixation of quota, there were no licenses issued to accommodate the market's need for intermediaries. In these cases many local officials acquiesced to the operation of private brokers, who were usually called *jingji*—a term still used today for intermediaries in general. In Hunan, *jingji* had become the term for unlicensed yet locally permitted brokers. Some county magistrates even set quotas for the number of *jingji* in addition to the central quota on *yahang*.[20]

Another goal of the reform, to prohibit local state offices from arbitrarily extracting resources through licensed brokers, had only limited success. Outright extortions without any compensation seemed to have been curtailed. Yet scheduled supplies to local government offices continued to be the licensed brokers' obligations, which allowed little flexibility in quantities or prices even when market conditions underwent violent fluctuations. For example, in 1799 licensed timber brokers petitioned to the Baxian County magistrate that because of the disturbance of the White Lotus rebellion, timber supplies to the city of Chongqing were cut off—the Yu Guan Customs only collected one-tenth of its normal timber taxes—and timber trade within the city had come to a standstill. They requested to postpone the obligated supplies to the Baxian County offices, only to be rejected by the magistrate even though their appeal to the superior Chongqing prefect earned some sympathy.[21]

The reforms on the licensed brokerage system in the first half of the eighteenth century aimed to prevent the local administration from meddling in the marketplace and trusted individual licensed brokers with the responsibility to promote fair transactions according to market principles. With its mixed record of success and failure, these regulations set the foundational market principles for the next century or so, during the period of which licensed brokers assumed the central positions in mediating nonlocal trade.[22]

TIMBER BROKERS

Timber brokers (called *muhang* or *muya*) opened lodges by the river to accommodate itinerant sellers and buyers. Specialized timber brokerages only mediated transactions in return for commission fees and conducted no proprietary trading. However, holders of brokerage licenses might establish a separate trading firm to deal with their own accounts.[23] Brokerage firms had a very simple organization, with one chief manager and a couple of assistant managers in charge of public relations and accounting, a few skilled workers specializing in timber measurement, and some handymen and apprentices. The primary task of the brokerages was to match sellers and buyers, which might take a long time when the purchase list of the buyer included a variety of products. The brokerages also helped lease the dock on the riverbanks to stock and inspect the tree trunks, act as arbiter of the quantity and quality of timber, hire laborers for transportation, negotiate the price, and manage the account books for both sellers and buyers. Short-term trade credit might also be extended to those sellers in need. In exchange for these services, a 3 to 5 percent commission fee out of the transaction price was charged.

The number of brokerage licenses for each market became largely fixed after the 1730s. The only occasion of significant adjustment happened after the pacification of the Taiping Rebellion in the 1860s. Other than that, the number of timber brokerages underwent little change. There were fewer than ten timber brokerage licenses even for larger timber markets such as Hangzhou and Chongqing and even fewer for smaller markets.[24] For the largest timber market at Nanjing, there was no definite information before the 1850s. When timber trade was recovered from the Taiping Rebellion in 1864, the number of timber brokers was set to forty.[25] In Hankou, until the end of the Qing, fifteen official brokerage licenses were issued, of which thirteen were allocated to Hubei locals and two to Hunanese.[26] In Hunan, after a round of consolidation in 1861, the numbers of brokerage licenses for each commodity were refixed until the end of the dynasty. As a major timber-exporting province, licenses of timber brokerages in Hunan were all distributed in the cities along the Xiang and Yuan Rivers and their tributaries, the main exporting routes for timber produced in eastern and western Hunan respectively.

The official regulation required that a brokerage firm could only be opened by the registered bearer of the license and the transfer of ownership should not be handled privately. If a son of the deceased holder wanted to inherit the license, he should pay the name-change fee and formally register his own name with the local state. If the holder intended to forgo the license, it should be retired to the government and reissued to another qualified applicant. In practice, however, private leasing of brokerage licenses was very common, a practice known as *dingtie* or *xietie*.[27] The evidence included in an 1804 case illustrates the complicated ownership and leasing practices on brokerage licenses.[28] The case involved five timber brokerage licenses. Four of the licenses were each registered under a real person; the fifth license, interestingly, was registered under a fake person, Feng Zhaoyuan—a name created to represent three persons (Feng Wanjin, Du Qizhao, and Liu Dianyuan) by taking one character from each person's name. Once discovered by the authorities, the name on the license was officially changed to Du Qizhao, but the license was still co-owned by the three parties according to their agreement in private. After the initial holders' passing, all the licenses had been inherited by their sons or grandsons without going through the formal procedure of name changes. To complicate it even more, an Imperial Academy student, Chen Zhengshu, had come to control all five licenses through leasing arrangements with the current license holders. To avoid the charge of being an illicit imposter, Chen and the five license-holding families claimed that Chen was hired to "help manage the business of the brokerages" (*banghang*).

The legal dispute was filed by another person, Tian Jinbang, who claimed that he had lent money to the five original license holders in return for the right to use their licenses in 1778 and sued their offspring and Chen Zhengshu in court for denying him that right. The authenticity of the two contracts presented by Tian as evidence was challenged by the defendants, and the incomplete case file failed to provide information on how the dispute was judged in the end. Nevertheless, in terms of styles and formats, these contracts are informative of how illicit license-leasing agreements might have been made under the guise of legally binding contracts of loans. Notice how the license leasers appear as loaners in this contract:

> Names of the loaners who signed this contract : Wang Hongren, Feng Zhaoyuan, Song Dazhao, Zhou Tianshun, and Gong Kaihou [the originally registered license holders]. Because the construction project of the prefecture and county *yamen* offices [demanded contributions and we are in need of funds], we use two out of ten shares of our brokerage firms as collateral to borrow one hundred strings of bronze coins from Tian Jinbang through an intermediary, with which we will fulfill our official obligations. We have made a clear decision on site that the borrowed amount should carry no interest, and [the collateral] bestows Tian the right to conduct brokerage business and demands no further leasing fees. From this borrowing date onward, Tian is free to [use our licenses to] broker transactions between buyers and sellers. In the future, if Tian makes a fortune and wants to leave the brokerage business, we five license holders shall return the one hundred strings of cash to Tian. This

agreement is reached at the two parties' free will, and there is no coercion. We are afraid that oral agreement carries no proof and establish this borrowing contract as evidence on record.

By the intermediation of Zhou Wanshun and Wang Denghou.
The forty-third year of Qianlong (1778), month 12, day 24.
Signatories of the loan contract: Wang Hongren, Feng Zhaoyuan, Song Dazhao, Zhou Tianshun, and Gong Kaihou.

Under the guise of a no-interest, indefinite term loan with shares of the brokerage firms as the collateral, the actual effect of the contract was essentially that Tian obtained the right to use the brokerage license for as long as he wished with a onetime leasing fee. Notice also the mentioning of "official obligations" as the legitimizing reason for the loan. From the case file, it was apparent that the 20 percent share of the brokerages was only a way to express Tian's right to use the license, not his claim on any share of profit. Of course, the money was never meant to be returned.

It is curious that in this case, both lessees—Chen Zhengshu and Tian Jinbang (or at least Tian claimed to be a lessee despite the defense's denial)—made the leasing arrangement with all five license holders, instead of dealing with one. If it was only to obtain the right to use a brokerage license, surely it was easier to reach an agreement with one license holder. Without further information from the case file, the following is purely my conjecture. Possibly what was happening here was a newcomer's entrance into the club—that is, he would need all the existing players' blessings. The club was in the pact together to circumvent the rigid fixation of license quota through such a semilegal leasing agreement and allow a new player into the business. Everyone had to be on board; otherwise one might breach it to the authority, who could very well question the contract's legality. Hence the "leasing fee" was shared by all the established brokerages in this trade. However, the new player who was allowed into the brokerage business in such a fashion could suffer from a precarious legal standing. Should some of the license holders change their minds, the new player could be denied his access out of the blue, which might be what happened to Tian Jinbang.

This and other cases reveal that the legally stipulated procedures for the registration, retirement, and reissuance of timber brokerage licenses were not always followed in practice. It might not concern the authorities very much if the only cases of breaching were those where a deceased broker's son inherited the license without bothering to change the registered name. But it became a concern when fake persons were used for registration, or when private leasing or title transfer were arranged so that people under no scrutiny of the state might be operating a brokerage business with all the pretense of licensed agencies. In the meantime, such private measures could also help circumventing administrative costs and introduce some flexibility into the seemingly rigid system.

Despite their exclusive legal standing, licensed timber brokerages were by no means the only available intermediaries in the timber trade. They shared the business of transactional matchmaking with various other forms of economic intermediaries. Take the timber market in Hangzhou, for example. The licensed timber brokerages in Hangzhou were dominated by Huizhou natives, who maintained close connections with timber sellers from their home prefecture. Apart from these official timber brokers, there was another group of intermediaries called "Mr. Timber" (*mu xiansheng*), who were more closely associated with the buying side. These were agents hired by timber retailers located in nearby consumption markets such as Jiaxing and Huzhou to help make purchases in Hangzhou and arrange for transportation. A Mr. Timber was usually an experienced practitioner in timber trade who had earned a good reputation and was well connected to licensed timber brokers. He acted as the local purchasing agent hired by extra-local buyers. Compensation to Mr. Timber was also on a commission basis. Therefore timber trade in Hangzhou was often conducted through two agents, with the licensed timber broker more aligned with the interests of the sellers and the Mr. Timber representing the interests of the buyers. There were similar purchasing agents in other timber markets too—for instance, those in Fujian were called *nantai xiansheng*.[29]

Part of the indispensability of timber brokerages derived from their mastery of the Longquan *ma* system of measurement and pricing, which is a dazzling system that does require some expertise and experience (see chapter 2). In addition to matching sellers and buyers, timber brokers also functioned as financial intermediaries. They obtained relatively cheap loans from urban financial institutions such as pawnshops and native banks (*qianzhuang*), with which they often shared overlapping ownership, and extended credit to timber sellers at higher rates, making a handsome profit from the interest gap. Such financial intermediation existed because native banks were reluctant to deal directly with small-scale sojourning sellers, whose reputation was unknown in the city. The timber brokers, by contrast, were established urban dwellers and business owners that merited cheaper loans. And as the mediator of timber transactions, a broker was in a much better position than a native bank to learn about a sojourning merchant's financial solvency and, if necessary, to demand his timber as collateral.

Moreover, if a seller borrowed capital from a timber broker to purchase timber from the mountains, it was a widely acknowledged custom that he should sell his commodities through the same broker when he brought the timber for sale the next year.[30]

A timber broker could employ further intermediaries to secure the loans. The manager of the workers who transported rafts along water routes (*baotou*) worked together with timber brokers to contract loans to sellers. Because most sellers would hire a *baotou* manager to transport their timber rafts, these managers could acquire detailed information about the seller's family, property, and credibility. A new seller who had not built enough credit history with a timber broker could obtain a loan with his *baotou* manager as the guarantor.[31] With extensive and regular credit extension to small sellers, a timber broker looked more like a wholesaler than an intermediary. A start-up seller without much capital would obtain loans from his broker each year to purchase and transport timber from the mountains. The turnover of the timber trade took at least a whole year (two years for those working the full Yangzi River route), with cutting and portering in the winter and spring, rafting in high waters during the summer, and sales in the late summer and fall. From the gross sales revenue, the broker would take out the principal and accumulated interest of the loan as well as his commission fee before paying the seller with the residual; meanwhile, the seller would have to borrow again from the broker for the following year's business. This way, the broker was quite like a wholesaler who sought to secure the next year's supply by extending loans to small producer-sellers. The more a seller relied on loans from his broker, the more he worked like an agent rather than a patron of the broker.

This was a common practice employed by licensed brokers of other trades as well. For example, the Association of Licensed Brokers of Mountain Products in Yiyang, Hunan, regulated that member brokers should not accept to deal the goods of a seller who had already contracted a loan from a member (and hence was expected to trade through him), which was to prevent the seller from intentionally defaulting on his loan after receiving the payment from selling his goods; moreover, members should report defaulted sellers to the organization so that when such a seller attempted to trade through another member broker, the organization could be notified to confiscate the seller's commodities to compensate his victim.[32] Although not exactly "licensed brokers" in the legal sense, late Qing to Republican treaty-port tea compradors, who worked as middlemen between foreign firms and inland tea merchants, followed similar strategies. They sought to better command the supply chain by forging a relationship of financial dependence with inland tea merchants through advance loans.[33]

Licensed brokerages and other intermediaries alike mitigated the frictions of transactions in two ways: they made the market by matching sellers to potential buyers; they also facilitated the flow of credit from urban capital centers to rural suppliers. They were able to perform these functions because of an informational edge. The knowledge of market price, customer base, source of capital, and solvency of traders was so essential in cross-local trades that informed intermediaries were indispensable. Their position of centrality in the commercial network was translated into financial power, channeling circulating capital into production and effectively rendering the small players among their clientele into their agents.

THE ZHAN FAMILY OF WUYUAN

Although "mountain guests," timber firms, and brokerages seemed to be separate entities, they could all play a part in a family's business operation. We can appreciate the professional and geographic scope of a timber-trading family from the autobiographical novel *My Little History* (Wo zhi xiaoshi), authored by the last-generation licentiate Zhan Mingduo.[34] The Zhan family was from the Lukeng Village in northeastern Wuyuan, Huizhou prefecture. Like many local elites in Huizhou, the Zhans pursued a mixed strategy of exam-oriented scholarly education and commercial enterprise. Mingduo's high-great-grandfather Fengrong, who lived during the Daoguang era, traded timber to Bozhou, Anhui, but unfortunately drowned in a flood, leaving behind three sons. With the help of his fellow kinsmen, the eldest son continued their father's timber practice in Bozhou. The second son, Xilu (Mingduo's great-grandfather), an Imperial Academy student, established new family business in Fuliang, Jiangxi. The youngest son, Fengyi, conducted trade in Hankou before the Taiping Rebellion and turned to trade timber and tea in Leping, Jiangxi, after the war.

Mingduo's father, Fanzhen, a tribute student with a fifth-rank title by contribution, traded timber and established several stores in Zhejiang. In 1894, Fanzhen partnered with his in-law, Jiang Fengqing, a famous gentry who later compiled the Republican Wuyuan Gazetteer, to open a De Chang Long Lumber Store in the Shimen township of Tongxiang County, Jiaxing. In 1896 the two partners opened a Long Ji Timber Brokerage in the Jianggan timber market of Hangzhou. The partnership dissolved in 1901; Fanzhen retreated from Long Ji and established his own Sheng Ji Timber Brokerage. In a different source dated to 1909, Sheng Ji and Long Ji appeared as two of the eight member brokerages in the Association of Huizhou Timber Merchants in Hangzhou, and Sheng Ji ranked top in terms of the number of sellers and trade value it brokered (analyzed in the next section).[35] Moreover, Fanzhen had a Fu Sheng Timber Brokerage in Lianshi Town of Gui'an County, Huzhou.

The four sons of Fanzhen all practiced timber trade at some point. The second son, Yaoxian, operated as a "mountain guest" in their home county of Wuyuan. In 1907 he amassed an inventory of more than four hundred Longquan *liang* with a thousand silver yuan of working capital borrowed from the Zhi Xiang Bank in Tunxi Town, which was the preliminary distribution center in Huizhou that gathered timber from the counties of Qimen, Wuyuan, Xiuning, and Yixian.[36] The third son, Lixian, followed Fanzhen to manage the family brokerage in Hangzhou, before Lixian eventually died of an opium overdose. Shaoxian, the youngest son, attended the Timber Academy (Muye Xuetang) in Hangzhou, which was a vocational school established by the timber trade association. Mingduo, the eldest son and author of the autobiography, had focused on the exams in his youth. After several attempts, in 1905 he obtained the licentiate degree at the age of twenty-three. That was also the last term of the civil service examination held in China before it was abolished. Thereafter, Mingduo turned to the family business as well. He managed the account books of the Fu Sheng brokerage in Lianshi, first spending a few months to "practice Longquan *ma* and other jargon in the timber trade, familiarize with the map of water routes, study the booklet of different raft styles, . . . , and speak fluently the dialect of the Jiaxing-Huzhou area." Mingduo's son, Zhishan, first apprenticed at the family Fu Sheng brokerage and later moved to learn at the Zhu Ji Ji Timber Brokerage of a family acquaintance in Huzhou.

The business operations of the Zhan family covered each segment of the supply chain, from "cutting-and-buying" logs directly from the mountains to the brokerages in Hangzhou and Huzhou, to the retail store in Jiaxing. When Yaoxian carried the logs to Hangzhou, buyers were arranged through the family Sheng Ji brokerage. The De Chang Long retail store in Jiaxing could obtain its supplies directly from Yaoxian's operation; in times of need, it could also approach sellers through the client list of the family brokerages. Such vertical integration of the sites of production, distribution, and retail provided the Zhan family with an upper hand in mobilizing its social capital and obtaining market intelligence, generating a synergy to all of its enterprises.

Thanks to a publication by the timber brokers' association in Hangzhou, we have a glimpse of the internal structure of the broker-seller network at this regional distribution center.[37] Since the Song dynasty, Hangzhou was the primary site of transactions for timber produced in Anhui and Zhejiang. It remained a major timber market during the Ming-Qing era, although the relative importance of Hangzhou's timber supply to the Jiangnan area diminished over time compared with the growing volume of timber transported down the Yangzi River. The Jianggan timber market was located south of the Tide Waiting Gate of Hangzhou, along the riverbank of the Qiantang River, which was connected to the Grand Canal by three south-to-north canals that ran through the city (figure 4.1). Timber produced in southern Anhui and a few western Zhejiang prefectures were floated along the Qiantang River to the Jianggan market, a trade route that had been

FIGURE 4.1 Hangzhou Wood Market and Canal, 1918. *Source*: Sidney D. Gamble Photographs Collection (167–938), David M. Rubenstein Rare Book and Manuscript Library, Duke University.

developed in the thirteenth century.[38] Sales of timber in the Hangzhou market targeted the core area of Jiangnan: Hangzhou, Jiaxing, and Huzhou in Zhejiang (the aforementioned Zhan family had establishments in all three locations), and Suzhou, Wuxi, and Changzhou in Jiangsu.

Hangzhou was different from Nanjing and Hankou in that it was located quite close to its source of timber supply. Although players in the markets of Nanjing and Hankou were mostly large capitalized timber-trading firms by the nineteenth century, many sellers in Hangzhou were small-time traders who worked a single route or only dipped occasionally in this business. Some were countrymen who were delegated with the timber produced in the mountains of his lineage; some tried their luck in this trade with the capital borrowed from the timber brokers. In this respect, Hangzhou was similar to other local markets in proximity to areas of production, such as Changde in Hunan, Ganzhou in Jiangxi, and Fuzhou in Fujian. In these markets, sellers were generally not very familiar with the customs of the timber trade and relied heavily on the services and capital provided by the brokers. Unlike the case in Nanjing and Hankou, where over the course of the nineteenth century licensed brokers became overshadowed by expansive trading firms that established their own branch offices in multiple localities, the economic and financial intermediation by timber brokers remained indispensable in the Hangzhou market well into the twentieth century.

In Hangzhou three organizations in the trade of timber were established representing different groups of interests. The Association of Huizhou Timber Merchants (Huishang Muye Gongsuo) was the organization of timber brokers who were originally from Huizhou as well as sellers from Huizhou. The Eastern Zhejiang Timber Association (Zhedong Muye Gongsuo) was the organization of timber sellers from the four timber-producing prefectures in eastern Zhejiang, including Chuzhou, Jinhua, Quzhou, and Yanzhou. The extant record of the activities of these two associations went back to the 1780s.[39] The Association of Tax-Paying Timber Merchants (Keshang Muye Gongsuo) was the organization of timber buyers from six Jiangnan prefectures: Hangzhou, Jiaxing, Huzhou, Suzhou, Wuxi, and Changzhou. The earliest extant mentioning of this organization was in 1876.[40] The association was so named because it was officially delegated the tax-farming responsibility of collecting levies from the timber buyers of these prefectures. This practice represented the common formula developed between local governments and merchant associations in the nineteenth century, especially in the post-Taiping era.[41]

Because of the large space required by the timber trade, moorage along the river bank was a constant cause for contention between different timber merchant groups and between timber merchants and the local residents. The two selling-side organizations, the Association of Huizhou Timber Merchants and Eastern Zhejiang Timber Association, were initially founded to safeguard the timber merchants' common property right over the sandy land along the Qiantang River and to fend off the intrusions by nearby villagers, who attempted to grow crops and build sheds to reclaim the land. The so-called Nanxin Customs sandy land (*Nanguan shadi*) referred to the strip of land of about two square kilometers produced by the alluvium of the Qiantang River, where the Ming-Qing Nanxin Guan timber tax station was located.

Despite the long-standing Qing policy of encouraging land reclamation, local and provincial officials valued the substantial income from transit timber taxes, which surely overshadowed the grain tax that could potentially be collected if the flood-prone land along the Qiantang River banks had been granted to the villagers. Government documents regarding the dispute between the merchants and the villagers (and its resolution in favor of the merchants during the Qianlong reign) was copied in a 1909 publication of the Association of Huizhou Timber Merchants. The remark by the financial commissioner of Zhejiang in 1785 reasoned:

> The sandy land is crucial for the timber merchants to stock their rafts when passing the Nanxin customs station . . . if pressed too close to the river, big loss could be incurred if the timber logs drifted away when water rose. . . . *It is unreasonable to risk thousands of teals of customs taxes just for a few hundreds of land taxes.* Comparing the effects on state income, the two options show great disparity. Without a doubt, the land in question should be permanently managed by the timber merchants, provided that they should *compensate the state for the forgone land tax.*[42]

The case was submitted all the way up the bureaucratic hierarchy, until the Board of Revenue presented it to the throne and obtained the Qianlong emperor's consent. The deal was for the timber merchants to compensate the local state for the forgone land tax, a responsibility that came to be called the "contribution for grain tax on the sandy land" (*shaliang juan*). A stele was erected as evidence in 1787 by the leaders of both the Huizhou and Eastern Zhejiang associations.[43]

The obligation to pay for the "contribution for grain tax on the sandy land" gave the two selling-side associations the legitimate reason to collect fees from their members. In addition to paying this "contribution," the two organizations hired security guards to patrol the riverbank to look out for thieves and fires, the cost of which was paid out of member fees. According to the regulation of the Association of Huizhou Timber Merchants, the fee was collected at 4.75‰ of the value of the timber dealt through each timber broker, in which 1‰ was for the security guard and 3.75‰ was for the land rent. The broker extracted this fee, together with other payables such as commission fee and repayment of previous loans, before releasing to the seller the residual amount from selling his timber (see table 2.3 for a representative bill).[44] Therefore the value of transactions conducted through each member broker of this organization can be inferred by dividing the amount of fees collected by each broker by 4.75‰ (table 4.1). It should be noticed that although the ad valorem fee was levied on the sellers in the name of the two specified causes, the total amount collected by the organization certainly more than covered these two items of expense and was used for all sorts of expenses of the association, including other miscellaneous obligations to local government agencies and providing other economic and ritualistic functions to its members.

In the year of 1909, 347 transactions of timber were conducted by 211 sellers through 8 timber brokers, generating a total of 1529.6 silver *yuan* as contribution to the organization, which meant an annual trading volume of 320,000 *yuan* by the members of the Association of Huizhou Timber Merchants (see table 4.1). While only this snapshot from 1909 is available from the sources, the following discussion about the brokers' network could, to some extent, be applied to earlier times. From the trade association's gazette, we know that their trade bounded back rather quickly after the Taiping Rebellion, during which the trade association hall was burned down. After its rehabilitation, previous practices resumed, and the total number of member brokerage firms remained stable. The trade association gazette left no remark about any systematic transformation in the timber market because of the Taiping interruption. Hangzhou's timber supply and distribution were not significantly influenced by the treaty-port system until the late 1920s, when imported timber started to flow into Hangzhou through Shanghai in volume. The 1909 data did show a few new expenditures of the association that were apparently added in the late Qing, such as contributions to the local police office, merchant protection association, chamber of commerce, and the bureau of lifeguard. To cover these additional costs, it is likely that the 4.75‰ levy as of 1909 was higher than the rate in the eighteenth century, although this speculation cannot be confirmed.

TABLE 4.1 Fee collection by the Association of Huizhou Timber Merchants, 1909

[1]		[2]	[3]	[4]	[5]	[6]	[7]
	BROKER	NUMBER OF TRANSACTIONS	NUMBER OF SELLERS	LAND RENT (SILVER *YUAN*)	SECURITY (SILVER *YUAN*)	TOTAL FEES (SILVER *YUAN*)	TRADE VALUE (SILVER *YUAN*)
1	Sheng Ji	64	50	247.83	66.09	313.92	66,088.00
2	De Chang Long	69	47	223.62	59.63	283.25	59,632.00
3	Xun Ji	49	29	161.82	43.15	204.97	43,150.93
4	Yu Da	32	26	148.76	39.67	188.43	39,669.33
5	Tong Yi Xing	47	28	137.65	36.71	174.36	36,706.67
6	Tong Li Xing	23	19	104.50	27.87	132.37	27,866.67
7	Long Ji	39	36	102.54	27.34	129.88	27,344.00
8	Tong Mao Xing	24	18	80.88	21.57	102.45	21,568.00
Total		347	211*	1,207.60	322.03	1,529.62	322,025.60

Source: Huishang gongsuo zhengxin lu.
Notes: Row numbers indicate rank (biggest broker, second biggest, and so on).
* The total number of sellers at the end of column [3] is not the sum of the number of sellers each broker served (253). The reason was that some sellers traded through more than one broker. Column [2]: The number of transactions each broker intermediated in 1909. Column [3]: The number of sellers who sold timber through each broker; because some sellers traded with the same broker multiple times, the number in column [3] is smaller than column [2]. Column [4]: The amount of "contribution for the grain tax on the sandy land" (*shaliang juan*) collected by each broker, which was 3.75‰ of trade value. Column [5]: The amount of contribution to cover the expenses in hiring security guards collected by each broker, which was 1‰ of trade value. Column [6]: The sum of columns [4] and [5]. Column [7]: The inferred value of trade intermediated by each broker, calculated by column [6] divided by 4.75‰.

The trade scale of different sellers varied very much, ranging from a minimum of 26 *yuan* to Zhan Maochun's 18,922 *yuan*, with a mean of 1,526 *yuan*, a median of 1,048 *yuan*, and a standard deviation of 2,001 *yuan*. About 80 percent of the sellers were small dealers who sold for less than 2,000 silver *yuan* during the year. The few top-ranked sellers were significantly larger than the others. The top three took up 13 percent of the total market share. The top fifteen traded for more than 4,000 *yuan*, whose collective share of trade volume reached 30 percent. Even with these disparities, the overall Herfindahl index derived from the data, which measures the level of competition and concentration in a market, was 0.013—a level that indicates a relatively unconcentrated and competitive market for the sellers.

Larger sellers tended to trade through more than one broker and trade more than once during the year. Among the 211 sellers, 32 (15 percent) transacted through more than one broker. The three largest sellers—Zhan Maochun, Song Zi, and Heng Faxiang—all did business with four different brokers and traded more than seven times this year. Four sellers traded with three brokers, and twenty-five with two brokers. Figure 4.2 illustrates the structure of the seller-broker network as reflected by the 347 transactions. The most distinguishing feature is the overall connectedness of the network. One might easily imagine a more segregated picture, where each broker controlled a distinct client base that was closed to each other. However, that was obviously not the case for the Hangzhou market. Admittedly, each broker did have a relatively independent client base, especially among medium-size to small sellers: eight communities are detected through the modularity algorithm, each centering around one broker. Yet the eight groups were not closed but were connected through the larger sellers, who traded with more than one broker.

Those sellers who dealt with more than one broker are placed by the algorithm in the relative center part of the figure because of their importance in bridging different groups. Notice that the volume of their trade was not evenly distributed among the brokers with whom they dealt—the thickness of the edges represents the scaled volume of trade between two connected nodes. Instead, they each had a primary broker and one or more minor ones. The trade volume through the primary broker overshadowed the volume with the others. This was true for most of the top ten sellers. For example, the largest seller, Zhan Mao Chun, was most close to the Yu Da brokerage, while also doing smaller businesses through Xun Ji, Sheng Ji, and Tong Li Xing. The second-largest seller, Song Zi, was most closely connected to the Tong Li Xing brokerage and then to Sheng Ji and Tong Yi Xing. Some of the large sellers were committed to a single broker, such as Cheng Qidong to Sheng Ji and Tong Fu Tai to Tong Mao Xing. Some of the brokers shared more customers than others. The communities surrounding the two largest brokers, Sheng Ji and De Chang Long, were well separated.

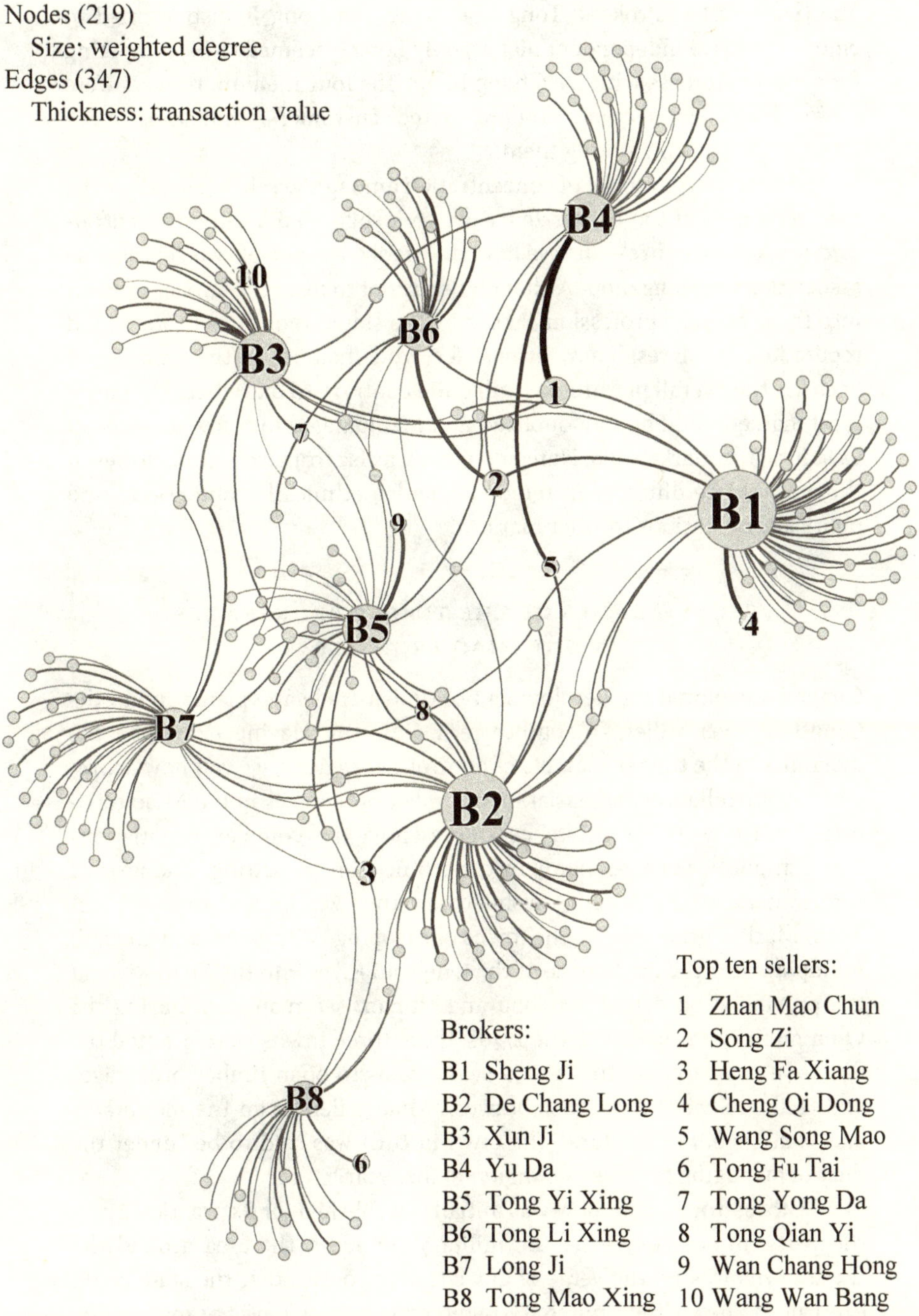

FIGURE 4.2 Network structure of timber sellers and brokers in Hangzhou, 1909.
Source: *Huishang gongsuo zhengxin lu.*

The two smallest brokers, Tong Mao Xing and Long Ji, also seemed to enjoy respective independent niches; only Long Ji seemed to be competing for some customers with De Chang Long. The four medium brokers were more closely connected through shared customers, indicating more intense competition among them.

The relatively low level of concentration among the sellers as well as the connectedness of the broker-seller network suggested a rather decentralized market structure—and we have only looked at one of two selling-side associations in Hangzhou. Although this is not to deny the barrier of entry into the brokerage profession caused by the state's requirement for sound reputation, local residency, license fee, and fixation of the number of licenses, the overall picture was still quite contrary to one where the entire local market could be monopolized and manipulated by a few players—at least for large markets like Hangzhou that was far from the truth. However, things could be different in remoter, smaller, ethnically contentious, and politically precarious frontier markets.

PECULIARITIES OF THE TIMBER BROKERAGES IN THE MIAO FRONTIER

Chapter 3 explored the development of timber trade and plantation in the Qingshui River valley in southeastern Guizhou. Having examined the dynamics in the timber markets of nonfrontier regions, we can now appreciate the installation and variation of timber brokerages in the Miao territories and how these differences represented the complex negotiations between politics and economy in the ethnic frontier setting. The nearest timber market to the lower Qingshui community was located at the "Three-Town Market" (referring to the towns of Maoping, Wangzhai, and Guazhi) in Jinping near the confluence of the Qingshui River into the Yuan River at the provincial border of Guizhou and Hunan (see map 2.2). During the Qing military campaign in the 1730s, these three towns were granted the exclusive right to take turns on a yearly basis to open timber brokerages and facilitate the transactions between Miao sellers from the mountains and Han buyers from afar.[45] The town in turn was said to be "under the duty of managing the river" (*dangjiang*) that year.[46]

The three-town monopoly was initially established for its practicality. In the years immediately after the military conquest, the area around the three towns was on the verge of any effective control that the state could exert in the newly incorporated Miao territory. In the eyes of many Qing officials, the Miao people of the three towns, who were bilingual in Chinese and Miao, were ready mediators of trade. The newly incorporated territories further to the west should be kept as a prohibited region from the entrance of downriver Han merchants so as to forestall ethnic conflicts.[47] In the following century and a half, concerns about ethnic tensions and social stability committed the state to the three-town monopoly system at this *perceived* Han-Miao border, despite recurrent challenges from downriver Han towns and gradual acculturation that rendered less relevant the initial rationale of mitigating cultural and linguistic barriers.

The timber brokers in the three towns were no different from the licensed brokerages in the nonfrontier provinces in terms of their actual business operations. They matched buyers and sellers, helped to arrange storage and transportation, and sometimes extended short-term credit to those sellers in need. Timber purchasers active in the three towns were composed of several merchant groups of different native place origins, the most dominant of which were referred to as the "three *bangs* and five assisting groups" (*sanbang wuxiang*). It was by no means surprising that the dominant "three *bangs*" here were the same as those in Nanjing: the *bangs* of Huizhou, Linqing, and Jiangxi. They were the first to have brought timber trade to this region in the early seventeenth century and sometimes worked concurrently as the agents to purchase tribute timber quotas for the provinces of Hunan, Jiangsu, and Jiangxi. The five assisting groups were merchants from nearby prefectures in Guizhou and Hunan along the water route who started as assistants or employees of the three *bangs* and later developed into independent timber merchants.[48]

The fight over the right to "manage the river" became an enduring theme almost as soon as the institution was established. Benchu, a Han-dominated town just a few miles downriver from the three towns, was the most insistent competitor that sought to overthrow the monopoly of the three towns. The residents of Benchu repeatedly applied to the authorities for official licenses to open brokerages. At the turn of the nineteenth century, the conflict between Benchu and the three towns escalated into a series of violent conflicts and lawsuits from 1798 to 1806. While I have analyzed the convoluting details of these conflicts elsewhere, the most striking outcome was that the rotating monopoly of the three towns' timber brokerages was reinforced despite the fact that the Benchu contenders presented a sound argument in line with the formal regulations of the licensed brokerage system and successfully won over broad and high-profile sympathies from both within and beyond Guizhou (including the faraway Longjiang Guan in Nanjing).[49]

Frontier policies, rather than economic principles, prevailed. The overriding consideration behind the officials' repeated rejection of Benchu's petition to normalize the three-town market was the political consequence of introducing competition from the Han of Benchu to the timber brokerage business, a livelihood that had been promised exclusively to the Miao people of the three towns. The disputes between the three towns and Benchu happened in the middle of a general Miao revolt in parts of Guizhou and Hunan that lasted from 1795 to 1806. Indeed, the loss of economic resources to Han settlers was the chief cause of the revolt. Advocates of immigration and assimilation learned the hard way that extensive acculturation of Miao individuals to Chinese ways did not necessarily carry with it a sense of loyalty to the Qing rule.[50] Although the Miao litigants involved in the three towns versus Benchu dispute were not part of that revolt, Guizhou officials nonetheless considered pacifying Miao resentment and protecting their economic interests as the first priority in preventing the spread of the unrest.

This official concern was used and further enhanced by the three-town residents' self-portrayal in their petitions. They appealed to officials that "we *impoverished Miao people* [*qiong* Miao] set up the brokerage business and depend on it for a living," and if Benchu's violent blockage of the river was not stopped, then "not only were we to suffer, all the Miao area along the river would be badly impacted as their timber could not find buyers. In sum, as long as those treacherous people are not eradicated, timber merchants would not come, and we poor Miao could have no reliance for life."[51] The upriver sellers, in support of the petition of the three towns, lamented their own loss over so many cut trees that could not be sold. They referred to the competitors from Benchu as the "treacherous Han Chinese" (*Hanjian*), while emphasizing their common Miao identity with the three towns' brokers, who "spoke the Miao language and understood the dialects of Huizhou and Jiangxi" and "always gave fair prices and stuck to the proper silver standard."[52]

In fact, by the 1800s cultural and language barriers were no longer as overwhelming as they were in the 1730s. Acculturation was in process. The Miao people in the lower Qingshui area had taken up lineage concepts, adopted Chinese-language contractual practices, and increasingly turned to the local administration for dispute resolution, especially when dealing with outsiders. Many of the large landowning families had produced degree-holders by taking advantage of the favorable Miao quotas in civil examinations.[53] This is not to say that the Miao had become fully assimilated but that their emphasis on the common Miao customs and languages in their appeals to Qing officials reflected less about actual communication difficulties with Han merchants than their strategic use of the state's ethnic policies to fend off Han competition.

In regular timber markets the Qing state usually upheld the principle of equal-and-fair market access (although the application of the principle to specific cases was subject to the interpretation of individual magistrates). In the Miao frontier, by contrast, concerns about ethnic tensions and social stability committed the state to a monopoly system at the perceived Han-Miao border even after the initial economic rationale withered away. The examination of the active timber trade in the Miao frontier reveals a more multifaceted picture of this contact zone than the simplistic understanding that economically unsophisticated natives were deprived of their land and other resources by encroaching outsiders. Episodes of fighting over the rights to open timber brokerages demonstrate that the state's ethnic policies and administrative priorities were all strategically used by the involved economic agents, including the Miao natives, to achieve their respective interests.

CONCLUSION

Along the timber supply chain a complete turnover could take a couple of years, from logging at mountain sites to purchases at preliminary local markets, to transshipments to regional and interregional distribution centers, and eventually to retail and consumption. "Mountain guests," itinerant traders, brokers, big wholesalers, and retailers operated different segments of the supply chain. Lumberjacks, porters, rafters, measurers, hawser manufacturers, and other specialized laborers animated this industry. As the Zhan family of Wuyuan exemplifies, a strategy of vertical integration and regional diversification could help a family enterprise spread its talent and capital to weave a synergistic business structure. Kinship and marriage ties, communal bonds, scholarly affinities, and business partnerships often overlapped in a nested social network that facilitated the making and sharing of profit as one of its many functions.

Among all the market players, licensed brokerages took on economic as well as administrative importance in the local marketplaces. The central-level reforms on the licensed brokerage in the first half of the eighteenth century aimed to preserve the integrity of the market space from excessive interferences of the local administrative framework and bestowed upon individual licensed brokers the responsibility to promote unhindered market exchange according to economic logic. These regulations set the foundational market principles for the next century, when licensed brokers assumed the central positions in mediating nonlocal trade.

The most important functions performed by licensed brokerages and other economic intermediaries alike in the trade of timber were informational: the matching of buyers and sellers as well as creditors and borrowers. What made these intermediaries essential to long-distance trades was their exceptional knowledge about sources of supply and demand, market tendencies, and the financial situation of individual firms and traders. Despite the usual accusations of licensed brokerages as monopolizers of local markets, the examination on the broker-seller network in big markets such as Hangzhou reveals a decentralized and connected market structure. Moreover, other than licensed brokerages, there were various economic intermediaries involved in the mediation of timber trade that occupied a legally recognized or customarily tolerated niche in the market. Both facts attested to the ample space for competition, at least in big markets. Frontier regions could have a very different story, however. The three-town monopoly of timber brokerages in the Miao territories arose more from the state's concern of protecting Miao livelihood and maintaining local stability than its normal calibrations of market regulation.

CHAPTER FIVE

Trade Associations, "Contributions," and Contract Enforcement

THE regulations made by the eighteenth-century Qing state regarding licensed brokerages were based on the basic imagination of market transactions as being conducted by individual itinerant traders through independently operating individual brokers. However, by the early nineteenth century, the individual-based landscape was increasingly replaced by a marketplace delineated by organized groups.[1] The increasing formalization of merchant networks into trade associations with permanent estates, written regulations, and registered members reduced the dependence on licensed brokers to match and guarantee deals, especially in the most developed interregional market centers. Indeed, the proliferation of trade associations in the Qing has been attributed to the merchants' efforts to free themselves of the licensed brokers.[2]

Some trade associations of timber merchants obtained a brokerage license under the name of a deceased founder or even the anonym of a deity worshiped by the group, in order to help their members circumvent the official requirement to trade through licensed brokers. For example, in Hankou the trade association of timber merchants from Changsha and Hengzhou of Hunan obtained a license under the name "Zou Gongyi"—not a real person but the anonym of a local god, Master Zou.[3] Such practices streamlined the separate obligations of licensed brokerages and trade associations to the local government into one. Member merchants registered their deals with the trade association and paid the charges of a few percentage in the name of "membership fees." The trade association, in turn, used the fund to pay for the brokerage license fee and other surcharges levied by various government offices as well as to keep the organization running and afford services to its members.

In response, licensed brokers tended to organize themselves into incorporated associations to collectively deal with the organized traders and defend their own legal privileges. In Suzhou, for example, the Xunzheng Association of Licensed Timber Brokers was founded in response to the establishment of the Daxing Association of Timber Traders, as members of the latter organization attempted to circumvent the brokers and sell to customers directly. Upon its founding, the Xunzheng Association petitioned to the Suzhou prefect that "all timber from Fujian, Zhejiang, Jiangxi, and Hunan should be taxed by the association at four coins per standard raft . . . a seller who transported timber to Suzhou must trade through us brokers and be forbidden to deal with customers directly," which was to ensure that "enough funds could be raised to cover our official duties [*chaiwu*] to the local government."[4] An association of timber brokers like Xunzheng, the Association of Huizhou Timber Merchants in Hangzhou shaped the landscape of timber transactions in nineteenth-century Hangzhou together with a timber sellers' association and a buyers' association in the city (see chapter 4). Similar trade associations of timber brokers also existed in Nanjing and Hankou, which engaged in constant negotiations with multiple organizations of timber traders that were founded on the basis of the merchants' native places or the origin, destination, or targeted customers of their timber.

Trade associations played important functions in commercial taxation, providing economic and social services to members, and making and enforcing trade regulations. Each of these aspects of trade association functions has been extensively recognized and studied in the existing literature. However, past studies tend to take a trade association's fiscal responsibilities toward the state and its economic functions toward the market as separate matters, largely neglecting the connections between the two.[5] By examining organized groups of timber traders and brokers in multiple marketplaces, I hope not only to provide a detailed depiction of these functions but also to elucidate the *complementarity* of these functions in facilitating a stable timber supply. This offers more relevance to our understanding of Chinese trade associations in general.

Notably, the very reason that a trade association could enforce its trade regulations and internal disciplines among its members was that it could provide appealing benefits that were *exclusive* to members in good standing—that is, should a member violate the association's rule, he would face the punishment of being excluded from such benefits. The exclusive services provided by a trade association to its members included (but were not limited to) storage, accommodation, charity (such as burying grounds for deceased itinerant merchants), business intelligence, legal assistance, and, most interesting for our purpose here, collective taxation coverage. It is somewhat counterintuitive that the inclusion in—instead of evasion from—a collective taxation plan should be something appealing to an individual merchant. The increased capacity of the state in direct commercial taxation after the mid-nineteenth century made the option of joining a trade association's collective taxation arrangement attractive to individual merchants. Not only did the collective taxation arrangement provide members with a shield from the nuisance of dealing with greedy tax clerks directly, but the association's membership fees (from which their collective taxes were paid) were often allocated at such a progressive rate that small traders would pay less than if they were to go through the direct taxation stops. The attractiveness of such a tax shield can be appreciated from the fact that the threat of being excluded from such coverage could do much in keeping a member in line with the trade association's other regulations, particularly its measures of contract enforcement based on reputation and collective actions. The same logic goes for the other member-only services. The exclusivity of these desirable benefits worked to increase the opportunity cost of breaching the association's rules, thus helping to enforce its internal regulations among members.

A crucial part of the trade associations' regulations was concerned with enforcing contracts and upholding credit agreements. Short-term trade credit in the form of chains of deferred payment was essential for the development of timber wholesale. This was not only because of the high monetary value of typical transactions (usually featuring the equivalence of hundreds to several thousand taels of silver) but also due to the long time it took for transporting timber to the destination for sale or finishing a large construction project. The grace period extended to construction contractors, in particular, was critical for the post-Taiping reconstruction in Jiangnan and the real estate boom in the new treaty ports. The risks of overdue payments and outright defaults had to be effectively combated to keep credit liquidity afloat; otherwise, the whole business would be forced to fall back on cash transactions in a credit crunch, causing earthquakes to the entire supply chain (as so happened in the aftermath of a couple of big fraud cases). To combat such risks, timber trade organizations relied on reputation mechanisms and information sharing to maintain intragroup solidarity and monitor outside trading partners. Horizontal communications among trade associations in different localities further enhanced their capability to respond promptly to cross-regional cases. When disputes escalated beyond the scope of a single merchant association, chambers of commerce (after 1904) and the court system became involved. Vertical communications among these organizations strengthened the continuity from informal norms of business practices to regulations in commercial organizations, and thence to adjudications in court.

Services provided by the trade associations can be understood from the framework of "club goods," a type of good in economics that exhibit high excludability in their provision and low rivalry in consumption (at least until reaching a certain level of congestion): a trade association could enroll a new member in such services at minimal marginal cost and could effectively block nonmembers from benefiting. The taxation arrangements with the government demarcated a more autonomous market space, and the features of club goods served to solidify collaborative actions, lending credibility to the association's enforcement measures. The obstacles of incessant tax stops and fraudulent trading were mitigated via these institutional arrangements to allow the smooth flow of timber logs and boards across the landscape.

COLLECTIVE TAXATION AND MARKET ACCESS

As merchant associations increasingly became the organizing framework in the market, local magistrates experimented with ways to incorporate them into the local framework of commercial taxation. By the first half of the nineteenth century, a balance was struck out of negotiations between merchant groups and local magistrates: officials lent their legal authorities to enforce customary practices in each trade as stipulated in trade association's regulations, as long as they did not object with basic principles of open market entrance and fair exchange. Other than that, officials maintained a noninterventionist position in the market. In return, trade associations offered their cooperation in securing the local government's fiscal objectives through collective taxation arrangements, which the magistrates promised to be limited to the basics and fairly allocated among different merchant groups. Such bottom-level negotiations between the merchants and local officials formed the underlying foundation of the overall trend that we have repeatedly seen during this period—namely that the state worked increasingly through the market and decreasingly through direct control of resources.

The reform on the licensed brokerage system in the 1730s had prohibited local offices and their employees from extracting supplies through licensed brokers without adequate compensation.[6] In principle, local governments were now supposed to make necessary purchases at the going market price, just like other market actors. However, this part of the new law was seldom followed in practice. Succeeding emperors attempted to abolish "official purchase prices" time and again, but all in vain.[7] For one thing, the annual procurement of imperial timber was still conducted at below-market official prices until the end of the dynasty. The fund-deprived local government had no means to obey this central law to its text.

How did local governments respond to their funding challenges? Historian Maura Dykstra's study on the state-building process in the city of Chongqing based on Baxian archives offers crucial clues to how local officials more generally may have gone about mobilizing the funds they needed and how these official actions supported the increased authority of merchant groups. During the second half of the eighteenth century, the local government began mobilizing resources in the name of "official duty," based on the concept of which collective taxation of merchant groups was arranged, negotiated, and contested. By assigning "exclusive responsibilities" to different merchant groups, the local state established an innovative framework to tap market resources. This local state-building process fostered the increased formalization of merchant groups.[8] Although it was not realistic for the local government to afford market prices, the allocation of official duties was by no means arbitrary. Local officials made a range of commitments to allocate duties in a fair and just manner in an effort to keep official purchases from ruining businesses, including opening the channel of negotiation with merchant groups to adjust official purchase prices—not high enough to cover the merchants' cost but at least to limit their losses caused by the official procurement system to a reasonable amount.[9]

Switching to the merchants' perspective, how was a merchant group's standing affected by the framework of performing exclusively assigned official duty? Being recognized as a proper merchant group and assigned an exclusive duty by the local government offices surely lent security and legitimacy to the group. Scholars have recognized that many petitions brought by merchant coalitions in a magistrate's court involved a delicate negotiation in which their official duties were used as the legitimate cause to press for the official's endorsement of the trade associations' attempt to suppress dissidents in the group or drive out competitors.[10] The previously quoted statement from the Xunzheng Association in the city of Suzhou was one example of making explicit connections between its claimed authority over timber traders and the official duties it performed. However, were these requests always granted in a magistrate's court? If not, what was the magistrate's consideration in making different decisions? More important, what was the implication for market structure and openness: Would all the traders in the same business be essentially forced to join the same trade association? Would it be possible to form a separate association of the same trade? The following legal cases provide insights into these questions.

The first is a simple lawsuit in which a merchant group brought suit against an individual merchant who refused to conform to the fee-collecting scheme of the group and, consequently, could offer more competitive prices in market exchange. The petition of the merchant group, which is representative of the genre, reads:

> The timber trading *bang* in the city of Chongqing, including the firms of Mei Rongxing, Tong Yiyuan, Li Daosheng, Wang Yongmao, Li Lisheng, Jiang Yongju, Xu Bingxing, and Wang Ruisheng, now collectively request Your Magistrate's judgment on the following matter of defying official duties [*chai*] and illicitly usurping the trade. We operate businesses of timber trade and shoulder the annual duty of supplying all the local government offices and examination halls in the provincial capital without any violations.
>
> Recently, an insubordinate Li Guisen has forcibly occupied a position in the Fushun Storehouse and illicitly made sales of timber. He vied to compete with us in the trade and defied the responsibility to contribute to the official duty. We have verified the truthfulness of this condition, with a former buyer [from Li Guisen], He Changfa, as the living testimony of Li's surreptitious sales. We have invited all the *bang* members to gather and reason with Li, who still did not repent and even threatened to sue us without fear.
>
> Our business is small, yet our official duty is heavy. Upon repeated urge from the magistrate's office to remit the required timber, we went to collect Li's share without any success. Now that Li Guisen conducts trade but shoulders no official duty, other members of our *bang* all have a wait-and-see attitude. It is for certain that others will follow suit and it will be more difficult to fulfill the duty. We collectively request Your Magistrate to open a court session to investigate this matter and make things right.[11]

In this case, because levies collected from group members were, at least partially, used to fulfill this trade's duties toward the local government, the legal authority of the magistrate was called upon to discipline the uncooperative individual. By expressing their concern that if left untended, others might follow this precedent, and the official duty could be in jeopardy, the merchant group subtly insinuated the magistrate's obligation of helping enforce their internal regulations in exchange of their performance of the duties. The magistrate's verdict at the end of the petition confirmed his overall priority in ensuring the timely delivery of the group's due amount of contribution:

> Verdict: Await the court's voucher to order Li Guisen to contribute to the official duty according to the group's regulations. Should he violate this order, bring him to court for punishment. As for this year's due payment of 40 taels for the timber needed for the Renwu-term Examination, which the provincial governor and administrative commissioner have repeatedly pressed for delivery within ten days, the group should follow the order to raise the full amount and submit it as soon as possible to the specialized agent for remittance. *Do not make other excuses to drag on anymore.* Otherwise, should any official business be adversely affected, you will be held accountable.[12]

From the magistrate's verdict, we may make some inferences about the initial cause of the lawsuit. It was possible that the sequence of events was just as the merchant group presented, that Li Guisen's refusal to chip in for the official duty obstructed the group's timely payment for their 40-tael due. Alternatively, it was also possible that Li's individual share of contribution would not make such a big difference, but the group simply used the provincial officials' urgent demand for an examination fund as an opportunity to press the magistrate into disciplining Li, possibly a long-term competitor who refused to join the group or failed to conform to the group's way. As the magistrate warning at the end indicated—"Do not make other excuses to drag on anymore"—he might have suspected the latter possibility.

While individual defiance like that of Li Guisen would often be straightened out by court verdicts, magistrates were more cautious when dealing with conflicts between groups.[13] Similar lawsuits brought by official-duty-bearing groups against competing groups of merchants seldom resulted in protected fiefdoms; instead, they resulted in a reallocation of official duties so that the defendant group was officially granted access to the market by being assigned a portion of the duty. The result was the projection of exclusively assigned official duties to officially recognized merchant associations. Any group of merchants that wanted to dissociate or remain separate from an existing trade association due to dissatisfaction with its trade rules or fee-collection schemes would be able to do so with official recognition by assuming an independently assigned official duty. Enrollment in some exclusive responsibilities to the local state became a merchant group's best shield against a competing trade association's challenge to its legitimacy as well as against local government subordinates' illicit exactions. From the perspective of market access, it did not attain the level of absolute free entrance but was still a much more decentralized structure than the one once imagined by earlier scholars, such as H. B. Morse, that Chinese "guilds" exerted a tyranny on market access and trade rules.[14] The following case illustrates such a decentralized structure.[15]

The timber-trading *bang* within the city of Chongqing that showed up in the previous case, also known as the Fir *bang* (*shanmu bang*), was assigned the annual official duty of 40 taels in the name of contributing the timber needed for examinations since 1864. Another timber-related group in the city, the Green Mountain *bang* (*qingshan bang*) of coffin materials, was not involved in the performance of this particular duty. Although the names of these *bangs* indicated different specializations, there were no clear-cut boundaries in their members' business scope. Neither group could claim a monopoly in the trade of a certain kind of timber. Firms in the Fir *bang* traded fir planks in addition to poles, which were good material for coffins, and members of the Green Mountain *bang* could sell their inventories for uses other than coffin making. Members of the Fir *bang* and the Cypress *bang* (*baimu bang*) certainly focused on fir and cypress, respectively, but did not necessarily limit their business to that particular variety.

In 1884, when the local government raised the "examination duty" by 20 taels, the Fir *bang* attempted to enlist the Green Mountain *bang* to share the responsibility. According to the former group's narrative, when the 40-tael duty was initially assigned to timber merchants in Chongqing twenty years earlier, the Green Mountain *bang* was able to shirk the duty and the Fir *bang* had to shoulder all the burden for the past seven triennial examinations. The Fir *bang* complained: "[The Green Mountain *bang*] is also a *bang* of timber trade, conducting the same business and making the same profit, how come they alone can escape from the official duty?" In their countersuit the Green Mountain *bang* refuted the charge by stressing the separate "official duties" they had been performing and referring to past magisterial adjudications in their favor as precedents:

> We always fulfill the official duty to supply seven government offices in the city with timber planks and pay the due amount of

> state taxes before we dare to make market sales. We have attempted no violations for decades. We and the Fir *bang* have *separate trades and separate official duties*, and there is no confusion to this fact.
>
> Back in 1879, Zhou Tongxing of the Fir *bang* attempted to use their examination duty as excuses to make extortions from us and falsely sued Wang Yuchun and others in our *bang* with the charge of defying official duties in court. Thankfully, the previous magistrate made the judgment that the two *bangs* should do separate businesses and undertake separate duties, [the Fir *bang*'s official duty] has nothing to do with ours. The record of the case can be checked in the Division of Works' dossier in the county government. Now that the provincial officials ordered their *bang* to pay more for the examination duty, Wang Yongmao [of the Fir *bang*] had the nerve to conceal the previous lawsuit and sue us in court with the charge of defying official orders and obstructing public duties.[16]

Here the Green Mountain *bang* invoked the basic principle of "separate trades, separate duties" (*gemao gechai*) regarding merchant groups and official duties—that is, separate groups should be allowed to conduct their businesses and handle their duties independently. Whereas the Fir *bang* was responsible for the duty related to provincial examinations, the Green Mountain *bang* assumed a different responsibility in supplying planks to seven offices in the city of Chongqing. Although both were timber-trading merchant groups, their independent organization was manifested in and guaranteed by their separate duties toward the local state. When the Fir *bang* attempted to impose their internal taxing scheme upon the Green Mountain *bang* in the name of allocating official duties five years earlier, their request was rejected by the previous county magistrate precisely for the principle of "separate trades, separate duties."

As for the current dispute, the magistrate acknowledged that the demanded 20-tael increase in the Fir *bang*'s duty was too heavy and eventually made the decision that the added 20 taels should be shouldered equally by three timber merchant groups: the Fir *bang*, the Green Mountain *bang*, and the Cypress *bang*. The Green Mountain and Cypress *bang*s were allowed to handle the increased amount according to their existing arrangement of fee collections from members and answer directly to the local state, instead of being subject to the Fir *bang*'s directions. This result was a reallocation of official duties among the different *bang*s of timber trade and a restatement of the boundaries between these groups as the merchants themselves saw fit. In addition to this incident, the Fir *bang* had made other similar attempts at taking over smaller timber merchant groups and subjugating them to its own fee-collecting formula but never succeeded. So long as these smaller groups petitioned to the local magistrate to assume a portion of the duty in question, their independence from the interference of the Fir *bang* was protected.[17]

The dynamics between various merchant groups and local government authorities as exemplified by this case point to a fundamental difference in the organizational principles of Chinese trade associations and European merchant guilds, despite the ostensible similarity that both relied on state support to delineate their sphere of authority.[18] Although scholars debate on how to evaluate the benefit and cost of medieval and early modern European guilds, there is consensus that they enjoyed the exclusive right to restrict participation in certain commercial activities by obtaining formal legal privileges from a ruler.[19] The monopoly of European merchant guilds rested in the distributional services they offered to two powerful groups: they enhanced the ruler's ability to extract extra revenues from the population, and the merchants' ability to extract profit by restricting the access to trade within a small group.[20] In a sense, chartered conglomerates like the British East India Company were an extension of this organizational principle from guilds to corporations.

Chinese trade associations also sought official recognition, but it was by no means the grant of a fixed fiefdom. Not only was it beyond a trade association's legitimate capacity to restrict market access to a small group, but its ability to force all newcomers to join the trade association was also severely limited. The sphere of authority of an officially recognized group was constantly challenged and modified. A dominant trade association's attempt to force the inclusion of newcomers through litigation could often end with the latter groups' petition to undertake a share of the responsibilities levied on this trade and the official recognition of this new association's independent standing. As a result, multiple merchant groups of the same trade could coexist in the same marketplace, all with official recognition and each shouldering a designated portion of this trade's tax or service obligations to the local government. Even in a second-tier timber market as Chongqing, there were at least three *bang*s of timber traders within the walled city and around a half dozen if counting those dotted in the suburban towns. The number of timber-related trade associations in larger markets such as Hangzhou, Hankou, and Nanjing was even more numerous, and their duties and authorities more finely delineated. When the midcentury fiscal crisis across the empire compelled the formal introduction of Lijin transit taxes on commerce, the local collective taxation arrangement between government offices and merchant organizations was not abandoned but incorporated and modified to facilitate the functioning of the new system.

THE LIJIN TAX

In response to the central and provincial fiscal crisis caused by the prolonged military involvement with the Taiping and other rebellious groups across the empire, the Lijin tax was introduced as a small percentage transit tax on commerce. The practice was first adopted in Jiangsu in 1853 and quickly spread all over the realm.[21] Although it was some provincial officials that initiated the collection of Lijin taxes, the tax income was increasingly mandated and controlled by the Board of Revenue and became a mainstay of formal government finance in the second half of the nineteenth century. The Lijin tax marked a significant shift in Qing taxation policy on commerce. Previously, just a dozen domestic customs stations were established along only major interregional trading routes to directly collect transit taxes. Commercial taxes collected from the domestic customs contributed around 10 percent to the national fiscal income before the 1850s.[22] Whatever collective taxation arrangements that existed between the local state and merchant communities remained shadowy practices in a legally gray area.

With the adoption of Lijin tax, the Qing state increased its capacity to directly and regularly tax commerce. The most visible change was the establishment of Lijin tax stops, the number of which counted to thousands, along the most traveled water and overland routes of transportation. Although some Lijin stations replaced previously existing domestic customs stations that were destroyed during the Taiping Rebellion (such as the Longjiang Guan in Nanjing), the vast majority were newly added tax stops. Contemporaries and later scholars lamented the dramatically increased burden on commercial exchanges, which was admittedly true. In the meantime, the number of reported Lijin tax stations in 1862 exceeded 2,500—only roughly on par with the density of commercial tax stations in the much smaller Northern Song dynasty (2,060 stations in 1077), an era that was not particularly criticized for its commercial tax policies but largely acclaimed for its synergistic state-market dynamics.[23] Seen in this vein, the late-Qing controversy over Lijin reflected more than anything the very low level of commercial taxation standardized during the High Qing era. By

1885 the Lijin tax was contributing about 20 percent to the fiscal income of the late Qing state, which had increased from 41 million to 77 million taels in forty years. The absolute amount of Lijin tax quadrupled between 1885 and 1911, rising from 12 million to 43 million taels.[24]

Take one of the main arteries of timber trade, the water route from Ganzhou to Nanjing, for example. In the pre-Lijin era a timber merchant traveling this route would pay a cumulative rate of roughly 12 percent by passing through Gan Guan, Jiujiang Guan, Wuhu Guan, and Longjiang Guan. Under the Lijin regime the total number of tax stops increased to eleven.[25] Taking into account the variations in the Lijin tax rate and collection method in Jiangxi, Anhui, and Jiangsu, this merchant would pay a 45 percent Lijin tax.[26] Although the assessed value for tax purposes was usually lower than the market price for which the goods would sell at the destination, the much-elevated tax rate as compared to the pre-Lijin era still stood out.

The nationwide layout of Lijin stations and personnel provided the basic infrastructure of direct commercial taxation. Upon arriving at a Lijin tax station, a timber merchant declared the kind, quantity, and value of his rafts. The declaration form was submitted to the Lijin station, and a clerk was dispatched to inspect the cargoes. Based on the verified volume of commodities, the amount of Lijin taxes was billed. Each merchant took his bill to the station and made the payment.[27] Three-part receipts were adopted in most provinces (although the exact design differed), with one part retained at the tax station, one issued to the merchant, and one part submitted to the provincial bureau for auditing. The receipt obtained was valid for a specified amount of time for the merchant to pass the inspections at the following stations on his itinerary.[28]

TRADE ASSOCIATIONS "UNDERTAKE CONTRIBUTIONS"

In addition to this formal structure of direct taxation, *renjuan* (or "undertaking contributions") was a common arrangement between Lijin bureaus and merchant organizations. Merchant organizations assessed themselves and undertook an organizational-level tax quota from the Lijin bureau or other taxation agencies; in return, individual members, with certificates issued by the organization, would not be subject to direct taxation when passing through the corresponding Lijin stations. Besides transit taxes, this arrangement was also commonly used for Lijin or its variants in other names levied on local marketplaces.[29] In Hankou, for example, the Bamboo-and-Timber Lijin Bureau delegated the collection of timber taxes to the native-place association of Hunan timber merchants (Lianghu Huiguan) and the Trade Association of Licensed Timber Brokers (Muhang Gonghui). These trade associations developed a scheme to collect a percentage fee from members' timber and submitted a portion of this income to the bureau as Lijin.[30] Similarly, the Association of Tax-paying Timber Merchants in Hangzhou (see chapter 4), a timber buyers' organization, assumed a quota of Lijin taxes on timber that was to be exported to six nearby prefectures in Zhejiang and Jiangsu, which legitimized its collection of fees from members and the mandatory requirement that all the timber buyers from these prefectures should join the organization.[31]

From the late Qing through the Republican period, two timber trade organizations in Shanghai—the South City Association of Domestic Timber Traders (Nanshi Mushang Gongsuo) and the Zhenxun Association of Imported Timber (Zhenxun Yangmu Ye Gongsuo)—applied the collective taxation practice for a series of duties and fees, including Lijin and similar transit taxes, levies on particular kinds of timber, duties at domestic and maritime customs, and the moorage rent payable to the Land Bureau.[32] Membership certificates issued by the organizations would ensure the cargoes' fast passage through tax stations and protect against harassment from the bribe-seeking clerks.[33] The arrangement featured either a monthly or annual quota payable by the organization to certain tax agencies, including the "contributions of imported timber" undertaken by the Zhenxun Association and the "contributions of Hunan timber" undertaken by the South City Association.[34] The South City Association designated a clerk, whose name was put on record with the maritime customs, to help members declare duties and mediate any issues that arose in their interactions with the customs.[35] Merchant organizations also put forward collective bargaining to fend off tax raises, as evidenced by the South City Association's resistance to increased levies on timber-transporting boats from Fujian, and the Zhenxun Association's constant bargaining on the total quotas of imported-timber contributions.[36]

In the case where merchant organizations undertook a lump-sum tax quota, the funds of course came from fees collected from member firms. The amount of membership fees usually varied according to the sizes of businesses but did not correspond exactly to a firm's estimated tax dues. In fact, it seemed that a few leading members would contribute an exceptionally large share to the funds of the organizations. For example, in the Shanghai Zhenxun Association, the largest firms each made an initial one-time contribution of 3,000 taels and subscribed to a monthly payment of 40 taels, whereas ordinary members paid a 30-tael joining fee and a monthly fee of less than 1 tael. Since the organizational regulations stipulated that voting rights were linked to monetary contributions, the mechanism meant that large firms shouldered tax burdens for smaller members in return for legitimized authority in decision-making.[37] The fund of the merchant organization also had a cushion effect: the various agency's frequent attempts to increase tax quotas, if not resisted successfully by the organization, would be absorbed by the collective fund first before resulting in higher membership fees. In 1925, when the Zhenxun Association had to elevate the monthly fees after the tax bureau's demand to increase their quotas by five times, it stipulated a 20 percent increase for ordinary members and a 30 percent to 40 percent increase for the top ten firms (from their already much higher base).[38]

There seemed to be a change of attitude toward trade associations' collective taxation among common merchants that was brought about by the state's increased capacity of direct commercial taxation after the introduction of Lijin. In the pre-Lijin era the state had little direct monitoring and control over traveling merchants. Direct transit taxes were only collected at a few domestic customs, and the tax rates were relatively low. Whereas organized groups were visible targets for the local government's exactions, individual merchants outside of any commercial organization had an easier time evading such demands and held considerable advantages in cost-saving. In other words, from individual merchants' perspective, despite other possible benefits from joining a commercial organization, the collective taxation arrangement was more often than not considered a burden.

The increasing implementation of direct commercial taxation after the mid-nineteenth century changed the situation. The middle and lower Yangzi area where timber trade flourished (including Hubei, Hunan, Jiangsu, Jiangxi, and Zhejiang) happened to be those provinces that established the thickest net of Lijin stations. A timber merchant had nowhere to hide with his bulky cargoes. The good news for him was that the long-established practice for a merchant organization to collectively pledge a quota of contribution was incorporated into the Lijin tax regime. From this individual merchant's perspective, the collective taxation regime had now become a more desirable service. The capacity of merchant organizations to negotiate with multiple agencies regarding tax rates was considered an attractive feature by potential members. If covered by the collective arrangement of a commercial organization, a merchant would be shielded from the unpleasantness of the long wait to be assessed at a tax stop, the volatile tax rates, and bribe-seeking clerks.

In its public letter to nonmembers, the Zhenxun Association mentioned its collective taxation arrangement as a major benefit to joining the organization: "Furthermore, the association undertakes annual contributions for the timber tax. Compared to each practitioner in this trade making his individual payment, [collective taxation] precludes the malpractice of harassment and extortions [at the tax stations] and reduces the economic cost greatly. The benefit to our business is indeed remarkable. Over the years the tax station negotiated with us seeking to take it back to be run by the government directly and attempted to increase the amount of our contributions. These were only fended off by the association's endless endeavors and utmost struggles."[39] Indeed, some nonmember merchants even chose to pay monthly fees to the Zhenxun Association to get covered by its collective taxation arrangement.[40]

This perspective furthers earlier endeavors in the literature to understand the rationale for the proliferation of trade associations in the late nineteenth century, which has been interpreted as an organized response to the state's increasing demand for "contributions" from the merchant community.[41] Although increased state solicitation was indeed an inducer, more precisely it was the *combined* effects of the expansion of direct taxation apparatus and its failure to completely replace the traditional indirect platform that made the option of collectively undertaking tax quotas more appealing to the merchant communities in the late Qing and Republican era.

COMBATING DEFAULT AND INFORMATION ASYMMETRY

In addition to facilitating the collection of commercial taxes to the benefit of both the state and their members, trade associations played a vital role in regulating trade behaviors and enforcing contracts, a function that was particularly essential for transactions spanning over time and distance. In a heavily credit-reliant trade like that of timber, the risks of default and information asymmetry constantly threatened to obstruct the flow of goods and capital. The system of contract enforcement constituted by the formal and informal institutions had to be effective enough to check excessive defaults in payment; otherwise, much of the long-distance exchanges would not happen in the first place.

Defaulting was the most common cause of commercial disputes, and it could take many forms beyond an outright refusal to pay. For example, there is the problem of merchants trying to exploit changes in market prices long after orders were placed. Such cases might arise when buyers refused to pay the previously agreed-upon price when market prices fell, or when sellers demanded extra payment if market prices rose after the conclusion of the deal.[42] Furthermore, how much time should be allowed for the buyer to pay up after delivery was another issue. Since its establishment in 1875, the South City Association of Domestic Timber Traders in Shanghai extended the time allowance after delivery several times, from seventy days to four months, as a reasonable interval for both sellers and buyers. The four-month term became a mutually recognized customary practice after 1898.[43] Delays beyond the fourth month should bear market interest.[44]

To some extent, the lengthening of credit terms between 1875 and 1898 reflected the relative ease with which Shanghai timber merchants could finance their business. Those were the years when Shanghai gradually rose as the new distribution center of Fujian timber for Zhejiang and Jiangsu. The area supplied by Shanghai's timber merchants expanded beyond the immediate vicinity of Shanghai to cover a larger hinterland. As buyers from more remote places came to Shanghai to buy wood, longer intervals were required for them to ship the purchased timber back, make sales, and earn the money to repay the sellers in full. The extension of the payment deadline tells us that Shanghai wholesalers essentially financed these delays. In contrast, the Shanghai-based timber merchants paid their Fujian suppliers upon signing the contracts—that is, long before the arrival of the timber at Shanghai.[45] In other words, Shanghai was not only the center of redistribution, but it also financed the operations of upstream and downstream traders.

This financing capacity was made possible thanks to Shanghai's financial institutions. Several documents mention that the timber merchants' ability to bear with the buyers' delay in payment depended on the liquidity situation in Shanghai's financial market.[46] In fact, close business connections between timber merchants and native banks can be found in other important centers of timber trade such as Nanjing and Hankou. Failure to repay bank loans was a common cause for a timber firm to be sued in court.[47] The interdependence between native banks and timber firms was further intensified by the cross-holdings of their shareholders.[48] Sometimes the bankruptcy of a large timber firm could drag down several native banks and start a financial crisis in the city, as was the case in Nanjing in 1875 and Zhenjiang in 1910.[49]

Although big firms based in high-order markets could accommodate some delays on the buyers' side in order to make more sales, there had to be a limit. Effective means to prevent excessive arrears were needed to protect the interests of members. An extra delay by one or two months would be unpleasant for individual sellers, but not worthwhile to be taken through the litigation process, which was uneconomical in terms of both time and money. However, occasional short-term delays, if left unpunished, would lead to a systematic extension of the customary time limit and compromise the common interests of the whole group. Moreover, what troubled the timber merchants the most was information asymmetry. They found it difficult to learn the solvency of a potential customer and were always cautious to avoid entering sales agreement with customers who were already deeply indebted to other members.[50] Some speculative customers placed new orders with no intention of repaying old debts, secretly transferred the revenue made through resale to their relatives, and suddenly announced bankruptcy to deny payments to creditors.[51] All of these pitfalls of delay, default, and fraud demanded intra- and trans-associational remedies.

REPUTATION AND GROUP SANCTIONS

Timber trade associations typically used information sharing and group sanctions to reduce the threat of payment defaults by both members and outsiders. Members were required to report any customer who failed to pay by the designated time limit, and the association would send a notice to all its members to stop doing business with the reported customer until the arrears in question were cleared. The pooling of information on defaults helped alleviate the information asymmetry that might cause members to enter into risky contracts with deeply indebted customers. The threat of exclusion of trade and the loss of reputation to a whole group of merchants increased the cost of default significantly. For example, the regulation of the South City Association from the 1880s stipulated that "should any member dare continue to trade with the reported customer upon receiving the organization's notice, he himself would be held responsible to repay the debt." This provision was preserved in the association's updated regulations of 1898 and 1916.[52]

Similarly, the 1911 regulation of the Zhenxun Association of Imported Timber in Shanghai prescribed that it would send a notice to all members when it learned of a defaulting customer. Every member involved with that customer had to report the amount of his outstanding debt. Then a leaflet containing the pooled information would be published, and all members should stop transactions with the defaulter. The group's sanction would only be lifted after all the outstanding accounts were cleared. Members who continued to trade with the defaulter after the notice would go without the association's support in any litigation following losses from those transactions. Moreover, the regulation stipulated specific rules about how to deal with construction contractors, the main customer base for members of the Zhenxun Association. The organization urged members to look out for those contractors who left debts unpaid by enlisting new partners and changing their firms' registrations. Whenever a member found such contractors working as partners of other construction firms, he should notify the association so that a warning could be sent out to all members. The 1925 and 1930 regulations of the Zhenxun Association kept all these articles and further added that the group sanction mechanism also applied to situations when customers attempted to take advantage of price decreases after orders were placed.[53]

The operation of these enforcement mechanisms can be seen in what has survived of the South City Association's correspondence with its members. Each month, the association asked members to submit detailed information on accounts receivable that had been outstanding for more than four months. The association's request came with the proviso that if a member firm neglected to report customers who did not pay on time, the firm could not request the trade association's assistance in future disputes about these transactions. The association added up each individual customer's debts to its members and took a first-step measure of writing to late debtors in the name of the organization pressing for immediate payment.[54]

The threat of group sanction was also invoked from time to time. For example, the council notified all members to stop trading with the Yi Tai Feng firm in Wujiang County after it ignored several letters from the South City Association demanding immediate payment to a member firm. The association published announcements in newspapers, urging debtors to clear outstanding accounts in time and threatening to impose group sanctions at the beginning of the next month. Letters from members demanding that the trade associations issue notice to stop trading with certain customers showed that the warning of a group sanction was considered a valuable weapon. Sometimes the organization led campaigns against groups of customers in particular places based on the common needs of members. Such a campaign directed at the Shahe group of timber merchants in the town of Qingkou was organized in 1929. Seven members of the South City Association submitted lists of Qingkou timber firms and the amounts owed by each. The organization produced an aggregate list and sent it to the Qingkou Chamber of Commerce to hasten payment.[55]

The timber trade associations also assumed the authority to adjudicate disputes between members. For bankruptcy cases, at the request of owners or creditors, the organizations could seize property, reckon accounts, and oversee the distribution of a bankrupt firm's liquidation to its creditors and shareholders. The trade associations required a timely report of any change in ownership or management at member firms. This information was critical to bankruptcy cases, for creditors usually only dealt with managers and lacked information about the owners and their respective shares. Partners in a dispute over each one's liability also sought the trade associations' adjudication.[56]

When a member was suspected of fraud, the associations investigated and audited account books to find evidence. For example, a member firm was accused of assisting an outsider in bilking large quantities of timber with voided checks. At the request of members, the Zhenxun Association looked into the accused firm's account books and found excessively low purchasing prices and inconsistencies in the invoices. Whereas the fraudster had escaped town and there was no means to locate and sue him in court, this member firm suspected of assisting in the crime was held responsible to compensate the victims for their losses. This was according to Zhenxun's regulation that "when strangers came with suspicious goods for sale, members should report to the organization. If any member accepted the suspicious goods without reporting, he should be held responsible to repay the victims when definite evidence showed that the goods in question were stolen from others."[57]

WHY PLAY BY THE RULES?

Effective measures were needed to ensure that members conformed to notices of group sanction, or else the threat would not be credible. Although it was in the common interest of all members to maintain the effectiveness of the sanction mechanism, there was a free-rider problem. A member might be tempted to take advantage of the opportunity when no other merchants would trade with the defaulting customer and negotiate a good deal for himself. If the defaulting customer could not pay cash, a higher price could be obtained to compensate for his higher probability of future default again and for the strong bargaining power of this single merchant who was still willing to sell to him. What would prevent the trade associations' members from ignoring the organizations' command and taking up such opportunities?

An effective instrument that helped reduce members' temptation to free ride was a security deposit. The trade association took a deposit of several hundred silver *yuan* from each member, the "security to uphold the agreement" (*jianyi zhi zhi*). The fund was deposited in native banks and generated interest at market rates to be distributed to members at the year-end clearing of accounts. Should any member disobey the order to cease trade with sanctioned customers or violate any other internal regulations of the organization, the deposit would be confiscated to tip the informer or saved as a collective fund to pay for holding festivals and other ritual events.[58]

The security deposit was only one component of what ensured members' conformity to organizational regulations. The trade associations also provided a series of exclusive benefits that could only be received by a member in good standing. The potential loss of the entitlement to such benefits would weigh against whatever profit that could be gained by violating the regulations. Indeed, a very important excludable benefit was the enrollment in the trade associations' collective taxation arrangement. Timber trade associations also provided valuable services related to the long-distance and wholesale nature of its members' businesses. For example, the South City Association handled issues with Fujian timber suppliers through the Fujian Peaceful Sea Association (Anlan Huiguan) and maintained moorage space along the bank of the Huangpu River for its member firms to stock timber.[59] It negotiated for transport services on its members' behalf, which involved contact and negotiation with several associations of commercial junks both in Shanghai and along the coastal route. The Renji Association of Commercial Junks in Ningbo provided regular reports to the South City Association about the arrival, departure, and occasional delay of the timber junks owned or rented by the Shanghai firms. It also arranged patrolling boats to sail with the timber junks at the request of the South City Association.[60] Moreover, the South City Association formed an alliance with the association of commercial junks to prohibit steamship transportation by members in return for significant discounts in junk rates.[61]

The different services provided by the trade associations—including contract enforcement, litigation support, collective taxation, transportation, and storage—may seem unrelated functions. However, the exclusiveness of such services banded them together into a mutually reinforcing system that promoted members' solidarity.[62] Only members in good standing could have access to these services. Violators would have to face the probability of losing their entitlement to not just one but all of these benefits. In addition to such preventative measures as the security deposit, these exclusive collective benefits added to the cost side should a member weigh the net benefit of violating a regulation or not cooperating in group sanctions.

Timber trade organizations were not alone in establishing information sharing, group sanction, and security deposit. Similar practices can be seen in many merchant organizations of different trades and localities. The Shanghai Tea Trade Association established similar stipulations in 1870.[63]

The Association of Native Banks in Shanghai registered the shareholders, managers, and invested capital of member banks, and made such information available to creditors in the event of a member bank's bankruptcy.[64] The Hankou Financial Association, established in 1871, demanded security deposits of several hundred taels from each member bank.[65] The Trade Association of Mountain Products in Changsha stipulated that members should share information regarding the creditworthiness of contracted suppliers; it also required the reporting of customers in default and listed group sanctions as a last-resort measure.[66] Although the exact combination of specific regulations varied, they constituted a set of commonly adopted strategies in trade associations that aimed to alleviate problems of information asymmetry and default.

COURT ADJUDICATIONS

The timber trade associations' internal enforcement mechanisms could by no means resolve all the default and bankruptcy cases. An issue of great interest is how merchants maneuvered between formal and informal platforms of dispute resolution. Evidence from Shanghai reveals old and new forces in the timber trade that came into play from the last decades of the Qing through the Republican period. Shanghai showcased the intermingling between domestic and international timber trade, between Chinese and foreign firms, and between native and Western legal practices during these transformative years. The question is to what extent these different platforms constituted a coordinated system of resolution that generated coherent expectations for potential litigants—otherwise speculative litigants would be able to take advantage of the divergent promises at different tribunals.

There were many courts in Shanghai. The standard Qing bureaucracy centered on the Shanghai County Magistrate. The magistrate, as the administrator of all aspects of local governance, heard cases in his *yamen* in the walled city. Appeal cases were heard by the Songjiang prefecture and then the provincial-level officials of Jiangsu. In the Republican period a local court was established as a separate entity from the local government. After the Opium War, foreign settlements were established north of the walled city, since 1843. Foreign nationals of treaty powers were subject to the consular courts of their home countries according to extraterritoriality.[67] With the growing Chinese population in the foreign settlements after the 1850s, a court was needed in the settlements to adjudicate disputes among Chinese people as well as those involving suits filed by foreigners against Chinese defendants. This need led to the Mixed Court of the British-American Settlement (later the International Settlement) and the Mixed Court of the French Concession, both formally established in 1869.[68]

The mixed courts dealt with the nationals of China and nontreaty powers who were accused of offenses or crimes committed within the limits of foreign settlement. While a Chinese magistrate sat for purely Chinese cases, a Western consular representative sat with the magistrate for cases where the plaintiffs were of treaty power nationalities.[69] In addition to these formal courts, some other entities could adjudicate small cases. In particular, the South-City Roadwork Bureau (Nanshi Malu Gongcheng Ju) was a proto-municipal organ established by Chinese gentry-merchants in 1895 in the Chinese city. The bureau was initially concerned with the construction of roads, but it came to take on broader responsibilities including maintaining public order and adjudicating small disputes. Since many timber firms were located in the South City, a number of cases involving them were decided by the Roadwork Bureau.

I have collected 255 timber trade debt cases that were brought to these different venues from 1878 to 1932 from *Shenbao*, the daily local newspaper. Foreign firms appeared as plaintiffs in twenty-five cases (9.8 percent), twenty of which featured the British firm China Import & Export Lumber Company, a member of the Zhenxun Association.[70] Most of the cases were local. Based on the cases where the occupations of both parties were known, the most common cause of a dispute in court was a contractor's failure to pay a timber firm (sixty-seven such cases in total). Because most of these construction projects were in the foreign settlements, these cases ended up in the mixed courts. A contractor often had the proprietor as his guarantor when he obtained timber and other construction materials on credit. It could also be the other way around, where the timber firm acted as the guarantor of the contractor to the proprietor, agreeing to see to the completion of the project should the contractor abscond. Some contracts stipulated that upon the completion of the project, the proprietor would pay the timber firm what it was owed directly. A dispute might thus arise among any pair of the timber merchant–building contractor–real estate owner triplet. Finally, because contractors and timber merchants belonged to different trade associations, disputes between them were beyond the influence of any single trade association and they were more likely to end up in court.

It is noteworthy that disputes between timber merchants, either in Shanghai or cross-regional, seldom showed up in court (ten such cases in total). When they did, it usually involved multiple litigants and/or complex ownership-creditor dispute in bankrupt cases. Litigation rarely arose from simple arrears in transactions between timber merchants. One reason for this rarity lay in the structure of the cross-regional flow of goods and credit. If a Shanghai merchant failed to pay his Fujian sellers, for instance, the most likely process would be for the sellers to sue the Shanghai firm's dispatched purchase office in the Fuzhou local court. If timber buyers who resided in another locality in Jiangsu or Zhejiang fell behind, it would be more effective to sue them in their locality than in Shanghai. Still, compared to the records of the South City Association, where arrears disputes between timber merchants are most commonly seen, the absence of such cases in the Shanghai courts, especially those between local merchants, points to the effectiveness of the trade associations in resolving simple disputes among members.

Despite the mixed court's peculiar status as a colonial institution and the political and legal tensions between China and the treaty powers it embodied, my examination of mundane commercial disputes shows that domestic courts and mixed courts were similar in their handling of such cases.[71] The two-dozen cases that involved foreign firms as plaintiffs, although a limited sample, indicate no deviation from the processes seen in purely Chinese cases. In principle, whether the Shanghai County Magistrate or the mixed courts had jurisdiction depended on the residential or business address of the defendant. In practice, litigants had considerable flexibility when the case involved only Chinese nationals. Some litigants, when unsatisfied with the result of the proceedings in one court, brought the same case to another court in the hope of a more favorable verdict. However, such attempts, once revealed by the counterparty to the magistrates, always led to the same outcome: the original verdict was usually upheld unless important new material evidence was presented or significant wrongdoing in the previous proceedings was detected.[72] For example, in 1878, Wu Yongpu agreed to guarantee the defendant's debt of 1,900 taels to the plaintiffs and signed a contract at the South City Association, which gave jurisdiction to the Shanghai County Court. Later, the creditors sued Wu at the French Mixed Court for failing to pay the remaining 400 taels on that debt. The Mixed Court Magistrate decided that Wu should come up with the payment within a week, or else be delivered to the Shanghai County Magistrate for further adjudication.[73]

Court proceedings and verdicts went through a noticeable change during the Republican era, departing from Qing practices. The domestic court and mixed courts seem to have evolved synchronously. Before the 1910s, courts were unlikely to issue a judgment that explicitly found the defendant guilty or innocent, or to decide the specific monetary amount payable to each plaintiff. Most often, the court simply urged the litigants to settle their dispute. Even in cases where the court decided that one party was at fault, it refrained from dictating the exact amount of compensation, but instead left it open for the litigants' negotiation. The magistrates' verdicts often read "settle by a certain date" or "find a reliable merchant to bail out the defendant and help them settle." When the litigants failed to resolve the case after several such orders, detention or physical punishments might be used to urge the defendant to settle. The involvement of trade associations was also more visible before the 1910s. The court upheld settlements that had been brought about by the trade associations, relied on the expertise of the associations' directors to reckon accounts and estimate values, and referred cases to trade associations and the Chamber of Commerce for out-of-court mediation.

So in late Qing Shanghai, the Shanghai County magistrate as well as the magistrates of the two mixed courts followed similar procedures in handling commercial disputes as their colleagues in other parts of China. The court's very admittance of a case was a strong enough signal in support of the plaintiffs that it could precipitate an out-of-court settlement and the case ended up never being heard—the goal of many was simply to get their case admitted rather than going through the full process of litigation. When the magistrate did hear a case, he often urged litigants to employ mediation platforms outside the court and limited his involvement to situations when out-of-court negotiations had been exhausted. But even then, besides ordering short-term detainment and light physical punishment, the court seldom mandated solutions other than those reached outside of the courtroom. Moreover, the court could not offer effective means to enforcing its solutions if one party was determined not to comply.[74] The magistrates were willing to intervene when a litigant claimed that the director of the trade association was partial or unfair in his mediation, but they did nothing more than appointing other merchants as mediators.[75] When everyone was willing to participate, the flexibility of the system produced compromises acceptable to all parties. But the system was virtually powerless if one or both parties refused to compromise, resulting in deadlocks that could endure for months and even years.

All this began to change in the 1910s. Both domestic and mixed courts became more willing to issue explicit verdicts and less likely to refer cases directly to trade associations. The improved capacity of the courts owed much to the establishment of a new position, the court accountant. This new office greatly reduced the court's reliance on commercial organizations for reckoning accounts. The result of the court accountant's auditing became the most important basis for judgment.[76] The courts' better grasp of a debtor's financial condition allowed the judge to decide the amounts debtors should pay. It also made the auction of the debtor's assets a more feasible option to the court, which was further facilitated in the mixed court by the introduction of court auctioneers.[77] Moreover, the employment of attorneys was no longer limited to Sino-foreign cases, but became a common practice among Chinese merchants as well. When defendants failed to show up in court, the judge now ordered the plaintiffs to publish a notice in local newspapers. If the defendant (or his representative) failed to register at the court within the specified period (typically two weeks), the judge had no hesitation in making verdicts in the absence of the defendant when the evidence presented by the plaintiff's attorney was considered strong enough.[78] Twelve cases from the Republican era, 11 percent of the cases with verdicts, were decided in the absence of defendants or their representatives.

While outright referral of cases to out-of-court forums of mediation became uncommon, the involvement of trade associations in court proceedings continued. Trade associations retained legal consultants for themselves and their members.[79] Most important, trade associations were often consulted by the court concerning customary practices in specific matters. For instance, in a typical case that concerned the triangle relationship between proprietors, hired contractors, and lumber stores, the Jiangsu Provincial Court asked the Zhenxun Association whether the proprietor or the contractor of the project should sign the receipt for the timber.[80] The legal basis for such consultations came from a 1913 decision by the Supreme Court of China that stated: "Civil cases are decided first according to express provisions of law; in the absence of express provisions, then according to customs, and, in the absence of customs, then in accordance with legal principles [*tiaoli*]."[81] The Chinese term *tiaoli* is best understood in this context as the idea of "the generally-acknowledged best principles to apply in such cases in the interests of regularity and order."[82] This decision, together with the collection of the Supreme Court's precedents, served as the de facto civil law before 1930, when the Republican Civil Code was finally promulgated. Regular and mixed courts often invoked as "customs" or "legal principles" both the principles delineated in the 1911 Draft Civil Code of the Great Qing and the short-lived 1906 Qing Bankruptcy Code as well as the regulations of trade associations.[83]

It was a common understanding that business customs, as enshrined in the regulations of trade associations, were enforceable principles in court as long as they were not contradictory to express stipulations of law. When Zhu Yaoqing, a Taicang merchant indebted to several members of the South City Association, lost a lawsuit over his debts in Taicang county court, he hired an attorney to appeal his case and accused his creditors of violating the association's own regulations regarding standardized measurements and fair pricing. In response, his creditors requested that a representative from the association testify that they had always conformed to the organization's regulations. In the end, Zhu's appeal was not accepted by the Jiangsu Supreme Court for lack of evidence (not for lack of grounds).[84] The significant point revealed by this incidence is that members of the association, nonmembers, and the court all agreed on the standards of conduct in the timber trade and that the formal court system had a role in supporting these private business norms.

CROSS-REGIONAL DISPUTES AND THE CHAMBER OF COMMERCE

Cross-regional disputes presented more severe informational and enforcement challenges. The network of chambers of commerce, established in 1904, proved essential for the resolution of cross-regional cases.[85] Previous studies have shown chambers of commerce inserted a more formal venue of vertical communication between merchant organizations and the court. Trade-based associations (and to a lesser extent native-place organizations) were brought under the umbrella of the chamber of commerce network. The chamber of commerce concentrated the strengths of long-established, noncourt social mediation and took on officially recognized authority in providing final resolution to commercial disputes. This newly integrated merchant forum remained the primary platform for settling contentious commercial disputes until the 1940s.[86] In addition to its role in narrowing the gap between local courts and private mediation embedded in trade associations, the nationwide system of chambers of commerce served the important function of facilitating cross-regional communications and negotiations between merchants and their trade associations in different localities.

Of two dozen cross-regional arrears cases collected from the Municipal Archives of Suzhou and Shanghai (1906–32), half of them involved one or more chambers of commerce. In disputes that involved timber merchants who were based in different localities, it was common to see the flow of information and request between the two localities' timber trade associations through their respective chambers of commerce. In cases where there was no specialized organization for timber trade, the local chamber of commerce would directly contact the timber firm in question. A chamber of commerce could also address county courts within its jurisdiction as an equal entity and request the magistrate's assistance in locating and detaining suspected defaulters.[87]

Take, for example, a case that started as a dispute between two local firms in the Yongjia County of Wenzhou, Zhejiang, which also involved merchants based in Shanghai.[88] Lin Zhensheng purchased lumber planks from Liu Zhenfeng in Yongjia with a void promissory note and soon announced bankruptcy. Lin absconded to Shanghai and sold the contested timber to Yin Ji and Sheng Da Long, two member firms of the Zhenxun Association. Liu and other creditors of Lin sent representatives to Shanghai to capture Lin. They sought help from the Yongjia Timber Trade Association, which forwarded their request to the Yongjia Chamber of Commerce. That chamber contacted the Shanghai Chamber of Commerce, requesting that the two Shanghai stores withhold their payment to Lin until Lin and his creditors reached a settlement agreement under the mediation of the Yongjia Timber Trade Association.

A month later, the Yongjia Chamber of Commerce updated the Shanghai Chamber of Commerce that the dispute had been resolved with all the creditors' agreement on a proportional settlement. It requested that the two Shanghai stores entrust the payment of about 1,500 silver *yuan* owed to Lin to the Yongjia Chamber of Commerce's account in the Bank of China, because the chamber had taken on the responsibility of distributing payment to Lin's creditors. Upon receiving the forwarded notice from the Shanghai Chamber of Commerce, the two stores sensed the potential risk of surrendering the money to the Yongjia Chamber of Commerce without Lin's written consent, for "although Lin is indebted to many others, he is a creditor to us. Without Lin's authorization and a legal procedure, we cannot deposit the money owed to Lin to other entities' accounts." To avoid being found fault by Lin in the future, the two stores entrusted the money to the Zhenxun Association, which contacted the Yongjia Chamber of Commerce and arranged the deposit.

The Yongjia-Shanghai case was representative of the cross-regional flow of information and requests through commercial organizations and chambers of commerce. These organizations dealt with complex issues when representing members to ensure fairness and help them avoid potential risks, such as the Yongjia Chamber of Commerce's distributing payment to Lin Zhensheng's creditors and the Zhenxun Association's dealings with the sensitive payment for the two Shanghai stores. The coordinated action of these organizations was far more flexible and effective than if the parties had to rely on the court system exclusively. The formal legal system reacted slowly to bankruptcies and thus could not act in a timely fashion to seize the properties of the bankrupt firm before its managers and shareholders appropriated any remaining assets and fled the city. In the above case, by having the two stores in Shanghai hold on to the money payable to Lin Zhensheng until further instruction, the trade associations in representation of the creditors effectively froze part of Lin's assets. The right to dispose of the frozen money was entrusted to a third party, the Yongjia Chamber of Commerce, to make sure that Lin's residual assets would be fairly distributed among his creditors.

The efficiency and effectiveness of this disposition owed much to a shared informal norm about how to deal with suspicious bankruptcies. This norm was exemplified by an article in the 1925 regulation of the Zhenxun Association, which stated: "If any indebted customer shows inclinations of fleeing town or his firm seems about to go bankrupt, it would be too much of a delay to go through all the formal legal procedures for the official agencies to act in time. With the universal consent of our members and in reference to the practices in other cities, [in future situations like this] we should gather local police officers and gentlemen jointly to impound the property of the suspicious party and take him into custody, while at the same time submitting formal petitions to the court."[89]

The operation of this informal procedure in cross-regional cases relied on the aforementioned chain of communication through chambers of commerce. Institutional arrangements at the organizational level helped remedy some limitations of the formal court system in resolving contradictory evidence, acquiring the knowledge of specific business customs in different trades, and enforcing judgments given the mobility of long-distance traders and the opacity of their property. Communications and collaboration between merchant communities in different localities, often through the mediation of chambers of commerce, could often bypass the slow hierarchical procedures in the formal bureaucracy and enable action in a more timely fashion to deal with cross-regional disputes. The role played by the network of chambers of commerce was particularly important given the lack of political unity and legal clarity in the early years of the Republican period. Chambers of commerce were able to mitigate the obstacles against solving cross-regional conflicts in a way that neither local magistrates/courts nor trade associations could have done, a function that was only taken up by a more fully constructed and connected legal system much later.

A case against the Yong Xing Shun Lumber Store in Wuxi (hereafter YXS) involved complicated trading relations among timber merchants of Shanghai, Changzhou, Wuxi, and Yixing. It exemplifies the complexities of an insolvency case resulting from a chain reaction to an exposed defaulting, the multitude of maneuvers and negotiations happening outside of the courtroom during the trial, and the measures taken by the timber trade associations to safeguard members' rights.[90] This is a case where all the institutions and channels of communications discussed earlier in this chapter were put into full operation and yet still failed, which makes it a good illustration of the capacity and upper limit of the system.

The incident started in 1932 with YXS's timber purchase from Yin Ji in Shanghai (figure 5.1). YXS paid 2,000 *yuan* with a guaranteed promissory note issued by a native bank in Changzhou, with the remaining 4,900 *yuan* left unpaid. When his entreaties for the remaining payment failed, Yin Ji brought a fraud lawsuit to the Wuxi County Court against the manager of YXS, Yu Pingfu, his nephew Yaoqing, and their accomplice Cheng Jinjian,

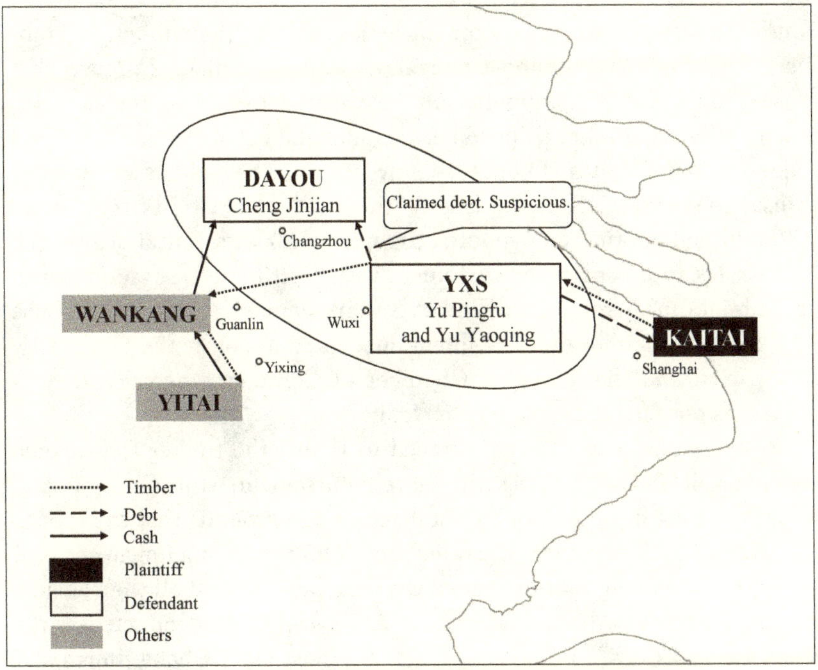

FIGURE 5.1 Kaitai versus Yong Xing Shun (YXS), 1932. *Source*: SHMA, S145-2-6.

the owner of the Dasheng and Dayou lumber stores in Changzhou, and won the case. The Zhenxun Association, upon receiving the news, immediately performed its information-sharing function and sent letters to all its members as well as to the South City Association and the timber trade associations in Wuxi, Changzhou, and Yixing, disclosing the defeat of YXS and demanding that all the noticed parties stop trading with the three fraudsters.

From the Zhenxun Association's interassociation notice, the Kaitai Lumber Store in Shanghai, a member of the South City Association, learned of Yin Ji's lawsuit against YXS. Kaitai's managers realized that his firm might suffer from YXS's insolvency since it had sold YXS 1,400 *yuan* worth of timber totally on credit. Kaitai sent an employee to Wuxi to conduct secret investigations on YXS. The employee found out that the timber purchased from Kaitai had already been resold to the Wankang Store in the town of Guanlin. Wankang had been directed by YXS to forward the proceeds of the sale to Cheng Jinjian to repay YXS's "debt" to the Dasheng and Dayou lumber stores. Finally, Wankang had sold the Kaitai timber to the Yitai Store in Yixing.

Believing that YXS would not be able to pay for its timber in full, Kaitai petitioned the Shanghai General Chamber of Commerce through the South City Association to ask for the assistance of the chambers of commerce in Wuxi, Yixing, and Changzhou. Kaitai's managers argued that these chambers should announce all these transactions void and canceled and have Kaitai's timber shipped back to Shanghai. Unfortunately, Kaitai's request was not legitimate because only two months had passed since its transaction with YXS. According to the trade association's regulation, YXS still had another two months to make good with Kaitai. Moreover, YXS's sales to downstream customers were legitimate transactions and could by no means be repudiated at Kaitai's demand. However, because YXS had been found guilty of intentional fraud at court, the South City Association and the Shanghai Chamber of Commerce deemed Kaitai's request as reasonable and supported it anyway.

As one would expect, Yitai refused to return the timber that it purchased legally from Wankang without reimbursement, while Cheng Jinjian refused to return the money to Wankang on the grounds that the money was to cover YXS's debts. At the same time, YXS and Cheng Jinjian accused each other of having masterminded the fraud and hogged all the benefits, leaving the other with no money at all. An investigation conducted by the Wuxi Chamber of Commerce suggests that most likely Cheng Jinjian and the two Yus conspired to fabricate YXS's huge debt to Dasheng and Dayou, the two stores owned by Cheng Jinjian. Proceeds from the resale of the timber obtained on credit from Kaitai and Yin Ji was transferred to Cheng Jinjian in the name of repaying YXS's debt. After embezzling whatever was left in YXS, Yu Pingfu and Yu Yaoqing announced the bankruptcy of YXS to deny payment to the two Shanghai stores and other creditors. Yu and Cheng then divided the profit from the fraud.

The conspiracy of Yu and Cheng was deliberately crafted, as the account books of YXS and the two stores of Cheng showed YXS's indebtedness to Cheng. As there was no priority of liability before the announced bankruptcy of YXS, it was fully legal to appropriate the funds from reselling the timber purchased from Shanghai to repay the "debt" to Cheng instead of paying the Shanghai stores immediately. When YXS's bankruptcy was announced, it had little left to compensate its creditors. Although Kaitai and Yin Ji won the lawsuit against Yu Pingfu and Yu Yaoqing in court, Cheng Jinjian was let off due to a lack of evidence. The judgment that Yu Pingfu should pay the two stores in full was difficult to enforce because on the books Yu Pingfu and his nephew were legally insolvent. In the end, the only real punishment meted out to Yu and Cheng was the disclosure of their fraud conspiracy by the timber trade associations and chambers of commerce in all three cities and the proclamation that no member should ever trade with them in the future.

That Yu and Cheng chose to do what they did despite their well awareness of such punishments shows that the effectiveness of reputation mechanisms has a limit. The ultimate limit is at the point where the potential gain from cheating could offset the present value of all the possible profit that one could make by trading with Shanghai timber firms in the future. The same could be said about the limit to the effectiveness of the court system. However, the YXS case illustrates another aspect of "limit"—that is, the limit of each individual institution of enforcement was extended by their communication and collaboration. Vertical communications from timber trade associations to the chambers of commerce to the court system strengthened the continuity from informal norms of business practices to semiformal regulations of commercial organizations to formal court adjudications. Horizontal communications, mainly through the chambers of commerce and sometimes trade associations in different localities, further strengthened the capability of informal institutions to promptly respond to cross-regional cases. Of course, this coordinated system still hit its limit in a case like YXS, but its capacity was undoubtedly higher than if each institution worked separately. Cases like that of YXS were rare enough that the Shanghai timber trade continued to flourish based on credit. What was significant was the continuity of the formal and informal systems of enforcement and the easiness at which merchants navigated between the two.

CONCLUSION

The nineteenth century saw the proliferation of self-directed merchant organizations, which were incorporated into the local framework of commercial taxation under the rhetoric of undertaking official duties. A merchant association's enrollment in some exclusive responsibilities to the local state lent legitimacy to its standing, strengthened its authority over individual merchants, and provided protection against random government underlings' illicit exactions. However, it is important to notice that a trade association could not claim a chartered fiefdom and force challenging groups to be subsumed under the association just because they shouldered some duties to the local government. Although an established merchant group would seek the support of the magistrate's court in forcing newcomers to join their association or disciplining members who refused to pay membership fees based on the argument that such measures were necessary for the trade association to fulfill its official duties, such attempts were not always successful.

While the prospect of an individual defiant was dim in such litigations, if the challengers formed a sizable group, they could volunteer to shoulder their own portion of exclusive duties and become a new officially recognized association independent from the existing trade association. In this manner the sphere of authority of any trade association could always be challenged and revised through a reallocation of official duties. In the first half of the nineteenth century, such collective taxation arrangements between merchant groups and local government existed in a legally gray area and the central state largely turned a blind eye to its increasing prevalence. These revenues supplemented the ill-funded local administration and were beyond the auditing and control of the central state.

The Qing state's capacity of direct commercial taxation was improved dramatically by the introduction of the Lijin tax in the 1850s. Provincial administrations gained immediate benefit from its collection, and the central state soon moved to impose regulation and assert claims on this new tax. The nationwide layout of more than two thousand Lijin stations provided the basic infrastructure to collect transit tax, a level of coverage that surpassed the Song system for the first time in centuries. However, this direct-taxation infrastructure did not replace the well-established collective taxation arrangements between merchant groups and local states. Rather, merchant organizations' practice of pledging contributions was incorporated into a scheme of Lijin tax farming and became even more prevalent in the second half of the nineteenth century. Merchant organizations assessed themselves and undertook an organizational-level tax quota from the Lijin bureau; in return, individual members, with certificates issued by the organization, would not be subject to direct taxation when passing through the Lijin stations. If covered by the collective arrangement of a commercial organization, a merchant would be shielded from the unpleasantness of the long wait at tax stops, inconsistent tax rates, and bribe-seeking clerks. In a way the expansion of the state's direct taxation apparatus made the alternative of joining a collective taxation program offered by merchant organizations a more appealing option in the late Qing and early Republican era.

Besides their interactions with the local state and their tax-related functions, merchant organizations performed important market functions through their regulations on business practices, internal enforcement mechanisms, and connections to other formal and informal platforms of dispute mediation. The taxation and market functions of trade associations were not separable. Indeed, the collective taxation coverage had become such a benefit that a trade association could use it as leverage to enforce the association's other regulations among its members, the most important of which dealt with defaults and frauds. In addition to the private-order solutions at the trade associations such as reputation mechanisms and group sanctions, the court system's backing of business customs lent more formal support to a coherent system of enforcement. The continuum from informal to more formal mechanisms was further strengthened by the network of the chambers of commerce since the first decade of the twentieth century, which opened reliable channels for vertical interinstitutional communication as well as horizontal cross-regional dispute resolution. By curbing fraudulent transactions, this web of complementary institutional arrangements enhanced the use of credit and facilitated the smooth flow of timber.

Epilogue

UNTIL 1890, timber supply had remained predominantly domestic in China. The Yangzi River valley drew timber from Jiangxi, Hunan, and Guizhou. Lowlands of the Pearl River delta tapped timber from the upriver highlands of the West River valley. Timber shipped by sea from Fujian supplemented the coastal areas of Zhejiang and southern Jiangsu but remained small in scale. China fir was the dominant timber variety in all these interprovincial flows, followed by pine. North China, especially the capital area, obtained some timber from the Yangzi trade system through the Grand Canal, but the Yellow River valley relied mostly on bricks as construction materials as well as cave houses in the Loess plateau. The old-growth forests in Manchuria remained largely untouched and exported little timber.[1] This basic structure began to change toward the end of the nineteenth century.

The structure of the overall timber market underwent significant reshuffling from 1890 to 1937. The Yangzi River timber trade system experienced some periods of prosperity, thanks to booming demands from the new industrial sectors, but was constantly frustrated by disturbances to river transportations during this turbulent era and ultimately lost considerable market shares to new sources of supply. Lumbering in Manchuria took off under competing Chinese, Japanese, and Russian interests, with a significant portion of its products arriving at Tianjin through coastal shipment and supplied eastern China from there. Timber from Fujian and southern Zhejiang, also transported by sea, took a stronghold in the rising metropole of Shanghai and the hinterland. With the significant cost reduction of transpacific shipment, high-quality, machine-processed foreign timber began to flow into China. Colloquially known as "American pine" in Chinese (*huaqi song* or *yang song*), Douglas fir (*Pseudotsuga menziesii*) from the Pacific Northwest swept the market of construction materials in the newly rising treaty ports.

During this period, annual turnover of the domestic market in Nanjing was around 4 million to 5 million taels, which was of comparable scale to the estimated level in the second half of the eighteenth century. The smaller timber (1–1.8 feet in circumference, dbh 0.3–0.6 foot, *fen ma* and *xiaoqian ma* in the Longquan *ma* categories) came from both Hunan and Jiangxi, with western Hunan timber priced higher than those from eastern Hunan and Jiangxi. Poles that were bigger than 1.8-feet in circumference (*zhongqian ma, daqian ma, qibajiu ma,* and *danliang ma*) were mostly from western Hunan. The timber market was traditionally dominated by the small *fen ma* and *xiaoqian ma*.[2] The price difference between Hunan and Jiangxi timber converged after the fall of the Qing dynasty, as the premium for western Hunan timber dropped sharply when the Dazhi *bang* merchants from Hubei, as compradors of Japanese conglomerates Mitsubishi and Mitsui, marched into the Qingshui River valley with abundant capital and aggressively expanded its timber output. This destabilized the long-term equilibrium between planting and logging and caused a round of premature cutting in this area.[3] Prices of bigger timber from western Hunan increased more steadily. Before foreign timber started to pour in, domestic fir enjoyed a period of prosperity by supplying the constructions of the new treaty ports and railroad sleepers. When modern urban planning took off in the Chinese cities in the 1920s and the call for supporting domestic products was high, they were purchased by the government to be used for the poles of street lights and telegraph wires and for the piles of hydraulic structures and high-rise buildings.[4]

Meanwhile, competition from imported timber began to intensify from the turn of the twentieth century. While the total value of timber import hovered around 1 million taels in the 1890s, it had multiplied by five times by 1910—already on par with the annual turnover of domestic fir at Nanjing. In the next decade, timber import continued to soar, though with a bigger annual variation. The year 1920 saw an all-time high of 12 million taels.[5] Douglas fir, with its appealing quality and sawed into lumber of all sizes, seized the treaty port markets and squeezed out the unprocessed domestic fir poles. Even though some domestic entrepreneurs in Fuzhou, Shanghai, and Wenzhou started to build industrial sawmills in the 1920s and claimed some share of the processed lumber market, they were not able to overhaul the whole system.[6]

The establishment of the Nationalist capital in Nanjing in 1928 spurred an ephemeral prosperity of this traditional timber market center. But soon the timber market was adversely affected by the worldwide Great Depression and a disastrous flooding of the Yangzi River. Ensuing political incidents and military actions in the 1930s further contributed to the disintegration of the Yangzi system of timber trade. Traffic to the southwest was constantly blocked, and export from Jiangxi was completely cut off during the anti-Communist campaigns. The traditional network of timber trade along the Yangzi River system was already in demise on the eve of the Sino-Japanese War in 1937 and came to a complete standstill during the war. One might wonder whether the waning of market appetite for domestic timber might have allowed forests to regrow. However, given that the domestic timber supply mostly came from managed plantations rather than natural forests, the decline of timber demand meant that specialization in timber production became less profitable. More generally, the disintegration of interregional markets propelled former tree growers to cultivate grains for subsistence, leading to shrinking forested areas. In the postwar era the consecutive advent of bureaucratic capitalization, nationalization, and collectivization changed the fundamental aspects of forest management and timber distribution beyond recognition.[7]

CHINESE REPLANTATION FORESTRY IN COMPARATIVE ENVIRONMENTALISM

When scholars started to approach the *longue durée* environmental history of China over the past three millennia, the issue of ecosystem sustainability attracted the most attention. "Three-thousand years of unsustainable development," as historian Mark Elvin put it, characterizes the development of Chinese state, population, and economy as a disaster in slow motion, leading "inexorably toward the weakening or even destruction of the systems of the natural infrastructure."[8] Synthesis works paint an overall picture that short-term gains in productivity or military advantage locked the state and the society into a situation demanding constant vigilant maintenance to prevent sharp ecological degradation and compromised ecosystem resilience in the long run.[9] The Chinese environmental pattern as a slow but steady move toward anthropogenic landscapes has been broadly comparable with other great urban-agrarian civilizations, with the particularities being more of matters of relative scale than of overall structure.[10]

While the replantation forestry studied in this book might seem an outlier to the general world-historical patterns of conversion of forests to cropland and pasture, it was still an integral part of the process of anthropogenic management and alteration of the natural landscape. Only, in this case, the selected "crop" was not rice, maize, or tea, but trees. Although China fir is indeed a native plant in southern China, biologists suspect that the currently observed broad range of this genus might not be natural, but a result of centuries of human selection.[11] There are landscapes that are self-sustainable, like natural rain forests. There are landscapes that could be sustainable only if humans put in constant and appropriate efforts, such as rice paddies, terraces, embankments, canals, and dams. The world environmental history could be simplified as a conversion of the former to the latter. In the current era of Anthropocene, when there is no going back to the "natural status," the only kind of sustainability that human society could aspire to achieve requires careful and efficient management: to prevent human negligence, overexploitation, and overalteration of nature that would render the human-made landscapes irrevocably unsustainable; and to put in effective maintenance at reasonable cost, with "cost" denoting not only direct monetary expenses but all the compromises that the involved groups have to make.[12] In this sense the Chinese replantation forestry was a valuable model of sustainable management.

Like other anthropogenic landscapes, tree plantation requires maintenance. What are the conditions necessary for durable private management, instead of unsustainable clear-cutting, to take place? One necessary, though not sufficient, condition is the capacity to enforce property rights and regulate access to the resources. In late imperial China, ownership of mountain lands was supported by written evidence such as contractual documents, genealogies, and graphs of grave groves—all of which, together with witness testimonies, were considered legitimate forms of proof in the court of law. However, property security per se was not enough to persuade the mountain owner to choose tree planting among the many options he had, some of which had direr ecological consequences than others.

This book further examines how private forest management could be profitable, flexible, and sustainable in the long term. The decades-long turnover period for planting timber trees was a serious obstacle for household finance and an often-cited reason to promote state forestry and public planning. This problem was mitigated in the Old South as corporate entities such as lineage trusts became the primary claimants of woodlands. The persistent structures and long investment horizons of corporate lineages made them well-adapted for production forestry. Instead of dividing the woodland into individual plots, members of the lineage were entitled to shares. When the system was first developed during the Ming, such shares were in principle inalienable and the profits from the forests were retained for lineage-wide activities. Over time the shares became increasingly tradable and more like private properties of individual households. During the Qing era, similar share-holding practices were seen in the southwest where powerful lineage organization was virtually absent. Rather than a lineage-dominated landscape, shares were claimed by individuals, divided up to be inherited by multiple heirs, and transferable to kin and nonkin alike, resulting in a woodland share-holding structure that functioned similarly to a prototype corporation. The remarkable similarity of silvicultural techniques and contractual practices between the two well-studied regions of Huizhou and eastern Guizhou suggested the possibility of knowledge transfer from the Old South to the frontiers when Jiangxi and Huizhou merchants marched westward to expand their supply networks.

How does the Chinese case compare to the rest of the world? Across Eurasia, from Japan and Korea to Italy, Spain, and France, the development of state forestry was closely linked to the rise of early modern states and their need to secure timber supply for the military.[13] The invention of scientific forestry in late eighteenth-century Prussia and Saxony further established the central role of the state in modern forestry management and brought bureaucratic administration of forests to a new level. With the goal of delivering the greatest possible constant volume of wood, forests were abstracted into elaborate tables and transformed from the diverse old-growth to monocultural, even-age, rigorously gridded plantations.[14] The practice later became the basis of forest management in France, England, British India, the United States, Japan, and throughout imperial colonies and aspiring modern states around the world.[15] Several sacred assumptions lie at the center of this body of scientific forestry thought and practice: that agencies of experts are better suited to design and direct the development of the landscape than untrained, self-interested peasants; that coordinated public planning is essential to solving the haphazard and exploitative practices common in the laissez-faire approach; and that scientific methods must become the foundation on which environmental plans should be built.[16]

What is surprising by the theories of "modernistic" environmental thinking is that replantation of considerable scale was achieved by self-interested households following silvicultural technologies transmitted intergenerationally in the context of a laissez-faire private property regime in late imperial China. The fate of these private plantations in socialist and reform-era China offers a counterexample. Similar to what happened to agricultural lands, socialist collectivization in the 1950s confiscated formerly private forests and put them under collective ownership. The level of collective ownership and management, however, underwent frequent swings between people's communes, production brigades (advanced cooperatives), and production teams (elementary cooperatives). Between 1956 and 1980, radical and frequent policy reversals regarding forest tenure defeated the communities' confidence in the security of the property rights granted to them and led to overexploitation and reluctance to invest.[17]

Several rounds of panic cutting occurred when ownership was about to shift, worsening the already severe industrialization-induced deforestation during this period. Entering the 1980s, paralleling changes in the agricultural sector, the use rights of collective forestlands were often contracted back to households, although the exact measures varied for different regions and land types. Yet still, policy shifts regarding the division of rights and profits between the collective and the households caused insecurity and overcutting, until some stability was achieved by the early 1990s. Interestingly, when some officials and academics became concerned that the household-based operation fragmented forests and increased management costs, they called on the government to promote shareholding systems. Similar to their late imperial predecessors, the shareholding systems do not divide the forestlands physically; rather, they distribute dividend-bearing shares to the villagers. Compared to the shareholding systems that were established under the directives of state forest bureaus or timber companies, which seemed merely a disguised form of former collective management, self-initiated shareholding systems by farmers attracted more engaged participation and exhibited more promise of sustainable success.[18] Especially in southern China, where such practices had a long historical root, their revival and successful adaption to the contemporary framework demonstrate the resilience of local institutions and the importance to co-opt, rather than supplant, voluntary local initiatives in official policies.

From these experiences the central issue is not simply whether public, common, or private property is best for preservation or afforestation—history has shown that any system could work or fail. The key is whether the specific dimensions of a particular system could coordinate to make sure the interests of the people with direct access to the forests are aligned with the more general interest of maintaining forest coverage. Macro-level factors and policy designs are always filtered, negotiated, and modified on the ground. It is the fine print of local institutions, which are forged out of constant adaptations to ecological and social conditions and in turn shape human incentives and behaviors, that lies at the heart of forest use and condition.

MARKET: THE DOUBLE-EDGED SWORD

Market demand for timber has always been blamed as a major factor leading to the exhaustion of natural forests—and with good reason. Not surprisingly, forestry regulations in most countries today include restrictions on the harvesting and marketing of timber trees, even when the trees are not state-owned. They follow the simple reasoning that the less consumption, the more trees would remain standing. Such regulations may help protect what remains of natural forests, but they could be counterproductive in societies like China, where sustainable forestry depends to a large extent on establishing new timber plantations. Experiences from recent decades illustrate this. From the reforms of the 1980s, household-based forest management returned to play a critical role. Despite changes in the tenure of forestlands that came to allow households more discretion and flexibility, their rights to timber trees remained rather limited, even when they "own" the trees. There are heavy restrictions on the harvesting and marketing of timber trees in the form of cutting permits, cutting quotas, transport permits, and the monopsony of state-owned lumber companies. By contrast, rights to nontimber trees on family croplands or around homesteads are much more secure and can be exercised with few restrictions. Not surprisingly, farmers are more enthusiastic to grow fruit trees than timber trees.

While these regulations on timber cutting and marketing were meant to preserve standing trees, they failed to recognize that rather than "ownership" in name, farmers need the complete rights to harvest, cut, sell, and mortgage at their discretion to make a profit from growing trees—and a reliable profit is essential to make private plantations sustainable. As the social scientist Dachang Liu has emphasized: "A distinction needs to be made between regulations on existing natural forests and regulations on artificially established plantations, as these forests differ in the relative importance of protection and production. Only full rights to trees, however, will be effective in encouraging farmers to grow more trees on lands of low forest production."[19] This is not a simplified call for the full privatization of forests—which is far from the panacea that a previous generation of scholars and policy makers made it seem—but for a careful deliberation over how to delineate and assign the bundle of rights (control, profit, mortgage, division, transfer, etc.) that constitute the abstract notion of "property" to different entities to achieve the desirable outcome of environmental sustainability and social prosperity.

The market could be both devouring and enabling, and a delicate balance is required to translate market appetite for a scarce resource into economic incentives for long-term investment in forest management. In this regard, the role of the market in the late imperial system of timber production and supply offers some important insights—although by no means an ideal model to copy. The interregional timber trade system was open and profitable to diverse groups of players along the supply chain, from mountain owners and planters to lumberjacks and rafters, from itinerant merchants to brokers and retailers. The state retreated from direct resource management and market control but relied on indirect means to procure materials and monitor market activities. All levels of the government tapped this trade for timber and taxes, but neither exerted excessive interferences to market operations nor extracted the lion's share of available supplies. The trade institutions and layers of formal and informal platforms of contract enforcement, not unique to the trade of timber, provided the channels to resolve disputes and encourage faithful transactions. The system's sustainability rested on the smooth cycling of trees, logs, people, and capital. Obstruction to any segment of the cycle, whether it was a blocked transportation route or a financial crisis that eroded the merchants' working capital, would ultimately factor into the decision of when to cut trees and whether to replant.

While the system as a whole proved to be rather resilient to the normal disturbances of business cycles and occasional natural or financial disasters, the ultimate challenge came from two sources. The first was the chronic deterioration of the general ecological landscape, particularly the accumulating disturbances to the hydraulic system that was the vital veins to interregional exchanges. Commercialized forestry was only one small aspect in the macro forces of social and demographic changes. It could not redress all the damages done to natural ecozones and waterways by unrestricted land and lake reclamations. In addition to the state's inability to rein in excessive reclamations even when it had the intention to do so, slacking maintenance of the water system, which had been so altered by human designs that it required constant intervention to work properly, further exacerbated the problem in times of political and fiscal difficulties.[20] These are problems that the market cannot solve but can only make worse, where higher authority and coercive capability would be necessary.

The second challenge was structural changes to the market system that threatened to cut off the flow of profit from the timber trade to local tree growers. The close ties between the market and forestry were manifested in the early twentieth century when the shrinking demand for domestic timber and disintegrated interregional connections did not lead to forest regrowth but the conversion of timber plantations to the cultivation of other crops. Further down the line, the monopolistic attempts by state-owned lumber companies, which came to dominance during the 1940s as part of the Nationalist state's effort to mobilize resources during the Anti-Japanese War, not only encroached upon the space of private timber merchants (who had already lost their traditional markets in East China to Japanese occupation) but also disturbed the sites of timber plantation by stripping the local tree growers of their discretion and bargaining power. The replacement of the open market and individual household growers by state-planned distribution and collective forest management was completed in the socialist era, only to be partially reverted to household management since the 1980s.

If there is any valuable lesson from this history for sustainable resource management, it is probably the appreciation that public efforts are better spent coordinating with existing institutions and practices than trying to invent wholly new institutions from scratch. The late imperial state's limited profile could certainly be expanded as an overall steward and regulator, but it would not be desirable to supplant what already worked well. Adjustments would be necessary to address some of the problems faced by the market and individual growers. Some carefully designed subsidies and restrictions might be good tools to strengthen the resilience of the system. With appropriate institutional and administrative support, practices that had a deep root in late imperial China, including flexible responses to market incentives, voluntary self-organization through shareholding systems, and inexpensive and rapid methods to resolve minor conflicts, could prove to be useful legacies toward the contemporary goals of resource conservation and regeneration.

APPENDIX A

Estimation of Timber Tax and Trade Volume at Longjiang Guan

Timber was the biggest taxable item at the Board of Works customs of Longjiang Guan in Nanjing, Jiangsu, and Wuhu Gong Guan in Wuhu, Anhui, and it also accounted for most of the variations in their revenues from 1720 to 1850. Although their taxation methods were slightly different and their fiscal terms ended in different months, the two customs stations shared a similar revenue base in upriver timber rafts and usually saw their revenues move synchronously.

From a handful of cases where we know the exact amount of timber taxes within total customs revenues, we can confirm the officials' remark that at least more than half of Longjiang Guan's revenue came from timber (*daban ziyu muzhi*). For example, in 1755 the total customs revenue of Longjiang Guan was 109,564 taels, with 82,005 taels (75 percent) coming from timber and coal. The total revenue of 1756 dropped to 76,805 taels because of a sharp decrease in timber and coal taxes by 37,383 taels (which was offset slightly by a minor increase in other miscellaneous taxes).[1] In another case, from the twelfth month of 1769 to the eleventh month of 1770 (a leap year), Wuhu Gong Guan collected 72,061 taels from timber, contributing 63 percent to its total revenue of 113,861 taels. During the same period, Longjiang Guan collected 67,240 taels from timber. The total customs revenue of Longjiang Guan for the term of 1770 (the ninth month of 1769 to the eighth month of 1770) was 123,507 taels.[2] Although the months do not exactly match, timber tax contributed about 54 percent to the annual revenue of Longjiang Guan. Moreover, since timber accounted for most of the variations in customs revenues, it can be deduced that, most likely, the higher the total revenue, the higher the proportion contributed by timber taxes.

Based on this, we could make the conservative estimation that 50 percent of Longjiang Guan's revenue was taxed from timber. The average annual revenue of Longjiang Guan from 1725 to 1850 was 123,188 taels, so the estimated average timber tax during this period would be 61,594 taels. At the high levels of the 1760s to the early 1780s, the estimated annual timber taxes could reach 70,000 to 85,000 taels. With the estimated timber taxes, we could further gauge the volume of timber in a rough manner. Before we proceed, some explanation of the method of timber taxation is in order. Instead of counting the exact number of different varieties of timber logs, big stations such as Longjiang Guan, Wuhu Gong Guan, and Jiujiang Guan (Jiujiang, Jiangxi) all estimated the number of logs after measuring the size of timber rafts. At Longjiang Guan some rules applied to raft measurement to account for the fact that timber rafts were thicker toward the central axis, especially for bigger rafts.[3]

While width was measured in a straightforward way, a special tool called *pagan* was used to measure the depth of a raft on the side. This tool was made of a straight pole and a horizontal hook toward the end. A big one (*da pa*) is 25 feet long with an 8.5-feet hook; a regular one (*ping pa*) is 8 feet long with a 3.5-feet hook. Given the shuttle shape of timber rafts, a *da pa* would return a bigger number than a *ping pa*. Measurement rules differed by raft sizes. Use *d* to denote the measured depth of a raft on the side using the appropriate *pagan*; use *x* to denote the difference in height between the center and the verge of a raft.

> For a "big raft" (width above 60 feet, depth above 10 feet), use the big *pagan* to measure depth. The finalized depth would equal
>
> $d + \frac{1}{2}x + 2.8$ feet;
>
> For a "medium raft" (depth between 6 to 10 feet), use the big *pagan* to measure depth. The finalized depth would equal
>
> $d + \frac{1}{2}x + 1.4$ feet;
>
> For a "small raft" (depth below 6 feet), use the regular *pagan* to measure depth. For every foot, add 0.1 foot.

Once the depth and width of a raft were determined, the number of logs was estimated by assuming a uniform size and shape. Notice that this was for the purpose of tax assessment only and did not correspond to the actual sizes of timber logs. For fir rafts, for example, it was assumed that one layer was 1.5 feet in depth and every 10 feet in width would be 12 logs. Therefore a raft segment of 10 feet deep and 60 feet wide could be estimated to include 480 logs. In practice, multiple segments were linked end to end to form a super raft. According to Republican-era social scientist Wu Chuanjun, "The rafts from the Yuan River were hundreds of feet long, more than a hundred feet wide, with a draft depth of 7 feet. . . . The rafts from Jiangxi were hundreds of feet long, 60 feet wide, with a draft depth of 10 feet."[4] Robert Dollar's description of seeing rafts floating on the Yangzi River in 1921 was similar: "The rafts were over a hundred feet wide and about four hundred feet long, and as they were six feet out of the water they must have been eight feet under the water, making a mass fourteen feet deep."[5] According to the calculation above, such rafts would include more than 10,000 logs.

With the rules of raft measurement and methods to approximate the number of logs, we now turn to the tax rate per log. From a series of official memorials from 1739 to 1741 debating the tax methods for timber at Longjiang Guan and a late-Ming gazetteer of the nearby Wuhu Gong Guan, we learn that fir was taxed at 0.007 taels per log and *qingliu* at 0.25 taels per log, before taking into account a 10 percent surcharge of *huohao* (meltage fee). *Qingliu* seems to be used as an abstract tax category, instead of a botanical term, to account for very big logs that were likely cut from old-growth forests.[6] The rate for fir could be corroborated by the rates at Jiujiang Guan, where small rafts were counted and taxed at 0.003 taels per log for those smaller than 1 foot in circumference, 0.007 taels for those between 1 and 2 feet in circumference, and 0.04 taels for those above 2 feet in circumference. Based on price information from the late nineteenth century, these rates largely corresponded to a per valorem rate of 3 percent to 4 percent, which would be in line with the rate at Chen Guan, Jing Guan, and Yu Guan.[7]

Again, the number of different varieties of logs were not counted directly. Instead, it was assumed that rafts from Jiangxi contained only fir, while rafts from Huguang contained some *qingliu* in addition to fir. For Huguang rafts they would first assess the tax of a shipment according to the fir rate. If the resulted tax payable was below 15 taels, they were not required to pay any taxes at the rate of *qingliu*; if the assessed tax was above 15 and below 100 taels, assume 3 percent of the logs were *qingliu* and recalculate the tax payable; if above 100 taels, assume 4 percent of the logs were *qingliu* and recalculate. Not considering surcharges, it approximately means that while a shipment from Huguang of 1,000 logs would pay a tax of 7 taels, a shipment of 10,000 logs, regardless of its actual composition, would pay 143 taels instead of 70 taels, and 20,000 logs would pay 334 taels instead of 140 taels. Besides fir and *qingliu*, other varieties constituted a small quantity and were taxed by counting individual logs.

For the purpose of estimating timber volumes, let's only consider fir and *qingliu*. Suppose, for simplicity, half of the logs passing through Longjiang Guan were from Jiangxi and the other half from Huguang, and on average 3 percent of the Huguang logs were taxed as *qingliu*. Take the previous estimation that the average timber tax at Longjiang Guan between 1725 and 1850 was 61,594 taels and take into account the 10 percent surcharge, then the average volume of timber reaching Nanjing annually would be about 5.2 million logs. At the high levels of the 1760s to the early 1780s, the estimated annual timber volume could reach 6.0 to 7.2 million logs. With our conservative estimation of the share of timber tax in Longjiang Guan's revenues, this estimation of the volume of timber logs is likely to be a lower bound as well. For reference, the Maritime Customs Service estimated that from 1882 through 1891, more than 18 million poles from Guizhou, Hunan, and Jiangxi, worth of 1.8 million taels, passed through the Inland Custom House of Wuhu annually.[8]

This estimation could be verified from a different angle. Annual timber shipments reaching the lower Yangzi customs stations in the 1760s are estimated to be about five hundred. One shipment, defined by a single tax declaration, could include multiple rafts and might well include the merchandise of multiple merchants. In the term of 1763 (QL28), the total customs revenue of Longjiang Guan was 150,906 taels, with 543 timber shipments arriving at the station. The next term of 1764 (QL29) saw the total revenue decrease to 144,947 taels, with 461 timber shipments arriving at the station. The difference of 82 shipments caused a tax decrease of 7,849 taels (on average 96 taels per shipment), which was offset by an increase in other miscellaneous taxes by 1,890 taels, resulting in a total revenue decrease of 5,959 taels from the previous term.[9] In 1768 the total customs revenue was 150,685 taels, and the number of timber shipments was 513. In 1769 the total revenue dropped to 124,423 taels, which was explained by a sharp decrease in the number of passing timber shipments by more than 320. This situation can be cross-checked with the upriver Wuhu Gong Guan, whose total revenue in 1768 was 133,061 taels, with 621 timber shipments declaring taxes. In 1770 there were only 228 timber shipments and the total customs revenue dropped to 113,861 taels.[10]

Keep in mind that such detailed explanations would only be offered in memorials when the customs revenues decreased significantly from the previous year. The average customs revenue of Longjiang Guan during the

1760s was above 140,000 taels, and that of Wuhu Gong Guan was about 130,000 taels. Compared with the examples above, it seems that an estimation of five hundred timber shipments annually would be appropriate for this decade. With the estimated timber tax level during this decade, the average tax levied on each shipment would be about 140 taels (meaning about 20,000 logs per shipment if from Jiangxi, or 10,000 logs per shipment if from Huguang).

While the size of each shipment could vary greatly, with the tax from a single shipment ranging from some dozens of taels to a couple of thousands of taels, an average of 140 taels of tax and 10,000 to 20,000 logs per shipment seem to be in line with the sparse information from the sources, lending support to the previous estimation of timber taxes and volume.[11] According to the taxation methods at Wuhu Gong Guan, surcharges were applied to different shipments by three tiers of their normal taxes: below 50 taels, above a 100 taels, and above 300 taels. From this division of three tiers, an average of 140 taels of tax per shipment would not be unreasonable. From the difference between 1763 and 1764 at Longjiang Guan, 82 timber shipments accounted directly for a tax decrease of 7,849 taels, indicating an average tax of about 96 taels per shipment, not differing in magnitude from 140 taels.

With these corroborations we can be fairly confident with the estimation that on average about 5 million logs reached Nanjing annually between 1725 and 1850, and the peak level reached 6 million to 7 million logs during the 1760s to the early 1780s. The magnitude, rather than the precise numbers, can be taken as a solid lower-bound estimation.

APPENDIX B

Estimation of Timber Tax at Jiujiang Guan

In Jiujiang Guan, in addition to boat levies, commercial taxes were collected on salt, tea, and timber.[1] Jiujiang Guan's revenues averaged 400,000 taels in the 1750s, increased by more than 70 percent to 740,000 taels in the mid-1780s, and gradually decreased to fluctuate between 500,000 and 600,000 taels in the first half of the nineteenth century. Evidence from the 1750s, 1820s, and 1830s indicated that the number of salt boats fluctuated around 1,200 to 1,300 in normal years, generating customs revenues of 130,000 to 150,000 taels, including levies on salt boats, taxes on salt, and taxes on commodity-bearing returning salt boats.[2] Data from the 1750s to the 1760s indicated that boat levies (other than those on salt boats), about 200,000 taels annually collected from more than 45,000 to 60,000 boats, accounted for about 40 percent to 55 percent of Jiujiang Guan's revenues.[3] In 1818 Jiangxi governor Qian Zhen remarked on the composition of Jiujiang Guan's average revenues of 540,000 taels. By then, the number of passing boats had reached 90,000, and boat levies 300,000 taels, contributing 55 percent of total revenue. Taxes from salt were 150,000 taels, and taxes from tea and other miscellaneous fees were about 10,000 taels. The rest was timber tax, fluctuating around 80,000 taels.[4]

Based on the customs superintendents' memorials, it is clear that taxes from salt and tea were very stable, while changing numbers of passing boats and timber rafts were always cited as reasons for revenue fluctuations. From 1796 to 1850 there were thirty-eight instances of revenue decreasing from the previous years and/or falling below the quota. It was customary for officials to offer explanations for such decreases in their memorials, which were available for thirty-two of these instances. Among the reasons offered, "fewer passing boats," usually due to unfavorable price trends or natural disasters that discouraged interregional trade, were mentioned nineteen times; "fewer passing timber rafts," either because of upstream supply shortage or downstream sluggish demand, were mentioned twenty times; and salt was only listed as a reason for three times, twice of which were as a supplementary cause besides the former two.[5]

Based on this information, I adopt the following strategy to estimate the timber taxes for Jiujiang Guan from the 1757 to 1850 (no information is available regarding the composition of customs revenues prior to 1757). First, I assume salt and tea taxes remained at 160,000 taels from 1750 to 1850. Second, for a few years in the 1750s and 1760s when the amount of boat levies was known, I take the residual of the total revenue as timber taxes. The estimated timber taxes for these years should represent relatively accurately the situation in the mid-eighteenth century. From 1770 to 1850, I assume that boat levies took up 55 percent of total revenues and that salt and tea taxes remained at 160,000 taels, and calculate the residual as the timber tax.

Then I adjust the estimated timber tax with descriptive information in the aforementioned memorials. Specifically, for a given year, if the reasons for decreased customs revenues included both boat levies and timber, then the estimated timber tax is kept. If "fewer passing boats" was given as the only reason, then the estimated timber tax, if lower than the level of the estimated amount for the previous year, is set to be the same as the previous year's level. If "fewer logs" was given as the only reason, I assume that the boat levies for this year were the same as the estimated boat levies of the previous year, and I adjust the estimated timber tax accordingly, sometimes with the help of occasional information in the memorials that mentioned the scale of the decrease of timber tax compared to the previous year.

For example, for 1823 the estimated timber tax using the general method is 100,731 taels. The total customs revenue in 1823 was about 5,000 taels lower than that in 1822. Sluggish demand for timber in Jiangnan due to a flood was given as the explanation, and boat levies were not mentioned. So I assume that boat levies in 1823 stayed about the same as those of 1822, which are estimated to be 321,510 taels (55 percent of the 1822 total revenue of 584,565 taels). Then I estimate the 1823 timber tax by subtracting the estimated boat levies of 321,510 taels and salt and tea taxes of 160,000 taels from the total revenue of 579,403 taels, resulting in 97,892 taels. This would be the estimated timber tax of 1823 if no other information was available. In this case, however, the memorial reported that the timber tax was about 20,000 taels lower than the previous year's level. The estimated timber tax for 1822 minus 20,000 taels is 83,054 taels, lower than the estimation of 97,892 taels. Therefore the final estimation of timber tax for 1823 is 83,054 taels.

A piece of circumstantial evidence from 1780 lent support to the above estimation method. The estimated timber taxes for Jiujiang Guan for 1780 and 1781 are 131,489 taels and 149,201 taels, respectively. A memorial by Jiangxi governor Hao Shuo in 1780 revealed that timber taxes collected at a branch station of Jiujiang Guan, Gutang, which taxed timber shipped up from Jiangxi, amounted to 82,364 taels in 1780 (from the fourth month of 1779 to the fourth month of 1780). This was considered very low; in fact, Hao Shuo mentioned that in the fifth and sixth months of 1780 alone, timber taxes collected at Gutang already reached 95,223 taels and expressed his optimism for revenues of 1781. Gutang only taxed timber from Jiangxi, so the timber from Hunan and other upper Yangzi regions was taxed at the main station. In these two years timber taxes at Chen Guan, which accounted for only timber from the western part of Hunan, were 14,611 taels and 16,473 taels, respectively. Timber taxes at Jing Guan, which accounted for timber from Hubei and Sichuan, were 10,211 taels and 14,065 taels. Comparing these numbers (and keeping in mind that timber from eastern Hunan was not accounted for), putting the estimated timber taxes of Jiujiang Guan at 131,489 taels and 149,201 taels seems reasonable. Moreover, the estimations for the 1800s and the 1810s are in line with Qian Zhen's 1818 description that timber taxes averaged 80,000 taels. The estimated timber taxes at Jiujiang Guan from 1757 to 1850 are shown in figure 2.1 together with the total customs revenues (including but not limited to timber taxes) from Longjiang Guan and Wuhu Gong Guan.

APPENDIX C

A Methodological Note on Land Contract Analysis

Chapter 3 is built on the analysis of my database drawing on more than a thousand timberland contracts from the lower Qingshui River valley in southeastern Guizhou. Previous studies by Chinese and Japanese scholars on the lower Qingshui area and its vicinities, based on both historical documents and anthropological fieldwork, have generated thick descriptions of the local society, ethnography, silvicultural technologies, contractual practices, marketplaces, local authorities, and state involvement, from which I have benefited enormously.[1] For the tree-planting industry, the works of Zhang Yingqiang and Aihara Yoshiyuki are especially helpful at delineating the division of shares and the intricate relations involved in contractual transactions. My contribution to this literature, and more generally to the study of contracts and land tenure, derives from a methodological approach that benefits from a combination of close textual analysis on historical materials as well as systematic statistical analysis on a large amount of homogeneous data. In this case, research methodologies in the disciplines of history and economics are not only put into tandem but also inform each other.

Because the titles of the contracts, either the curt original titles or the titles/categories given by the compilers of the published materials, are often misleading, irrelevant, or even wrong, the understanding of the complex economic relationships involved in these contracts requires careful textual analysis and categorization. This categorization, based on my analysis of a large portion of the sample collection, informs the design of a database, according to which all sample contracts are examined again and coded. The construction of a database with variables that are not predetermined but finalized through the trials and errors of text-based analysis enables me to show effectively the supporting statistics for changing patterns over time, albeit very basic ones. I would particularly caution against rushing into data collection without carefully analyzing individual documents, an omission that usually leads to statistical results that are either misleading or historically inconsequential. Textual analysis reveals the internal logic of the contracts and informs the kinds of variables we should trace, while statistical analysis allows us to go beyond descriptions of examples and demonstrate temporal and spatial patterns of change.

Combining categorical and statistical analysis in the same study is both feasible and beneficial, although it has become increasingly rare in the field of economic history, with the growing separation between the two disciplines of history and economics. This methodological approach makes possible the systematic study of land contracts, a genre of historical material that is abundant in Chinese history yet proves challenging for systematic analysis. Enormous amounts of local documents have recently been discovered, collected, and published by academic institutions in China, of which the Qingshui River material used in this book is just one example. A model of historically informed database construction and scholarly collaboration is crucial for the digitalization, sharing, and more efficient use of this large pool of materials.

CHINESE CHARACTER GLOSSARY

Anlan Huiguan 安瀾會館

baimu bang 柏木幫
baiqi 白契
bang 幫
banghang 幫行
baogao 包告
baojia 保甲
baotou 包頭
Benchu 坌處
Bulantai 布蘭泰
bumao 不毛
Buxi 補熙

caoyun 漕運
chaiwu 差務
Chen Guan 辰關
Chen xing gongshan 陳姓公山
chenglin 成林
Chenzhou 辰州
choufen ju 抽分局

da pa 大扒
daban ziyu muzhi 大半資于木植
dagu 大股
dangjiang 當江
danliang ma 單兩碼
daqian ma 大錢碼
dingtie 頂帖
dizhu gu 地主股
dong-Hu mu 東湖木

e'mu 額木
e'wai yingyu 額外盈餘

fei ma 飛碼
fen ma 分碼
fencheng hetong 分成合同
fengjin 封禁
fengshui lin 風水林
fenshan hetong 分山合同

gaitu guiliu 改土歸流
Gan Guan 贛關
gemao gechai 各貿各差
gongshan 公山
gongsuo 公所
gongtou 工頭
gu 股
Guang Hou 廣厚
guang mu 廣木
guanshan 官山
guansi yaren 官私牙人
Guazhi 掛治
Guo Mingzhu 郭明珠

Guo Weijing 郭維經
Gutang 姑塘

Hanjian 漢奸
Hao Shuo 郝碩
hongqi 紅契
Houchao Men 侯潮門
huangdi 荒地
huangmu 皇木
huaqi song 花旗鬆
hui 會
huiguan 會館
Huishang Muye Gongsuo 徽商木業公所
humu 護木
huohao 火耗

jiaji 加級
jiamu 架木
Jian Yuanji 剪元吉
Jiang Yinghui 姜映輝
Jianggan 江幹
jianyi zhi zhi 堅議之質
jiao 脚
Jing An 景安
jingji 經紀
Jisi Hui 祭祀會
Jiujiang Guan 九江關

kan qingshan 坎青山
Keshang Muye Gongsuo 課商木業公所

Li Ba 李拔
Li Daoyuan 李道遠
liang 兩
Lianghu Huiguan 兩湖會館
Longjiang Guan 龍江關
Longquan ma 龍泉碼
Lukeng 盧坑

mai mu 賣木
mai pingshui 買平水
mai shanchang 賣山場
mai shanchang shanmu 賣山場杉木
Maoping 茅坪
mawei song 馬尾鬆
Miao mu 苗木
mindi 民地
minzu 民族
Mu Li Ju 木釐局
mu xiansheng 木先生
muhang 木行
Muhang Gonghui 木行公會
muhao 木號
Mulan Weichang 木蘭圍場
muya 木牙
Muye Xuetang 木業學堂

Nanguan shadi 南關沙地
nanmu 楠木
Nanshi Malu Gongcheng Ju 南市馬路工程局
Nanshi Mushang Gongsuo 南市木商公所
nantai xiansheng 南臺先生
Nanxin Guan 南新關
Nanyue Gong Hui 南嶽宮會
nianli muzhi 年例木植

pagan 扒竿
pengmin 棚民
ping pa 平扒
Ping'ao 平鰲
pinmai 拼買

qianzhuang 錢莊
qibajiu ma 七八九碼
qinding yingyu 欽定盈餘
qingbai zi 清白字
qingliu 青柳

Qingming Hui 清明會
qingong limu 欽工例木
qingshan bang 青山幫
qinzi dianzai 親自佃栽
qiong Miao 窮苗

Randugan 冉度敢
renjuan 認捐

sanbang wuxiang 三幫五勷
shaliang juan 沙糧捐
shan 杉
shan gao 杉槁
Shangxin He 上新河
shanke 山客
shanmu 杉木
shanmu bang 杉木幫
shuangliang ma 雙兩碼
shuike 水客
shuiyan 水眼

tanchi 灘尺
tiaoli 條理
tongjin shuijiao 銅斤水腳
tongpi gao 桐皮槁
tuntian 屯田
Tusi 土司

Wang Rou 王柔
Wangzhai 王寨
weimu 桅木
Wendou 文斗
Wuhu Gong Guan 蕪湖工關
wutou chuwei 吳頭楚尾
wuzhu 無主

xiaogu 小股
xiaoqian ma 小錢碼
xietie 寫帖
xi-Hu mu 西湖木
Xixin Guan 西新關

yahang 牙行
yang song 洋鬆
Yang Xifu 楊錫紱
yanglian yin 養廉銀
yanshang muke 鹽商木客
yi zhumu paiba wei dazong 以竹木簰把為大宗
yijia huo 一家貨
yingyu 盈餘
yinliang 銀兩
yinyuan 銀元
Yu Guan 渝關

zaishou gu 栽手股
zhaqi guansi qucai 詐欺官司取財
Zhedong Muye Gongsuo 浙東木業公所
zheng'e 正額
Zhenxun Yangmu Ye Gongsuo 震巽洋木業公所
zhesuan tianbu 折算添補
zhongqian ma 中錢碼
zhongsu zaishan 種粟栽杉
zimu 子木
Zou Gongyi 鄒公義
Zu Zhiwang 祖之望

NOTES

FOREWORD

1 Totman, *Green Archipelago.*
2 Fedman, *Seeds of Control.*

MEASURES AND RELATED TERMINOLOGY

1 Aihara, "Shindai chūki Kishū tōnanbu Seisui Kō ryūiki," 550.
2 For a detailed explanation of the Qing currency system and the different units of account, see Lin, *China Upside Down*, xxiii–xxv.

INTRODUCTION

1 Margary and Alcock, *Journey of Augustus Raymond Margary*, 126.
2 For example, see the constant fire threat and preventative measures in Hankou in Rowe, *Hankow: Conflict and Community*, 158–68.
3 Tang Lixing, "Ming Qing Huizhou mushang kao"; Li Linqi, "Huishang yu Ming Qing shiqi de mucai maoyi"; and Wang Zhenzhong, "Taiping Tianguo qianhou Huishang zai Jiangxi."
4 For an overview of the process of China's deforestation and its regional variations over two millennia, see Elvin, *Retreat of the Elephants*, 19–85. For the environmental transformation in frontier areas over the late imperial period, see Marks, *China: An Environmental History*, chap. 5.
5 For a similar transition in the late imperial state's procurement of materia medica, see Bian, *Know Your Remedies*, chap. 2.
6 For the various definitions of "sustainability" and priorities used in different disciplines, see Foy, "Economic Sustainability and the Preservation of Environmental Assets"; Turner, *Sustainable Environmental Economics and Management*; Rubenstein, "Science and the Pursuit of a

Sustainable World"; Ludwig, "Environmental Sustainability"; and Gatto, "Sustainability: Is It a Well Defined Concept?"

7 Elvin, "Three Thousand Years of Unsustainable Growth"; Elvin, *Retreat of the Elephants*; and Elvin and Liu, *Sediments of Time*.

8 My approach is largely in line with that of the World Bank. See the works of Ismail Serageldin, the World Bank's first vice president for Environmentally Sustainable Development, "Making Development Sustainable" and *Sustainability and the Wealth of Nations*.

9 For the ecological problems caused by the intensified reclamation of the lower Yangzi upper lands (especially the devastating impacts of maize cultivation), see Osborne, "Highlands and Lowlands."

10 North, *Institutions, Institutional Change, and Economic Performance*, 3–4.

11 Marks, *China: An Environmental History*, 228–31; Osborne, "Local Politics of Land Reclamation"; and Averill, *Revolution in the Highlands*, 23–30.

12 Dollar, *Memoirs of Robert Dollar*, 72–73. Regarding Dollar's reference to "small timber," note that "small" is in comparison to the centuries-old natural Oregon pine (i.e., Douglas fir) that his company specialized in.

13 With state-led efforts of reforestation in recent years, by 2010 China's forest coverage had bounced back to more than 20 percent. Despite some overstatement in the official data, there is no doubt that more of China is now more forested than in 1950 or 1990. See Marks, *China: An Environmental History*, 288; and Robbins and Harrell, "Paradoxes and Challenges for China's Forests in the Reform Era."

14 McNeil, "China's Environmental History in World Perspective."

15 For tree plantation in the Old South, see McDermott, *Making of a New Rural Order in South China*, 369–429; Menzies, *Forest and Land Management*, 89–104; Averill, *Revolution in the Highlands*, 25–27; and Miller, *Fir and Empire*, chap. 4. For similar practices in southwestern China, see Zhang Yingqiang, *Mucai zhi liudong*; and Daniels, "Seisui ryūiki no Byōzoku ga shokurin."

16 An exception is Joseph McDermott's study on the development of "timber futures" in southern Anhui. See McDermott, *Making of a New Rural Order in South China*, chap. 6. I make comparisons between similar practices in Anhui and Guizhou in chapter 3.

17 Holling and Meffe, "Command and Control."

18 Anderson and Libecap, *Environmental Markets*. For related scholarship on environmental markets, see Freeman and Kolstad, *Moving to Markets in Environmental Regulation*; and Stavins, "Experience with Market-Based Environmental Policy Instruments."

19 For an overview of such commercial organizations, see Kwang-Ching Liu, "Chinese Merchant Guilds."

20 For a recent elaboration of this view, see Zhou Lin, "Bianshang yihuo haishang." For a short review of the Chinese-language studies on *yahang*, see Lin Hongzhuang, "Ming Qing ji jindai yahang yanjiu zongshu."

21 For reviews of the scholarly debate on the economic functions of merchant organizations, see Moll-Murata, "Chinese Guilds," 223; and Rowe, "Ming-Qing Guilds," 47–60.

22 For *yahang*, see Chen Zhongping, "Ming Qing shiqi Jiangnan shizhen de yaren yu yahang"; and Dykstra, "Complicated Matters," 142–71. For merchant associations, see Chen and Myers, "Coping with Transaction Costs"; and Rowe, *Hankow: Commerce and Society*, 252–321.

23 The genus of *Cunninghamia* also includes *Cunninghamia konishii*, a species native to Taiwan. The Chinese character *shan* could also refer to other species, including Japanese cedar (*Cryptomeria japonica*), which is called *sugi* in the Japanese language and written with the same Chinese character. However, historical texts rarely contain enough details for us to differentiate the specific species. Integrated Taxonomic Information System, "ITIS Standard Report Page: Cunninghamia"; and Fu, Yu, and Mill, "Cunninghamia."

24 Yang Yusheng, *Shanmu lin ke chixu jingying de yanjiu*; and Yu Xintuo, *Shanmu zaipei xue*.

25 Liu Mingguang, *Zhongguo ziran dili tuji*, 87.

26 Bello, *Across Forest, Steppe, and Mountain*, chap. 2.

27 For the Qing invention and restoration of "nature" in Mongolia and Manchuria, see Schlesinger, *World Trimmed with Fur*.

28 Reardon-Anderson, "Land Use and Society in Manchuria and Inner Mongolia," 510–14; and Menzies, *Forest and Land Management*, chap. 3.

29 Millward, *Beyond the Pass*, 201.

CHAPTER ONE: OBTAINING TIMBER FOR THE COURT

1 Menzies, "Forestry," 563; and Shiba Yoshinobu, *Commerce and Society in Sung China*, 91.

2 Shiba Yoshinobu, *Commerce and Society in Sung China*, 92.

3 Mao Qiling, "Hangzhou zhihuo yi"; and Gan Xi, *Baixia suoyan*, *juan* 1.

4 Li Bozhong, "Ming Qing shiqi Jiangnan diqu de mucai wenti," 87.

5 Shiba Yoshinobu, *Commerce and Society in Sung China*, 93.

6 Shiba Yoshinobu, *Commerce and Society in Sung China*, 95–96; and Miller, *Fir and Empire*, chap. 1.

7 Fan Chengda, *Canluan lu*, entry for 1173.1.3.

8 *Chunxi Xin'an zhi*, *juan* 1, "fengsu."

9 Zhang Haipeng and Wang Tingyuan, *Ming Qing Huishang ziliao*, 180.

10 Shiba Yoshinobu, *Commerce and Society in Sung China*, 91.

11 Fan Chengda, *Canluan lu*, entry for 1173.1.3.

12 Tan Qixiang, "Zhongguo neidi yimin shi: Hunan pian"; and Ge Jianxiong, Cao Shuji, and Wu Songdi, *Jianming Zhongguo yimin shi*, 271–393.
13 Li Bozhong, "Ming Qing shiqi Jiangnan diqu de mucai wenti," 89.
14 For the early Ming decommercialization and physiocratic policies, see von Glahn, *Economic History of China*, 285–93.
15 The Chinese word *nanmu* refers to a precious softwood that is unique to southern China and Vietnam, which could come from several evergreen species, with the highest grades coming from the *Phoebe* genus (*Phoebe hungmaoensis*, *Phoebe nanmu*, and *Phoebe zhengnan*). For the large-scale procurement of *nanmu* in southwestern China during the Yongle reign for several grand imperial constructions, see Campbell, *What the Emperor Built*.
16 Lan Yong, "Ming Qing shiqi de huangmu caiban"; and *Dongzu shehui lishi diaocha*, 6–7.
17 Campbell, *What the Emperor Built*.
18 For an overview of the two commercial revolutions, see Rowe, "Approaches to Modern Chinese Social History."
19 For the gradual revival of timber markets and the Ming state's shifting methods of timber requisition, see Miller, *Fir and Empire*, chaps. 5–7.
20 Lan Yong, "Ming Qing shiqi de huangmu caiban."
21 For studies of the late imperial incorporation of southwestern borderlands and the vibrant local histories of choices and resistance, see Herman, *Amid the Clouds and Mist*; Giersch, *Asian Borderlands*; Bello, "To Go Where No Han Could Go for Long"; Atwill, *Chinese Sultanate*; and Shin, *Making of the Chinese State*.
22 For the centuries-long endeavors at weakening the native chieftains by the Ming-Qing state, see Herman, "Cant of Conquest"; Herman, "Empire in the Southwest"; and Sutton, "Ethnicity and the Miao Frontier."
23 For how the Qing state acquired empirical knowledge about the southwest through cartography and ethnography to pursue its imperial ambitions, see Hostetler, *Qing Colonial Enterprise*. For the spread of knowledge about travel routes and local conditions through commercial publishing during the Ming-Qing period, see Chen Xuewen, *Ming Qing shiqi shangye shu*.
24 Marks, *China: An Environmental History*, 198–207.
25 The non-Han groups in this area, officially categorized today as Miao, Dong, Yao, and other minority nationalities (*minzu*), were often collectively labeled as "Miao" or classified with varying adjectives of specificity ("Flower Miao," "Cave Miao," and so forth) in both official and popular usages during the Qing. See Diamond, "Defining the Miao"; and Deal and Hostetler, *Art of Ethnography*. I use the term "Miao" in accordance with its general Qing usage instead of its contemporary meaning of one particular "nationality" per official usage.

26 Liang Cong, *Qingshui Jiang xiayou cunzhai shehui*, 212–17; and Zhang Yingqiang, *Mucai zhi liudong*, 28–35.
27 Jiang Shunyuan, "Ming-Qing chaoting Sichuan caimu yanjiu."
28 In 1906 the newly established Ministry of Civil Affairs assumed control. Aihara Yoshiyuki, "Shinchō ni yoru mokuzai chōtatsu," 22.
29 GX_HDSL, *juan* 875 and 877, "mujia"; Aihara Yoshiyuki, "Shinchō ni yoru mokuzai chōtatsu," 25.
30 GX_HDSL, *juan* 875.
31 Xing, Zhang, and Baker, "Age and Radial Growth Pattern."
32 Aihara Yoshiyuki, "Shinchō ni yoru mokuzai chōtatsu," 23–24.
33 GX_HDSL, *juan* 58.
34 Aihara Yoshiyuki, "Shinchō ni yoru mokuzai chōtatsu," 25.
35 Lu Yin, "Shangxin He shanmu ye wushi nian gaikuang."
36 Aihara Yoshiyuki, "Shinchō ni yoru mokuzai chōtatsu," 28–29.
37 *Jiaqing Hunan tongzhi*, *juan* 175; and FHA 04-01-35-0953-040, 04-01-35-0954-056, 04-01-37-0090-038.
38 GZD 000840.
39 Aihara Yoshiyuki, "Shinchō ni yoru mokuzai chōtatsu" n. 45.
40 Aihara Yoshiyuki, "Shinchō ni yoru mokuzai chōtatsu" n. 46.
41 SYD, QL30 (1765).
42 GX_HDSL, *juan* 875.
43 Activities of Jiangsu and Jiangxi timber merchants who were delegated the task of purchasing large timber for those two provinces were mentioned in a number of legal cases in 1806, which are reprinted in *Dongzu shehui lishi diaocha*, 39–41.
44 The National Science Library in the Chinese Academy of Sciences in Beijing, Call No. 260664. For more on this manuscript, see Aihara Yoshiyuki, "Shindai chūki Kishū tōnanbu shimizu kō ryūiki"; and Qu Jian, "Wenben yu chaoben."
45 Ying'an, *Caiyun huangmu andu*, 4a.
46 This data is obtained from *Wuliao jiazhi zeli Databases*.
47 GZD 4020009317.
48 Aihara Yoshiyuki, "Shindai chūki Kishū tōnanbu shimizu kō ryūiki," 555.
49 Ying'an, *Caiyun huangmu andu*, 107b.
50 Tuokou was a timber market in the Miao region where large tribute timber was often purchased. Ying'an, *Caiyun huangmu andu*, 91b.
51 Ying'an, *Caiyun huangmu andu*, 35a.
52 Aihara Yoshiyuki, "Shindai chūki Kishū tōnanbu shimizu kō ryūiki," 553, 557–59.
53 Aihara Yoshiyuki, "Shindai chūki Kishū tōnanbu shimizu kō ryūiki," 557–59.
54 FHA 03-2235-020.
55 Ying'an, *Caiyun huangmu andu*, 88b–89a.

56 Aihara Yoshiyuki, "Shindai chūki Kishū tōnanbu shimizu kō ryūiki," 552.
57 Aihara Yoshiyuki, "Shindai chūki Kishū tōnanbu shimizu kō ryūiki," 558.
58 Ying'an, *Caiyun huangmu andu*, 87a and 88a.
59 Longquan *ma* was the measurement and pricing system for timber, explained in chapter 2. Ying'an, *Caiyun huangmu andu*, 72a.
60 Ying'an, *Caiyun huangmu andu*, 86b and 87b.
61 A short survey of Hankou's timber market in English can be found in Rowe, *Hankow: Commerce and Society*, 269–73.
62 Ying'an, *Caiyun huangmu andu*, 82b.
63 Ying'an, *Caiyun huangmu andu*, 108b.
64 Aihara Yoshiyuki, "Shindai chūki Kishū tōnanbu shimizu kō ryūiki," 563.
65 GZD 000840.
66 Such a dispute between Nanjing and Suzhou brokers that reached the provincial government can be found in *Ming Qing Suzhou gongshang ye beike ji*, no. 73.
67 The details of this case are included in FHA 03-2235-020.
68 Aihara Yoshiyuki, "Shindai chūki Kishū tōnanbu shimizu kō ryūiki," 562.
69 For the Hunanese's increasing participation in long-distance timber trade by the nineteenth century, see Rowe, *Hankow: Commerce and Society*, 270.
70 FHA 03-2235-020.
71 Aihara Yoshiyuki, "Shindai chūki Kishū tōnanbu shimizu kō ryūiki," 558.
72 For examples of such instances, see Aihara Yoshiyuki, "Shindai chūki Kishū tōnanbu shimizu kō ryūiki," n. 90.
73 Ying'an, *Caiyun huangmu andu*, 82a.
74 For general survey of the late imperial grain tribute system, see Hinton, "Grain Tribute System of the Ch'ing Dynasty"; Fan Shuzhi, "Ming Qing caoyun shulue"; and Li Wenzhi and Jiang Taixin, *Qing dai caoyun*.
75 Hinton, "Grain Tribute System of the Ch'ing Dynasty," 348–52.
76 Chen Feng, "Jianlun Song Ming Qing caoyun," 121–22.
77 Chen Feng, "Jianlun Song Ming Qing caoyun," 123–25.
78 FHA 04-01-35-0137-005.
79 FHA 04-01-35-0162-007 (1772), 04-01-35-0220-028 (1813), 04-01-35-0265-011 (1834), 04-01-35-0379-052 (1843); DGSL, *juan* 146, DG8 (1828).11.*renyin*; DGSL, *juan* 252, DG14 (1834).5.*yihai*; and DGSL, *juan* 255, DG14 (1834).8.*jiyou*.
80 For the essence and effect of such ideals in Ming-Qing China, see Wong, "Taxation and Good Governance in China."
81 Similar strategies of bureaucratic funding and official compensation (in altered forms but in the same spirit) proved important for building the market in the early stage of China's reform and opening up, see Ang, *How China Escaped the Poverty Trap*, chap. 4.

82 Earlier historiography in environmental history tends to patch up all available sources from poetry, literature, and gazetteers to generate general timelines about the process of deforestation in China. Elvin, *Retreat of the Elephants*, 19–85. Such efforts are indeed valuable and necessary as a first step and further inspire more careful examinations as this book attempts to do.

83 For discussions on the Ming-Qing procurement of timber for imperial construction projects, see Vermeer, "Population and Ecology along the Frontier," 247–51; Adshead, "An Energy Crisis in Early Modern China"; and Lan Yong, "Ming Qing shiqi de huangmu caiban."

CHAPTER TWO: THE INTERREGIONAL TIMBER MARKET

1 Liao Shengfeng, *Qingdai changguan yu quyu jingji yanjiu*, 18–23.

2 *Da Ming huidian, juan* 35.

3 For early Ming monetary policies and the ultimate demise of the paper money system, see von Glahn, *Fountain of Fortune*, 70–82.

4 Liao Shengfeng, *Qingdai changguan yu quyu jingji yanjiu*, 22; and *Da Ming huidian, juan* 204.

5 For institutional histories of individual customs stations during the Ming-Qing transition, see Deng Yibing, "Qingdai qianqi shuiguan de shezhi."

6 KX_HD, *juan* 16.

7 QL_HDZL, *juan* 47 and 136.

8 QL_HDZL, juan 47 and 136.

9 QL_HDZL, *juan* 47 and 136; and QSG, *juan* 125.

10 Qi Meiqin, "Guanyu Qingdai queguan eshui de kaocha," 62.

11 QL_HDZL, *juan* 47 and 136; and GX_HDSL, *juan* 235 and 941.

12 Qi Meiqin, "Guanyu Qingdai queguan eshui de kaocha," 64–65; and QL_HDZL, *juan* 48.

13 Qi Meiqin, "Guanyu Qingdai queguan eshui de kaocha," 65.

14 QL_HDZL, *juan* 47.

15 GX_HDSL, *juan* 237.

16 GX_HDSL, *juan* 237.

17 GX_HDSL, *juan* 237; and Liao Shengfeng, *Qingdai changguan yu quyu jingji yanjiu*, 217.

18 GX_HDSL, *juan* 238.

19 For the secular decrease of customs revenues in the first half of the nineteenth century, especially post-1820, see Ni Yuping, *Qingchao Jia Dao guanshui yanjiu*.

20 Liao Shengfeng, *Qingdai changguan yu quyu jingji yanjiu*, 245–98.

21 For the revenue compositions of Gan Guan, see Liao Shengfeng, "Qingdai Gan Guan shuishou de bianhua."

22 *Nanjing wuzi zhi*, 19–21.

23 One issue is that *Nanjing wuzi zhi* and some other publications of the 1980s and 1990s have associated Xi *bang* with the Shanxi or Shaanxi merchants. For example, see Yang Yougeng, "Qingdai Qian dongnan Qingshui Jiang liuyu muhang chutan," 49; and Jin Qin, "Qing mo sanda hangye zhiyi de Shangxin He mushi." However, there does not seem to be clear sources to support this claim. Although Shanxi and Shaanxi merchants were indeed referred to as "Xi *bang*" in salt and other trades, no source whatsoever indicated that they were a significant group in the trade of timber in Jiangnan or other parts of southern China. I have based my understanding on the writings of Republican-era practitioners who clearly explained that "Xi *bang*" in the timber trade referred to merchants from Jiangxi. For example, see Wu Chuanjun, "Nanjing Shangxin He de mushi"; and Yin Qing, "Jiangxi zhi mucai ye."

24 Such stories abound in merchant biographies in *Guangxu Wuyuan xian zhi*, *juan* 33–35.

25 *Nanjing wuzi zhi*, 21.

26 Dai Yuan, "Nanjing Shangxin He mucai maoyi zhuangkuang," 237.

27 Liu Peiliang and Fan Jingyu, "Nanjing shi mucai shikuang diaocha shang," 21.

28 For similar remarks, see FHA 02-01-008-000367-0006, 04-01-35-0315-030, 04-01-35-0329-032, 03-0593-030, 03-0607-006; and GZD 40212, 001409, 005748, 403006452, 014090, 040641, 086080.

29 Inspector General of Customs, *Decennial Reports*, vol.1 (1882–1891), 238. Since the timber trade was not taxed by the Maritime Customs, these figures were offered as estimates rather than exact statistics.

30 This price was for logs between 1 and 1.5 feet in circumference (dbh 0.3–0.5 feet) from Hangzhou in 1900, see Liu Boshan, *Huizhou wenshu di san ji*, vol. 7, p. 245. Similarly, in the 1890s, 1-foot-circumference logs were selling for 0.3 to 0.6 taels in Nanjing, see Lu Yin, "Shangxin He shanmu ye wushi nian gaikuang."

31 Population data is from Cao Shuji, *Zhongguo renkou shi.*

32 For the issues surrounding the Dongting Lake and the middle Yangzi hydrological system, see Perdue, *Exhausting the Earth*; and Marks, *China: An Environmental History*, 232–37.

33 Nineteenth-century officials remarked on mounting hydrological difficulties, the consequences of deforestation, and species extinction. See Vermeer, "Population and Ecology along the Frontier in Qing China," 272–77; and Marks, *Tigers, Rice, Silk, and Silt*, 331–32. Environmental historians identify a systematic environmental crisis building up in nineteenth-century China that was qualitatively more severe than in previous periods. See Marks, *China: An Environmental History*, 264–82.

34 For example, see Dai Yuan, "Nanjing Shangxin He mucai maoyi zhuangkuang"; and Wu Chuanjun, "Nanjing Shangxin He de mushi."

35 GX_HDSL, *juan* 941.

36 Liao Shengfeng, *Qingdai changguan yu quyu jingji yanjiu*, 123.

37 GZD 027882.

38 Lu Yin, "Shangxin He shanmu ye wushi nian gaikuang"; Yin Qing, "Jiangxi zhi mucai ye"; Lu Qizao, "Gannan mucai hangye shihua"; and Ouyang Tianxing, "Gannan mucai hangye shihua buji."

39 *Tongzhi Ganzhou fu zhi*, *juan* 20 and 21; and Lu Qizao, "Gannan mucai hangye shihua," 112.

40 *Qianlong Longnan xian zhi*, *juan* 13 and 25. See also *Guangxu Longnan xian zhi*, *juan* 2.

41 Yin Qing, "Jiangxi zhi mucai ye," 2–5.

42 Lu Yin, "Shangxin He shanmu ye wushi nian gaikuang," vol. 2, no. 1, 13.

43 *Guangxu Jiangxi tongzhi*, *juan* 49; Yin Qing, "Jiangxi zhi mucai ye," 5; Lu Qizao, "Gannan mucai hangye shihua," 112; and Ouyang Tianxing, "Gannan mucai hangye shihua buji," 166, 168.

44 Lu Qizao, "Gannan mucai hangye shihua," 114–15; and Ouyang Tianxing, "Gannan mucai hangye shihua buji," 167–68.

45 Yin Qing, "Jiangxi zhi mucai ye," 6.

46 Ouyang Tianxing, "Gannan mucai hangye shihua buji," 167–68; Wu Chuanjun, "Nanjing Shangxin He de mushi"; and Lu Yin, "Shangxin He shanmu ye wushi nian gaikuang," vol. 2, no. 2, 13–14.

47 My estimation of the timber volume for Jing Guan is much lower than that of Shi Ying because I have taken out estimated boat levies from Jing Guan's revenues, while Shi has assumed the total revenue to be timber tax. Apart from this flaw, the bigger problem in Shi's approach is that she uses the estimated volume of timber through Jing Guan as the indicator of the scale of Hankou's timber trade. As I explain in this book, however, Jing Guan only accounted for timber from Sichuan and Hubei, a shrinking portion of Hankou's timber supply. Shi's conclusion, based on Jing Guan's revenue data, that the timber market in Hankou became stagnant in the first half of the nineteenth century, is contradictory to historical accounts of the rapid development of Hankou's Parrot Island timber market since the 1800s. The reason lies in Shi's omission of the rising amount of timber from Hunan, which more than compensated for the declining supplies from Hubei. See Shi Ying, "Qingdai Hankou de zhumu shichang"; and Chen Xing and Chen Lilian, "Hanyang Yingwu Zhou zhumu shichang shihua."

48 Chen Xing and Chen Lilian, "Hanyang Yingwu Zhou zhumu shichang shihua."

49 *Guangxu Wuyuan xian zhi*, *juan* 30, 34.

50 A comprehensive account of the historical development of Hankou's timber market and the customary practices in this business is written by Chen Xing and Chen Lilian, two timber merchants who had traded in Hankou since the early twentieth century for several decades: "Hanyang Yingwu Zhou zhumu shichang shihua."

51 *Jiaqing Wuhu xianzhi*, *juan* 6; and *Minguo Wuhu xianzhi*, *juan* 13.

52 Chen Xing and Chen Lilian, "Hanyang Yingwu Zhou zhumu shichang shihua," 116–17.

53 Rowe, *Hankow: Commerce and Society*, 269–72; and Chen Xing and Chen Lilian, "Hanyang Yingwu Zhou zhumu shichang shihua," 123.

54 Chen Xing and Chen Lilian, "Hanyang Yingwu Zhou zhumu shichang shihua," 121–24.

55 Rowe, *Hankow: Commerce and Society*, 272–73; and Chen Xing and Chen Lilian, "Hanyang Yingwu Zhou zhumu shichang shihua," 124–26.

56 Chen Xing and Chen Lilian, "Hanyang Yingwu Zhou zhumu shichang shihua," 125. William Rowe mentioned that the Lianghu Huiguan became inclusive toward Hubei merchants after the settlement of this dispute at the pressure of the two prominent Hunanese officials Zeng Guofan and Zuo Zongtang, and thereafter became an all-encompassing timber trade organization. The source is unclear, however. Rowe, *Hankow: Commerce and Society*, 273.

57 Ni Yuping, *Qingchao Jia Dao guanshui yanjiu*, 99–104.

58 GX_HDSL, *juan* 941.

59 The 1686 mentioning of Chen Guan is found in an entry in QL_HDZL, *juan* 146. However, it was not included in the formal list of Board of Works customs in the Kangxi edition of *Collected Statutes*, which covered up to 1686, or in the Yongzheng edition, which covered up to 1727. See KX_HD, *juan* 136; and YZ_HD, *juan* 201.

60 Chen Xing and Chen Lilian, "Hanyang Yingwu Zhou zhumu shichang shihua," 118–19.

61 Dai Yuan, "Nanjing Shangxin He mucai maoyi zhuangkuang"; and Liu Peiliang and Fan Jingyu, "Nanjing shi mucai shikuang diaocha shang," 20–21.

62 GZD 402016499.

63 GZD 402013901; and FHA 02-01-04-12848-003.

64 FHA 02-01-04-12848-003.

65 GZD 402002884.

66 FHA 02-01-04-18334-018, 02-01-04-18335-028. See also GX_GBZL, *juan* 80.

67 FHA 03-1768-039.

68 Since the 1860s, memorials started to report timber and salt taxes separately. From a dozen of these memorials, it can be inferred that the quota for salt taxes was set at 3,255 taels in 1732, which remained stable,

except for an addition of 10 percent meltage fee in 1807. Annually collected salt taxes seemed to be around the quota level until after the 1850s, when shortages of a few hundred to more than a thousand taels became normal.

69 Lu Yin, "Wo ye laitan Longquan ma," 12. For descriptions on how the Longquan *ma* system worked in a number of markets, see *Dongzu shehui lishi diaocha*, 82; Tang Bingnan, "Hankou ce mucai zhi fa"; Wang Boxin, "Nanjing shi mucai maoyi jijia fangfa gaiyao"; and Yin Qing, "Jiangxi zhi mucai ye," 9–11.

70 Menzies, "Forestry," 633.

71 Wang Zhenzhong, "Taiping Tianguo qianhou Huishang zai Jiangxi," 151.

72 Aihara Yoshiyuki, "Shindai chūki Kishū tōnanbu shimizu kō ryūiki," 555.

73 Liu Boshan, *Huizhou wenshu di san ji*, vol. 7, 245.

74 Lu Yin, "Shangxin He shanmu ye wushi nian gaikuang," vol. 1, no. 4, 10.

75 Lu Yin, "Shangxin He shanmu ye wushi nian gaikuang," vol. 2, no. 1, 13.

76 Zhan Mingduo, *Wo zhi xiao shi*, 187–88.

77 *Dongzu shehui lishi diaocha*, 82. Information about discount practices can also be found in Lu Yin, "Bo xinding shichi muma."

CHAPTER THREE: SUSTAINING THE RESOURCES

1 Nicholas K. Menzies has been motivated by this very question in his pioneering study on the forest management systems in Chinese history, *Forest and Land Management*, 2.

2 Menzies, *Forest and Land Management*, 123–37.

3 A study on Kenya between 1930 and 1990, for example, finds that increased market opportunities and labor availability, combined with technological knowledge and appropriate institutions, have led to more sustainable resource practices through the planting and husbandry of more trees. See Tiffen, Mortimore, and Gichuki, *More People, Less Erosion*.

4 Miller, *Fir and Empire*, chap. 1.

5 Marks, *China: An Environmental History*, 286.

6 Songster, "Cultivating the Nation in Fujian's Forests," 457–58.

7 Rotation lengths for fir cultivation seem to be longer in earlier periods. The late-Ming gazetteer of Kaihua County recorded a duration of thirty to forty years (see *Chongzhen Kaihua xian zhi*, *juan* 3, 4a). Similar rotations were recorded for the eighteenth and nineteenth centuries (see *Qianlong Kaihua xianzhi*, *juan* 5; and *Guangxu Chun'an xian zhi*, *juan* 5). Nowadays, rotations in intensively managed, fast-growing fir plantations range from twelve to thirty years depending on the desired size (see Guojia Linye Ju, "Shanmu susheng fengchan yongcai lin").

8 *Guangxu Chun'an xian zhi*, *juan* 5.

9 It is not clear that problem has been fully solved, as there is uncertainty whether the locals will continue to replant the trees after the subsidies end. See Trac et al., "Environmental Reviews and Case Studies."
10 For patterns of the internal migration to the southwest during the late imperial period, see Tan Qixiang, "Zhongguo neidi yimin shi"; and Ge Jianxiong, Wu Songdi, and Cao Shuji, *Jianming Zhongguo yimin shi*, chaps. 6 and 7.
11 For the diverse contractual practices in land transactions by the late imperial period, see Long Denggao, "Qingdai diquan jiaoyi xingshi"; and Long Denggao, "Diquan jiaoyi yu shengchan yaosu zuhe."
12 Von Glahn, *Economic History of China*, 324.
13 Appuhn, *Forest on the Sea*.
14 Totman, *Green Archipelago*; and Lee, "Postwar Pines."
15 Totman, *Green Archipelago*, chaps. 4 and 6.
16 McDermott, *Making of a New Rural Order in South China*, chaps. 5 and 6; and Miller, *Fir and Empire*, chap. 4.
17 For imperial foraging in Manchuria, see Bello, *Across Forest, Steppe, and Mountain*, chap. 2.
18 Von Glahn, *Economic History of China*, chap. 6.
19 For the Mulan Weichang imperial hunting enclosure, see Menzies, *Forest and Land Management*, chap. 3. For the laws governing the gradient access to concentric forest zones around the Qing imperial mausoleums, see Xue Yunsheng, *Dulü cunyi*, *juan* 25, *xing lü* 1, *zeidao shang* 1, "dao yuanling shumu."
20 For an example in Guizhou, see *Daoguang Renhuai zhili ting zhi*, *juan* 1.
21 For an example in Guangxi, see *Jiaqing Guiyang xian zhi*, *juan* 1.
22 *Qianlong Qingyuan xian zhi*, *juan* 4, 240–41.
23 *Kangxi Nancheng xian zhi*, 171–82; and *Jiaqing Xuancheng xian zhi*, *juan* 4, 152.
24 For examples of the state's encouraging poor people to settle and cultivate *guanshan*, see *Zeli bianlan*, *juan* 17, 76–77. Regulations about the registration and security control of mountain settlers (*pengmin*) are included in Xue Yunsheng, *Dulü cunyi*, *juan* 22, *bing lü* 3, *guanjin*, "panjie jianxi."
25 *Qianlong Heyuan xian zhi*, *juan* 10, 653.
26 For examples of references to *guanshan* as *huangdi*, *bumao* (uncultivated; not vegetated), *wuzhu* (without owners), and generating no tax revenues, see *Qianlong De'an xian zhi*, *juan* 11, 690; *Daoguang Lanzhou fu zhi*, *juan* 2, 134; *Daqing Guangxu xin faling*, 1791; and Zhuang Lunyi, *Lu xiang gongdu*, *juan* 1, 38.
27 *Qianlong Heping xian zhi*, *juan* 2, 155.
28 For examples of the state's explicit rejections and denunciations of privatization schemes to keep the *guanshan* in question as open-access

resources, see Zhuang Lunyi, *Lu xiang gongdu, juan* 2, 67–68; and *Xing'an huilan, juan* 56, 1965.

29 *Xing'an huilan, juan* 29, 1006–1007. For other references to the open-access nature of *guanshan* in this source, see *juan* 31, 1076–77; and *juan* 56, 1965.

30 *Daoguang Renhuai zhili ting zhi, juan* 20, 1509; *Guangxu Baise ting zhi, juan* 3, 165–66; *Qiannan shilüe, juan* 7, 216; *Guangxu Guangzhou fu zhi, juan* 70, 4231; *Xing'an huilan, juan* 30, 1052; and *Bo'an xubian, juan* 2, 41.

31 *Tongzhi Dehua xian zhi, juan* 13, 944.

32 This concept refers to situations where shared and unregulated resource systems collapse due to overuse, which could happen to overexploited open-access regimes or poorly managed common-property regimes (the word "commons" in the concept could be misleading as it does not distinguish between open-access and common property). See Hardin, "Tragedy of the Commons." It is worth noting that the "tragedy" does not necessarily happen for all common-resource systems. Indeed, many examples exist where communities with access to a common resource cooperate to regulate the use of those resources in a sustainable way. Local institutions could be effective in sustainable common-resource management without top-down regulations or privatization (see Ostrom, *Governing the Commons*). In this book I use the "tragedy of the commons" concept in its basic meaning that shared and unregulated resources tend to be overexploited. I distance my usage from those who see the "tragedy of the commons" as proving the superiority and necessity of the Lockean private property, which historically justified the dispossession of Indigenous people and hastened colonization. For some criticisms of the conceptualization and usage of the "tragedy of the commons," see Ciriacy-Wantrup and Bishop, "Common Property as a Concept in Natural Resources Policy"; Feeny et al., "Tragedy of the Commons: Twenty-Two Years Later"; and Harvey, "Future of the Commons."

33 *Qianlong Funing fu zhi, juan* 12, 739–41.

34 This memorial is analyzed in Aihara Yoshiyuki, "Qingchao zhongqi de senlin zhengce."

35 The prototype and variations of this basic family property system is explained in Shiga Shuzo, "Family Property and the Law of Inheritance in Traditional China."

36 For temple and monastic forests, see Menzies, *Forest and Land Management*, chap. 4.

37 Allee, "Status of Contracts in Nineteenth-Century Chinese Courts."

38 Some examples of community regulations on forest and woodlots are discussed in Menzies, *Forest and Land Management*, 78–79.

39 Ostrom, *Governing the Commons*; and Poteete and Ostrom, "In Pursuit of Comparable Concepts."

40 One example of such lineage regulation is "Cheng Yanxi Tang hezu jinyue" (1832) in the *Huizhou wenshu* collection at the Institute of History and Philology, Academic Sinica, Taipei (call no. 63-1-688-116061203011). Two renewed versions with additional clauses were issued in 1901 (63-4-116092710004) and 1903 (63-5-689-116092909001).

41 *Xing'an huilan, juan* 56, 1965.

42 *Xing'an huilan, juan* 21, 737.

43 Daniels, "Seisui ryūiki no Byōzoku ga shokurin," 11.

44 *Dongzu shehui lishi diaocha*, 15.

45 "Sanjiang muye jianshu."

46 The current sample includes all the documents included in two compilations: JYZ and GZM.

47 Zhang Yingqiang, *Mucai zhi liudong*, 200–202.

48 *Qiannan shilüe, juan* 13, 11b.

49 *Qianlong Qingjiang zhi, juan* 1, 79.

50 *Qiannan shilüe, juan* 9, 9b–10a.

51 *Qiannan shilüe, juan* 13, 6a; *juan* 23, 14b.

52 Wu Zhonglun, *Shanmu*, chap. 13.

53 Daniels, "Seisui ryūiki no Byōzoku ga shokurin," 27–28.

54 Xu Guangqi, *Nongzheng quanshu, juan* 37.

55 *Qiannan shilüe, juan* 21, 8b; and Daniels, "Seisui ryūiki no Byōzoku ga shokurin," 29–30.

56 Menzies, *Forest and Land Management*, 96; and *Guangxu Guzhou ting zhi, juan* 4, 224.

57 Menzies, "Three Hundred Years of Taungya."

58 For a detailed discussion of the variety of crops available for intercropping in the different stages of China fir growth and their properties, see Yu Xintuo, "Shanmu de hunnong linye." For more comprehensive introductions to the contemporary practices in the silviculture of China fir, see Yu Xintuo, *Shanmu zaipei xue*.

59 Wang et al., "Development of Chinese Fir Plantations"; and Bi et al., "Yield Decline in Chinese-Fir Plantations."

60 See *Chunxi Xin'an zhi, juan* 1, 5a.

61 For a sampling of such contracts over a millennium, see Zhang Chuanxi, *Zhongguo lidai qiyue*.

62 In a rare contract of the sale of ready-to-fell trees, price per tree and the number of trees were specified, which was different from contracts selling growing trees that always omitted such information. See JYZ 102.

63 To my knowledge, the earliest tenancy contract was from 1780, as recorded in *Dongzu shehui lishi diaocha*, 15.

64 GZM B0120, B0136, B0141. It was also common for planters to sell their shares to buyers other than the landowner—for example, see GZM B0140, B0185, and B0203.

65 The initial tenancy contract usually specify that the tenant could "grow millet and plant fir" (*zhongsu zaishan*). For example, see JYZ 69. In the Qingshui River valley the crop of millet was not shared with the landowner, which was different from the custom in Huizhou, where sometimes the tenants were required to pay additional annual rent from supplementary crops such as grain, sesame, mushrooms, or other plants that they grew on the same mountain land site. See Cheng Zeshi, *Qingshui Jiang wenshu zhi fayi chutan*, 69; and McDermott, *Making of a New Rural Order in South China*, 402–403.

66 JYZ 173, 174b, 196–97.

67 For example, large landowner Jiang Yinghui invested in tenancy shares of several plots on which he did not have ownership shares. See JYZ 142, 148, 149, 150, 155.

68 For example, a merchant from Jiangxi purchased tenancy shares; see GZM B0143.

69 This point is in line with recent attention to the more independent and entrepreneurial characters of tenant farmers as compared to hired wage labor. See Long Denggao and Peng Bo, "Jinshi diannong."

70 GZM B0131, B0132, B0144, B0160.

71 For examples of resale of purchased tenancy shares, see GZM B0178, B0201.

72 For examples of the use of this set phrase, see JYZ 194, 195, 206.

73 For instance, see GZM B0159.

74 See GZM B0115, B0127, B0202, B0166.

75 For an example that specifically explained that the whole usufruct rights for sale was acquired through two previous purchases of landowner's share and tenant's share, respectively, see GZM B0167.

76 See GZM B0115.

77 The role of land transactions in mitigating intertemporal liquidity issues and the primitive securitization of some land rights in late imperial China have been discussed in Long Denggao, Ren Zhiqiang, and Zhao Liang, "Jinshi Zhongguo nongdi chanquan."

78 See JYZ 172, 433, 483.

79 For examples of such cases, see GZM B0133; and JYZ 191.

80 JYZ 392. For an example of multiple sources of one person's holding of landowners' share, see GZM B0161.

81 See GZM B0005.

82 JYZ 114. See also JYZ 131, 138; and GZM B0135, B0138.

83 See JYZ 169.

84 Zhang, "Financing Market-Oriented Reforestation," 132. For the level of social network complexity that had resulted from such frequent transactions, see the ego network of Jiang Yinghui (active c. 1774–1836) compiled by the author at https://youtu.be/Z-NlAn1xbcY.

85 JYZ 554, 555, 559, 566, 583.

86 Agreements on share division after disputes were sometimes called "clarification agreements" (*qingbai zi*), a genre that was also used in the private resolution of other kinds of disputes. For an example, see Zhang Yingqiang and Wang Zongxun, *Qingshui Jiang wenshu di er ji*, 3: 28.

87 JYZ 554.

88 For an example of a physical division of a mountain plot, see JYZ 58.

89 Some examples include GZM A0020, A0062, A0069, A0245, C0008. Aihara Yoshiyuki has made the same argument regarding such *gongshan*; see Aihara Yoshiyuki, "Shindai Chūgoku Kishū Shō Seisui Kō ryūiki," 141–42.

90 *Jinping xianzhi*, 2:1519.

91 *Jinping xianzhi*, 2:1521–22.

92 Menzies, *Forest and Land Management*, 78–80.

93 Coggins et al., "Village Fengshui Forests of Southern China."

94 For a discussion on lineage-owned timberland, see Menzies, *Forest and Land Management*, 76–78. For regional variations in Chinese descent groups' control over properties, see Watson, "Anthropological Overview."

95 Kishimoto Mio has made the same observation that the so-called *zushan* or *gongshan* in the lower Qingshui area were not collectively owned; see Kishimoto Mio, "Kishū no sanrin keiyaku bunsho," 188.

96 Liang Cong, *Qingshui Jiang xiayou cunzhai shehui*, 54.

97 JYZ 461, 562, 572, 568.

98 GZM E0039, E0060; and Aihara Yoshiyuki, "Shindai Chūgoku Kishū Shō Seisui Kō ryūiki," 126–27, 138.

99 See GZM B0201; and JYZ 468.

100 JYZ 360, 365, 486.

101 For an example of land used as collateral for loans from a *hui*, see JYZ 468.

102 Cheng Zeshi, *Qingshui Jiang wenshu zhi fayi chutan*, 135–46.

103 For forestry practices in southern Anhui, I rely mostly on McDermott, *Making of a New Rural Order in South China*, chap. 6.

104 McDermott, *Making of a New Rural Order in South China*, 382–83.

105 McDermott, *Making of a New Rural Order in South China*, 370–73.

106 For a comparison between the timberland practices in Guizhou and Huizhou, see Kishimoto Mio, "Kishū no sanrin keiyaku bunsho."

107 McDermott, *Making of a New Rural Order in South China*, 374–76.

108 McDermott, *Making of a New Rural Order in South China*, 418.

109 Kishimoto Mio, "Kishū no sanrin keiyaku bunsho," 181–88.

110 *Chunxi Xin'an zhi*, *juan* 3, 4b. For state efforts to record forests in governmental land registers from the Southern Song to the early Ming period, see Miller, *Fir and Empire*, chap. 2. To the extent these policies were implemented, they were carried out mostly in the Old South and had little impact in the southwest.

111 *Ming Qing Huizhou shehui jingji ziliao*, 561–610; and McDermott, *Making of a New Rural Order in South China*, 387–89.

112 For the importance of land registration in establishing private forest ownership between 1100 and 1400, see Miller, *Fir and Empire*, chap. 2.

113 For an example of taxation responsibility being transferred together with agricultural land, see JYZ 47.

114 *Minshi xiguan diaocha baogao lu*.

115 Bao Weimin, Wu Zhengqiang, and Du Zhengzhen, *Longquan sifa dang'an xuanbian di yi ji*, cases 4, 13, and 17.

116 *Minshi xiguan diaocha baogao lu*, 347.

117 For lake shares, see Liu Shigu, "Ming mo yijiang Poyang Hu diqu 'shuimian quan'"; and Xu Bin, *Zhidu, jingji, yu shehui*, 47–81. For shareholding-coalitions for tax purposes, see Cohen, "Writs of Passage in Late Imperial China."

118 Zelin, "Firm in Early Modern China."

119 Zelin, *Merchants of Zigong*; and Zelin, "Rise and Fall."

120 Zelin, "Eastern Sichuan Coal Mines in the Late Qing."

121 Watson, "Corporate Property and Local Leadership in the Pearl River Delta."

122 For strategies of effective management of common-pool resources, see Ostrom, *Governing the Commons*; and Gibson, McKean, and Ostrom, *People and Forests*.

123 Appuhn, *Forest on the Sea*.

124 Lee, "Postwar Pines," 10.

CHAPTER FOUR: MERCHANTS, BROKERS, AND MARKET DYNAMICS

1 For evidence of this practice from contracts, see JYZ 461, 572. For Huizhou merchants' *pinmai* in Anhui and Zhejiang, see Zhang Haipeng and Wang Tingyuan, *Ming Qing Huishang ziliao*, 181; and McDermott, *Making of a New Rural Order in South China*, 427.

2 Menzies, *Forest and Land Management*, 112; and *Dongzu shehui lishi diaocha*, 87–89.

3 *Jinping xianzhi*, 1513–14.

4 Menzies, "Forestry," 642–43.

5 "Liangjiang mucai piaoliu shuqu bei" in *Jinping xianzhi*, 1514–15.

6 "Wangzhai piaoliu mucai qingshu bei" in *Jinping xianzhi*, 1517–18.

7 Wu Chuanjun, "Nanjing Shangxin He de mushi."

8 Inspector General of Customs, *Decennial Reports*, vol.1 (1882–1891), 174–75.

9 Wu Chuanjun, "Nanjing Shangxin He de mushi."

10 Wu Chuanjun, "Nanjing Shangxin He de mushi," n. 6; and Dai Yuan, "Nanjing Shangxin He mucai maoyi zhuangkuang," 238.

11 Yin Qing, "Jiangxi zhi mucai ye," 8–9; and Liu Peiliang and Fan Jingyu, "Nanjing shi mucai shikuang diaocha shang," 17.

12 Wu Chuanjun, "Nanjing Shangxin He de mushi"; and Chen Ruizhi, "Hangzhou mucai ye de neimu."

13 For long-term trends in the modes of imperial market management from the Tang dynasty down to the Qing dynasty, see Mann, *Local Merchants and the Chinese Bureaucracy*, chap. 3; and von Glahn, *Economic History of China*, chaps. 6–8.

14 For this section in the Ming Code, see Lei Menglin, *Dulü suoyan*, 200. Although references to "official and private brokers" (*guansi yaren*) also appeared in Song-era materials, it is important to notice that the connotations of *si* (private/unlicensed) were significantly different from the licensed brokerage system of Ming-Qing times. During the Song, the majority of brokers were "private," and being "private" did not mean illegal. By contrast, under the licensed brokerage system of the Ming-Qing era, only officially licensed brokers were licit agents; "private brokers" referred to those unlicensed (thus illicit) brokers. See Miyazawa Tomoyuki, "Sodai no gajin," 8–9; Kobayashi Takashiro, "Tō Sō gajin ko," 53–69, and "Tō Sō gajin ko hosei." Another view is that the difference between "official" and "private" brokers during the Song lay in whether written contracts and taxes were required for the deal in question, which is still divergent from the Ming-Qing usage. See Shiba Yoshinobu, *Sōdai shōgyō shi kenkyū*, 392, and *Commerce and Society in Sung China*, 165.

15 Ch'iu Pengsheng, *Dang falü yushang jingji*, chap. 1.

16 GX_HDSL, *juan* 106, 370–31. It was also added to the Qing code as a substatute in 1706. See Xue Yunsheng, *Dulü cunyi*, *juan* 17, *hu lü* 9, *shili*, "sichong yahang butou."

17 YZSL, YZ11.10.*jiayin*. The law was reinforced by the Qianlong emperor when he noticed the resurgence of newly issued licenses by county officials in Jiangsu in 1739 (see QLSL, QL4.6.*dingyou*).

18 Xue Yunsheng, *Dulü cunyi*, *juan* 17, *hu lü* 9, *shili*, "bachi hangshi" 8.

19 The restrictions on yamen employees and degree holders were issued in 1740 and 1743, respectively. See QLSL, QL5.9.*wuyin*; and QL8.6.*jimao*.

20 *Hunan shangshi xiguan baogao shu*, 117.

21 BX 006-005-04602 (1799).

22 For the role of licensed brokers in court adjudication of commercial cases in the city of Chongqing, see Dykstra, "Cross-Jurisdictional Trade and Contract Enforcement in Qing China."

23 Dai Yuan, "Nanjing Shangxin He mucai maoyi zhuangkuang," 237.

24 *Huishang gongsuo zhengxin lu*; and Dykstra, "Complicated Matters," 143.

25 Liu Peiliang and Fan Jingyu, "Nanjing shi mucai shikuang diaocha shang"; Wu Chuanjun, "Nanjing Shangxin He de mushi"; and *Nanjing wuzi zhi*, tables 1–4.

26 Chen Xing and Chen Lilian, "Hanyang Yingwu Zhou zhumu shichang shihua," 127.

27 Chen Xing and Chen Lilian, "Hanyang Yingwu Zhou zhumu shichang shihua," 109.

28 BX 006-004-03018 (1804).

29 "Zhejiang zhi mucai," 13–14; Chen Ruizhi, "Hangzhou mucai ye de neimu," 92; and *Minshi xiguan diaocha baogao lu*, 604–5.

30 The inside story of Hangzhou's timber brokers and customary practices in timber trade were revealed most vividly in the memoir of Chen Ruizhi, a Wuyuan merchant who succeeded his father to practice the business of timber brokerage in Hangzhou for more than thirty years and became the director of the Association of Timber Trade in the late 1940s. See Chen Ruizhi, "Hangzhou mucai ye de neimu," 111–12.

31 Chen Ruizhi, "Hangzhou mucai ye de neimu," 113.

32 Peng Zeyi, *Zhongguo gongshang hanghui shiliao ji*, 215–16.

33 For the practices of treaty-port tea compradors and Republican-era criticisms of them as parasitic and unproductive financial capital, see Liu, *Tea War*, chap. 7.

34 The materials for this section, if not otherwise indicated, are from Zhan Mingduo, *Wo zhi xiaoshi*.

35 *Huishang gongsuo zhengxin lu*.

36 Wang Zhen, "Tunxi shangbu yu Huizhou mushang."

37 *Huishang gongsuo zhengxin lu*.

38 Specifically, timber-producing prefectures included Huizhou in southern Anhui, and Chuzhou, Quzhou, Yanzhou, and Jinhua in western Zhejiang. See "Zhejiang zhi mucai."

39 *Huishang gongsuo zhengxin lu*, 184–92.

40 *Huishang gongsuo zhengxin lu*, 200–201.

41 Chen Ruizhi, "Hangzhou mucai ye de neimu," 94–95.

42 *Huishang gongsuo zhengxin lu*, 184–86 (emphasis added).

43 *Huishang gongsuo zhengxin lu*, 184–86. Frequent regime changes during the Republican period reignited waves of contest over the property of the sandy land. When the two associations of Huizhou and Zhejiang timber merchants were reestablished in 1946 after the Sino-Japanese war, it was again listed as the top priority of the two organizations to reclaim and

clear up the sandy land. Chen Ruizhi, "Hangzhou mucai ye de neimu," 96–97; and "Huishang yu Zhedong muye fulishe cailiao," 1947–48, HMA L010-001-196.

44 *Huishang gongsuo zhengxin lu*, 180–83.

45 Wu Zhenyu, *Qian yu, juan xia*, "Liping mu"; and *Dongzu shehui lishi diaocha*, 36.

46 *Guangxu Liping fu zhi, juan* 3a, 32b; and Liang Cong, *Qingdai Qingshui Jiang xiayou cunzhai shehui*, 216–17.

47 *Jinping xianzhi*, 1523–24.

48 Zhang Yingqiang, "Cong Guazhi 'Yishi Yongzun' shike."

49 For a full analysis of the controversies around the three-town monopoly, see Zhang, "Frontier Timber in Southwest China."

50 Sutton, "Ethnicity and the Miao Frontier."

51 *Dongzu shehui lishi diaocha*, 39–40 (emphasis added).

52 *Dongzu shehui lishi diaocha*, 41–42.

53 *Jinping xianzhi*, 1511–13, 1517; and Zhang Yingqiang and Hu Teng, *Xiangtu Zhongguo Jinping.*

CHAPTER FIVE: TRADE ASSOCIATIONS, "CONTRIBUTIONS," AND CONTRACT ENFORCEMENT

1 For the proliferation of new types of merchant organizations during the eighteenth and nineteenth centuries, see Ch'iu Pengsheng, *Shiba shijiu shiji Suzhou cheng.*

2 Liu, "Chinese Merchant Guilds," 8.

3 Chen Xing and Chen Lilian, "Hanyang Yingwu Zhou zhumu shichang shihua," 127.

4 *Ming Qing Suzhou gongshang ye beike ji*, 123–25.

5 For some overviews, see Moll-Murata, "Chinese Guilds"; Liu, "Chinese Merchant Guilds"; and Zelin, "Chinese Business Practice in the Late Imperial Period."

6 QL_HDZL, *juan* 18, 35; and Xue Yunsheng, *Dulü cunyi, juan* 17, *hu lü* 9, *shili*, "sichong yahang butou" 3.

7 See such attempts in JQSL, JQ8(1803).9.*guichou*; and GXSL, GX9(1884).2.*jiaxu.*

8 Dykstra, "Complicated Matters," chap. 5. My emphasis on the economic benefit of collective actions as a major rationale for merchants to form associations complements Dykstra's explanation of state initiative in formalizing merchant groups. They point to different factors that were simultaneously contributing to the proliferation of merchant organizations during this period.

9 Dykstra, "Complicated Matters," 240.

10 Zelin, "Chinese Business Practice in the Late Imperial Period," 785–86; and Dykstra, "Complicated Matters," 259–61.

11 BX 006-056-0868.

12 BX 006-056-0868 (emphasis added).

13 For similar cases in the timber trade where the magistrate supported merchant groups in disciplining unruly individuals, see BX 006-056-0905, 41, 51, 52.

14 Morse, *Guilds of China*, 28.

15 BX 006-6336.

16 BX 006-6336 (emphasis added).

17 The principle of "separate trade, separate duties" was invoked in several other instances of intergroup disputes in the Chongqing timber trade, see BX 006-4527; and 006-056-0905.

18 The discussion here concerns only merchant guilds. Craft/artisan guilds in both China and Europe are beyond the scope of this comparative discussion.

19 Some stress the economic benefits of European guilds in forming networks, fostering specialization, cultivating human capital, and so on. For example, see Epstein and Prak, *Guilds, Innovation, and the European Economy*; and Epstein, "Craft Guilds in the Pre-Modern Economy." Others see more problems in the guilds' price manipulation and restriction of market access. See Ogilvie, "Rehabilitating the Guilds"; and Ogilvie, *Institutions and European Trade*.

20 Ogilvie, "Economics of Guilds."

21 Mann, *Local Merchants and the Chinese Bureaucracy*, 103–105.

22 Shen Xuefeng, "Qingdai caizheng shouru," 87.

23 The numbers of tax stations are from Liu, "Making of a Fiscal State," 69; and Luo Yudong, *Zhongguo lijin shi*, 81. For positive assessment of the Song-era state-market dynamics, see von Glahn, "Modalities of the Fiscal State in Imperial China."

24 Shen Xuefeng, "Qingdai caizheng shouru," 84–85, 88.

25 Yin Qing, "Jiangxi zhi mucai ye."

26 For a complete list of average Lijin rates and collection methods in all provinces, see Luo Yudong, *Zhongguo lijin shi*, 62. For details on my calculation, see Zhang, "Timber Trade along the Yangzi River," 232–35.

27 Luo Yudong, *Zhongguo lijin shi*, 99–103.

28 Luo Yudong, *Zhongguo lijin shi*, 93–99, 625–40.

29 Luo Yudong, *Zhongguo lijin shi*, 109–17.

30 Chen Xing and Chen Lilian, "Hanyang Yingwu Zhou zhumu shichang shihua," 128.

31 Chen Ruizhi, "Hangzhou mucai ye de neimu," 94–95.

32 Taxation-related matters are mainly covered in SHMA, S145-2-5.
33 SHMA, S145-1-7.
34 SHMA, S145-2-5; and S145-1-33.
35 SHMA, S145-2-8.
36 SHMA, S145-1-33; and S145-1-7.
37 SHMA, S145-1-7.
38 SHMA, S145-1-7.
39 *Zhenxun Muye Gonghui baogao lu*, 39–40.
40 *Zhenxun Muye Gonghui baogao lu*, 19–22.
41 Negishi Tadashi, *Chūgoku no girudo*; and *Shanhai no girudo*, 243–47.
42 For examples of such cases, see *Shenbao*, 1898.8.31 (sec. 3), and 1906.1.17 (sec. 9).
43 These regulations can be found in SHMA, S145-1-2; and S145-1-3.
44 SHMA, S145-1-13; and S145-2-7.
45 SHMA, S145-2-7.
46 *Shenbao*, 1919.1.3 (sec. 10).
47 For example, see *Shenbao*, 1884.2.6 (sec. 3), 1899.2.4 (sec. 9), 1904.5.29 (sec. 3), 1909.1.7 (sec. 12), 1923.7.6 (sec. 16), and 1927.4.4 (sec. 15).
48 *Shenbao*, 1923.3.1 (sec. 14).
49 *Shenbao*, 1875.8.13, 1910.8.22 (sec. 12), 1910.8.26 (sec. 11), and 1910.8.31 (sec. 12).
50 SHMA, S145-1-2; and S145-1-7.
51 For examples of such cases, see SHMA, S145-2-6.
52 SHMA, S145-1-2; and S145-1-3.
53 All the regulations can be found in SHMA, S145-1-7.
54 SHMA, S145-2-7.
55 SHMA, S145-2-7.
56 SHMA, S145-2-4.
57 SHMA, S145-2-6.
58 SHMA, S145-1-2.
59 For prolonged negotiations between the association and the local state regarding the riverbank used for timber storage, see *Shenbao*, 1916.12.1 (sec. 10), 1917.1.4 (sec. 11), 1917.3.9 (sec. 10), 1917.3.16 (sec. 11), 1917.4.10 (sec. 11), 1917.4.26 (sec. 10), 1917.9.30 (sec. 10), 1918.1.30 (sec. 10), 1918.5.12 (sec. 10), 1918.6.12 (sec. 10), and 1918.7.28 (sec. 10).
60 For examples of regular reports and letters to arrange guarding boats, see SHMA, S145-2-8.
61 SHMA, S145-1-59.
62 Olson, *Logic of Collective Action*.
63 Du Xuncheng, *Jindai Zhongguo qianye xiguan fa*, 43.
64 Du Xuncheng, *Jindai Zhongguo qianye xiguan fa*, 58.
65 Rowe, *Hankow: Commerce and Society*, 174.
66 *Hunan shangshi xiguan baogao shu*, 192–94.

67 Yang Xiangjun, *Diguo zhi bian*, 46–56.

68 For the establishment of mixed courts, see Stephens, *Order and Discipline*, 44–47; and Yang Xiangjun, *Diguo zhi bian*, 67–73, 91–96.

69 For changes in the administration of mixed courts in the Republican era, see Stephens, *Order and Discipline*, 48–51, 64–65.

70 Foreign timber firms sent their Chinese compradors as representatives in the Zhenxun Association. SHMA, S145-1-7.

71 Existing studies on the Shanghai mixed courts have focused on the interplay of power relations and the tensions between two different legal cultures. The materials used in these studies are mainly documents that reflected different parties' diverging stances as well as legal cases that stood out as manifestations of underlying clashes. See Yang Xiangjun, *Diguo zhi bian*; and Stephens, *Order and Discipline*. My demonstration of the similarity of the mixed courts and domestic courts in dealing with commercial disputes complicates a widespread argument that portrays the mixed courts as a one-directional channel through with Westerners brought in new formal institutions, which consequently accounted for the economic growth in Shanghai. For such an approach, see Ma, "Law and Economy in Traditional China."

72 For example, see *Shenbao*, 1902.6.11 (sec. 9).

73 *Shenbao*, 1878.1.4 (sec. 3).

74 For Qing-era commercial litigation, see Fan Jinmin, Yao Yang, and Ni Yi, *Ming Qing shangshi jiufen yu shangye susong*; and Dykstra, "Cross-Jurisdictional Trade and Contract Enforcement in Qing China."

75 For example, see *Shenbao*, 1899.1.25 (sec. 9), 1899.2.6 (sec. 9), and 1899.5.12 (sec. 3).

76 For example, see *Shenbao*, 1918.11.12 (sec. 11), 1919.1.18 (sec. 11), 1918.11.25 (sec. 11), and 1922.1.8 (sec. 12).

77 Kotenev, *Shanghai*, 272.

78 For example, see *Shenbao*, 1919.11.27 (sec. 11).

79 SHMA, S145-2-7.

80 SHMA, S145-2-6.

81 *The Chinese Supreme Court Decisions*, no. 1, 2d year A.C. 64, in Kotenev, *Shanghai*, 431.

82 Stephens, *Order and Discipline*, 87.

83 Huang Yuansheng, *Minchu Daliyuan yu caipan*; Kotenev, *Shanghai*, 257–71; and Stephens, *Order and Discipline*, 88.

84 SHMA, S145-2-7; and S145-2-6.

85 For an account of the establishment of the chambers of commerce, see Chen Zhongping, "Origins of Chinese Chambers of Commerce."

86 Ma Min and Zhu Ying, *Chuantong yu jindai de erchong bianzou*; Ma Min, "Shangshi caipan yu shanghui"; and Dykstra, "Beyond the Shadow of the Law."

87 SZMA, I14-001-0817-068.
88 Details of this case are found in SHMA, S145-2-6.
89 SHMA, S145-1-7.
90 Details of this case are found in SHMA, S145-2-6.

EPILOGUE

1 Ai Zhongquan, "Zhongguo muye chanxiao zhidu de bianqian," vol.1, no. 2, 18–19.
2 Annual market information from 1888 through 1937 is from Lu Yin, "Shangxin He shanmu ye wushi nian gaikuang."
3 *Dongzu shehui lishi diaocha*, 31–32.
4 Lu Yin, "Shangxin He shanmu ye wushi nian gaikuang."
5 Data on imported timber is from Inspector General of Customs, *Decennial Reports.*
6 "Shanghai shi shehui ju muye shangqing diaocha"; and Ai Zhongquan, "Zhongguo muye chanxiao zhidu de bianqian", vol.1, no. 3, 15–16.
7 Wu Chuanjun, "Nanjing Shangxin He de mushi"; and Lu Yin, "Shangxin He shanmu ye wushi nian gaikuang."
8 Elvin, "Three Thousand Years of Unsustainable Growth"; and Elvin and Liu, *Sediments of Time*, 1–28.
9 Elvin and Liu, *Sediments of Time*; and Marks, *China: An Environmental History.*
10 McNeil, "China's Environmental History in World Perspective."
11 Menzies, "Forestry," 575.
12 "Anthropocene" is perhaps the most provocative concept to hit environmental history since its inception. I am sympathetic to the argument that the advent of the Industrial Revolution around 1800 is a logical starting date for the new epoch, with the climate, biological, and geochemical signatures of the human society becoming manifestly different from the preceding Holocene period by the mid-twentieth century. See Steffen et al., "Anthropocene"; and Waters et al., "Anthropocene Is Functionally and Stratigraphically Distinct from the Holocene." For major debates and critiques on the use of this term, see Moore, *Anthropocene or Capitalocene?*; Haraway, "Anthropocene, Capitalocene, Plantationocene, Chthulucene"; Malm and Hornborg, "Geology of Mankind?"; and Demos, *Against the Anthropocene.*
13 Totman, *Green Archipelago*; Lee, "Postwar Pines"; Appuhn, *Forest on the Sea*; Wing, *Roots of Empire*; and Matteson, *Forests in Revolutionary France.*
14 Scott, *Seeing Like a State*, 11–12.
15 Sivaramakrishnan, *Modern Forests*; Rajan, *Modernizing Nature*; Barton, "Empire Forestry and American Environmentalism"; and Fedman, *Seeds of Control.*

16 Worster, *American Environmentalism*, 2.

17 For an overview of the changes in forest management in the PRC, see Marks, *China: An Environmental History*, 322–37; and Liu, "Tenure and Management of Non-State Forests in China since 1950."

18 Liu, "Tenure and Management of Non-State Forests in China since 1950," 252–53.

19 Liu, "Tenure and Management of Non-State Forests in China since 1950," 254–56.

20 For discussions of excessive reclamations and the vulnerable water control system, see Osborne, "Local Politics of Land Reclamation"; Perdue, "Official Goals and Local Interests"; and Pomeranz, *Making of a Hinterland*.

APPENDIX A: ESTIMATION OF TIMBER TAX AND TRADE VOLUME AT LONGJIANG GUAN

1 FHA 02-01-04-15048-014; 04-01-35-0329-032.

2 GZD 014090; FHA 02-01-008-001708-0006.

3 Although the measurement rules as recorded in *Collected Statutes* are too terse to understand, detailed explanations of the rules and their rationales can be found in a round of concentrated discussion of the taxation methods at Longjiang Guan during 1739–1741 (QL4-6): FHA 04-01-35-0310-023, 04-01-35-0310-040, and 04-01-35-0312-007.

4 Wu Chuanjun, "Nanjing Shangxin He de mushi."

5 Dollar, *Memoirs of Robert Dollar*, 72–73.

6 Yan Sisheng, "Qingli guanwu jibi shu," in *Huangchao jingshi wenbian*, *juan* 51; FHA 04-01-35-0310-023, 04-01-35-0312-007, and 02-01-008-000292-0008; Liu Hongmo, *Wuguan quezhi, juan xia*.

7 The prices from the late nineteenth century are from Liu Boshan, *Huizhou wenshu di san ji*, vol. 7, 245; and Lu Yin, "Shangxin He shamu ye wushi nian gaikuang."

8 Inspector General of Customs, *Decennial Reports, 1882–1891*, 162.

9 FHA 03-0593-020; GZD 403021112.

10 GZD 014090.

11 FHA 04-01-35-0357-0507.

APPENDIX B: ESTIMATION OF TIMBER TAX AT JIUJIANG GUAN

1 GX_HDSL, *juan* 235.

2 Xu Tan, "Qingdai qianqi de Jiujiang Guan jiqi shangpin liutong," 89; and Memorial by Jiangxi Governor Qian Zhen on JQ23 (1818).4.27, quoted in Liao Shengfeng, *Qingdai changguan yu quyu jingji yanjiu*, 122.

3 Xu Tan, "Qingdai qianqi de Jiujiang Guan jiqi shangpin liutong," 87.
4 Liao Shengfeng, *Qingdai changguan yu quyu jingji yanjiu*, 122.
5 The counting is based on cited memorials in Ni Yuping, *Qingchao Jia Dao guanshui yanjiu*, 88–96.

APPENDIX C: A METHODOLOGICAL NOTE ON LAND CONTRACT ANALYSIS

1 Zhang Yingqiang, *Mucai zhi liudong*; Cheng Zeshi, *Qingshui Jiang wenshu zhi fayi chutan*; Liang Cong, *Qingshui Jiang xiayou cunzhai shehui*; *Dongzu shehui lishi diaocha*; Aihara Yoshiyuki, "Seisui Kō ryūiki niokeru ringyō keiei no ichi sokumen"; Daniels, "Seisui ryūiki no Byōzoku ga shokurin"; Kishimoto Mio, "Kishū no sanrin keiyaku bunsho"; and Takeuchi Fusaji, "Narukami to meikan no aida."

BIBLIOGRAPHY

ABBREVIATIONS

BX	Baxian Archives, Sichuan Provincial Archives, Chengdu
DGSL	*Daoguang chao shilu* 道光朝實錄, full text in Scripta Sinica
FHA	The First Historical Archives of China, Beijing
GJK	*Airusheng jiben guji ku* 愛如生基本古籍庫
GX_GBZL	*Guangxu qinding Gongbu zeli* 光緒欽定工部則例. 120 *juan.* 1884 edition. Taipei: Chengwen Chuban She, 1966.
GX_HDSL	*Guangxu Da Qing huidian shili* 光緒大清會典事例, full text in Scripta Sinica
GXSL	*Guangxu chao shilu* 光緒朝實錄, full text in Scripta Sinica
GZD	*Qingdai Gongzhong dang zouzhe ji Junji Chu zhejian ziliao ku* 清代宮中檔奏摺及軍機處摺件資料庫, National Palace Museum, Taipei.
GZM	Christian Daniels, Yougeng Yang 楊有庚, and Fusaji Takeuchi 武内房司, eds. *Kishū Byozoku ringyō keiyaku bunsho kaihen (1736–1950 nen)* 貴州苗族林業契約文書匯編. 3 vols. Tokyo: Tokyo University of Foreign Studies, 2001.
HMA	Hangzhou Municipal Archives
JQSL	*Jiaqing chao shilu* 嘉慶朝實錄, full text in Scripta Sinica
JYZ	Chen Jinquan 陳金全 and Du Wanhua 杜萬華, eds. *Guizhou Wendou Zhai Miaozu qiyue falü wenshu huibian: Jiang Yuanze jiacang qiyue wenshu* 貴州文斗寨苗族契約法律文書彙編——姜元澤家藏契約文書. Beijing: Remin Chuban She, 2008.
KX_HD	*Kangxi Da Qing huidian* 康熙大清會典, full text in Scripta Sinica

QL_HDZL *Qianlong Da Qing huidian zeli* 乾隆大清會典則例, full text in Scripta Sinica

QLSL *Qianlong chao shilu* 乾隆朝實錄, full text in Scripta Sinica

QSG *Qing shi gao* 清史稿, full text in Scripta Sinica

Shenbao *Shenbao* 申報, 1872–1949, full-text database digitized by Green Apple Data Center

SHMA Shanghai Municipal Archives

SYD *Junji Chu shangyu dang* 軍機處上諭檔, accessed at the First Historical Archives of China, Beijing

SZMA Suzhou Municipal Archives

YZ_HD *Yongzheng Da Qing huidian* 雍正大清會典, full text in Scripta Sinica

YZSL *Yongzheng chao shilu* 雍正朝實錄, full text in Scripta Sinica

LOCAL GAZETTEERS

Gazetters of provinces (*tongzhi*), prefectures (*fu zhi*), subprefectures (*ting zhi*), and counties (*xian zhi*) are accessed through the *Airusheng Zhongguo fangzhi ku* 愛如生中國方志庫. In this book's notes, I follow the original pagination whenever possible and use *Airusheng*'s pagination if the original mark is illegible.

Chongzhen Kaihua xian zhi 崇禎開化縣志. 10 *juan*.

Chunxi Xin'an zhi 淳熙新安志. 10 *juan*.

Daoguang Lanzhou fu zhi 道光蘭州府志. 12 *juan*.

Daoguang Renhuai zhili ting zhi 道光仁懷直隸廳志. 20 *juan*.

Guangxu Baise ting zhi 光緒百色廳志. 8 *juan*.

Guangxu Chun'an xian zhi 光緒淳安縣志. 16 *juan*.

Guangxu Guangzhou fu zhi 光緒廣州府志. 163 *juan*.

Guangxu Guzhou ting zhi 光緒古州廳志. 10 *juan*.

Guangxu Jiangxi tongzhi 光緒江西通志. 180 *juan*.

Guangxu Liping fu zhi 光緒黎平府志. 18 *juan*.

Guangxu Longnan xian zhi 光绪龍南縣志. 8 *juan*.

Guangxu Wuyuan xian zhi 光緒婺源縣志. 40 *juan*.

Jiaqing Guiyang xian zhi 嘉慶桂陽縣志. 10 *juan*.

Jiaqing Hunan tongzhi 嘉慶湖南通志. 219 *juan*.

Jiaqing Wuhu xian zhi 嘉慶蕪湖縣志. 24 *juan*.

Jiaqing Xuancheng xian zhi 嘉慶宣城縣志. 32 *juan*.

Kangxi Nancheng xian zhi 康熙南城縣志. 12 *juan*.

Minguo Wuhu xian zhi 民國蕪湖縣志. 60 *juan*.

Qianlong De'an xian zhi 乾隆德安縣志. 15 *juan*.
Qianlong Funing fu zhi 乾隆福寧府志. 44 *juan*.
Qianlong Heping xian zhi 乾隆和平縣志. 8 *juan*.
Qianlong Heyuan xian zhi 乾隆河源縣志. 15 *juan*.
Qianlong Kaihua xian zhi 乾隆開化縣志. 12 *juan*.
Qianlong Longnan xian zhi 乾隆龍南縣志. 26 *juan*.
Qianlong Qingjiang zhi 乾隆清江志. 8 *juan*.
Qianlong Qingyuan xian zhi 乾隆清遠縣志. 14 *juan*.
Qiannan shilüe 黔南識略(Qianlong). 32 *juan*.
Tongzhi Dehua xian zhi 同治德化縣志. 54 *juan*.
Tongzhi Ganzhou fu zhi 同治贛州府志. 78 *juan*.
Wu Zhenyu 吳振棫. *Qian yu* 黔語 (Xianfeng). 8 *juan*.

OTHER WORKS CITED

Adshead, S. A. M. "An Energy Crisis in Early Modern China." *Ch'ing-Shih Wen-t'i* [Now *Late Imperial China*] 3, no. 2 (1974): 20–28.

Ai Zhongquan 艾中全. "Zhongguo muye chanxiao zhidu de bianqian" 中國木業產銷制度的變遷. *Muye jie* 木業界 1 (1940): no. 2, 18–20; no. 3, 14–17; no. 4, 15–17; no. 5, 7–8.

Aihara Yoshiyuki 相原佳之. "Qingchao zhongqi de senlin zhengce: Yi Qianlong ershi niandai de zhishu taolun wei zhongxin" 清朝中期的森林政策——以乾隆二十年代的植樹討論為中心. In *Zhongguo lishi shang de huanjing yu shehui* 中國歷史上的環境與社會, edited by Wang Lihua 王利華. Beijing: Sanlian Shudian, 2007.

———. "Shinchō ni yoru mokuzai chōtatsu no ichisokumen: Shinchō zenki no reiki seido" 清朝による木材調達の一側面——清朝前期の例木制度. *Chūgoku-shi kenkyū ronsō* 中国史研究論叢 no. 3 (2003): 22–38.

———. "Shindai Chūgoku Kishū Shō Seisui Kō ryūiki niokeru ringyō keiei no ichi sokumen: 'Kishū Byōzoku ringyō keiyaku bunsho kaihen' Heikō Sai bunsho o jirei toshite" 清代中国貴州省清水江流域における林業経営の一側面——『貴州苗族林業契約文書匯編』平鰲寨文書を事例として. In *Kishū Byōzoku ringyō keiyaku bunsho kaihen (1736–1950 nen)* 貴州苗族林業契約文書匯編(1736–1950 年), edited by Daniels Christian, Yang Yougeng 楊有賡, and Takeuchi Fusaji 武内房司, 3:121–64. Tokyo: Tokyo University of Foreign Languages, 2003.

———. "Shindai chūki Kishū tōnanbu Seisui Kō ryūiki ni okeru mokuzai no ryūtsū kōzō: *Caiyun huangmu andu* no kijutsu wo chūshin ni" 清代中期貴州東南部清水江流域における木材の流通構造——「採運皇木案牘」の記述を中心に. *Shakai keizai shigaku* 社会経済史学 72, no. 5 (2007): 547–66.

Anderson, Terry L., and Gary D. Libecap. *Environmental Markets: A Property Rights Approach*. New York: Cambridge University Press, 2014.

Ang, Yuen Yuen. *How China Escaped the Poverty Trap*. Ithaca, NY: Cornell University Press, 2016.

Appuhn, Karl Richard. *A Forest on the Sea: Environmental Expertise in Renaissance Venice*. Baltimore, MD: Johns Hopkins University Press, 2009.

Atwill, David G. *The Chinese Sultanate: Islam, Ethnicity, and the Panthay Rebellion in Southwest China, 1856–1873*. Stanford, CA: Stanford University Press, 2005.

Averill, Stephen C. *Revolution in the Highlands: China's Jinggangshan Base Area*. Lanham, MD: Rowman & Littlefield Publishers, 2006.

Bao Weimin 包偉民, Wu Zhengqiang 吳錚強, and Du Zhengzhen 杜正貞, eds. *Longquan sifa dang'an xuanbian di yi ji: Wan Qing shiqi* 龍泉司法檔案選編第一輯: 晚清時期. 2 vols. Beijing: Zhonghua Shuju, 2012.

Barton, Gregory A. "Empire Forestry and American Environmentalism." *Environment and History* 6, no. 2 (2000): 187–203.

Bello, David A. *Across Forest, Steppe, and Mountain: Environment, Identity, and Empire in Qing China's Borderlands*. New York: Cambridge University Press, 2016.

———. "To Go Where No Han Could Go for Long: Malaria and the Qing Construction of Ethnic Administrative Space in Frontier Yunnan." *Modern China* 31, no. 3 (2005): 283–317.

Bi, J., J. A. Blanco, B. Seely, J. P. Kimmins, Y. Ding, and C. Welham. "Yield Decline in Chinese-Fir Plantations: A Simulation Investigation with Implications for Model Complexity." *Canadian Journal of Forest Research* 37, no. 9 (2007): 1615–30.

Bian, He. *Know Your Remedies: Pharmacy and Culture in Early Modern China*. Princeton, NJ: Princeton University Press, 2020.

Bo'an xubian 駁案續編. 7 *juan*. 1884 printed edition, GJK.

Campbell, Aurelia. *What the Emperor Built: Architecture and Empire in the Early Ming*. Seattle: University of Washington Press, 2020.

Cao Shuji 曹樹基. *Zhongguo renkou shi (di wu juan) Qing shiqi* 中國人口史（第五卷）清時期. Shanghai: Fudan Daxue Chuban She, 2001.

Chen, Fu-mei, and Ramon H. Myers. "Coping with Transaction Costs: The Case of Merchant Associations in the Ch'ing Period." In *Chinese Business Enterprise*, edited by R. Ampalavanar Brown, 4 vols., 2:252–71. London: Routledge, 1996.

Chen Feng 陳峰. "Jianlun Song Ming Qing caoyun zhong sihuo fanyun ji maoyi" 簡論宋明清漕運中私貨販運及貿易. *Zhongguo jingji shi yanjiu* 中國經濟史研究 no. 1 (1996): 120–27.

Chen Ruizhi 陳瑞芝. "Hangzhou mucai ye de neimu" 杭州木材業的內幕. In *Zhejiang wenshi ziliao xuanbian (di jiu ji)* 浙江文史資料選編 (第九輯), 90–120. Hangzhou: Zhejiang Renmin Chuban She, 1964.

Chen Xing 陳醒 and Chen Lilian 陳立廉. "Hanyang Yingwu Zhou zhumu shichang shihua" 漢陽鸚鵡洲竹木市場史話. In *Wuhan wenshi ziliao wenku* 武漢文史資料文庫, 3:362–78. 1964. Reprint, Wuhan: Wuhan Chuban She, 1999.

Chen Xuewen 陳學文. *Ming Qing shiqi shangye shu ji shangren shu zhi yanjiu* 明清時期商業書及商人書之研究. Taibei: Hongye Wenhua, 1997.

Chen Zhongping 陳忠平. "Ming Qing shiqi Jiangnan shizhen de yaren yu yahang" 明清時期江南市鎮的牙人與牙行. *Zhongguo jingji shi yanjiu* 中國經濟史研究 no. 2 (1987): 31–38.

———. "The Origins of Chinese Chambers of Commerce in the Lower Yangzi Region." *Modern China* 27, no. 2 (2001): 155–201.

Cheng Zeshi 程澤時. *Qingshui Jiang wenshu zhi fayi chutan* 清水江文書之法意初探. Beijing: Zhongguo Zhengfa Daxue Chuban She, 2011.

Ch'iu Pengsheng 邱澎生. *Dang falü yushang jingji: Ming Qing zhongguo de shangye falü* 當法律遇上經濟: 明清中國的商業法律. Taipei: Wunan Tushu, 2008.

———. *Shiba shijiu shiji Suzhou cheng de xinxing gongshang ye tuanti* 十八十九世紀蘇州城的新興工商業團體. Taipei: Taiwan Daxue Chuban She, 1990.

"Chōkō no ikada" 長江の筏. *Atō ingashū* 亜東印画輯 5, no. 79 (1930): 81. The Toyo Bunko.

Ciriacy-Wantrup, S., and Richard Bishop. "Common Property as a Concept in Natural Resources Policy." *Natural Resources Journal* 15, no. 4 (1975): 713–27.

Coggins, Chris, Joelle Chevrier, Maeve Dwyer, Lindsey Longway, Michael Xu, Peter Tiso, and Zhen Li. "Village Fengshui Forests of Southern China—Culture History and Conservation Status." *ASIANetwork Exchange: A Journal for Asian Studies in the Liberal Arts* 19, no. 2 (2012): 52–67.

Cohen, Myron L. "Writs of Passage in Late Imperial China: The Documentation of Practical Understandings in Minong, Taiwan." In *Contract and Property in Early Modern China*, edited by Madeleine Zelin, Jonathan K. Ocko, and Robert Gardella, 37–93. Stanford, CA: Stanford University Press, 2004.

Da Ming huidian 大明會典. Wanli edition prefaced 1587, full text in Scripta Sinica.

Dai Yuan 戴淵. "Nanjing Shangxin He mucai maoyi zhuangkuang" 南京上新河木材貿易狀況. *Zhongguo nongxue hui bao* 中國農學會報 no. 129–30 (1934): 230–40.

Daniels, Christian. "Seisui ryūiki no Byōzoku ga shokurin o kaishi suru made: Ringyō keiei e to karitate ta sho yōin" 清水流域の苗族が植林を開始するま

で—林業経営へと駆り立てた諸要因. In *Kishū Byōzoku ringyō keiyaku bunsho kaihen (1736–1950 nen)* 貴州苗族林業契約文書匯編 (1736–1950 年), edited by Christian Daniels, Yougeng Yang 楊有賡, and Fusaji Takeuchi 武内房司, 3:9–48. Tokyo: Tokyo University of Foreign Languages, 2003.

Daqing Guangxu xin faling 大清光緒新法令. 20 vols. 1910 Shangwu Yinshu Guan edition, GJK.

Deal, David Michael, and Laura Hostetler, eds. *The Art of Ethnography: A Chinese "Miao Album."* Seattle: University of Washington Press, 2007.

Demos, T. J. *Against the Anthropocene: Visual Culture and Environment Today.* Berlin: Sternberg Press, 2017.

Deng Yibing 鄧亦兵. "Qingdai qianqi shuiguan de shezhi" 清代前期稅關的設置. *Qingshi yanjiu* 清史研究 no. 2 (2007): 54–64.

Diamond, Norma. "Defining the Miao: Ming, Qing, and Contemporary Views." In *Cultural Encounters on China's Ethnic Frontiers*, edited by Stevan Harrell, 92–116. Seattle: University of Washington Press, 1995.

Dollar, Robert. *Memoirs of Robert Dollar.* San Francisco: W.S. Van Cott & Co., 1921.

Dongzu shehui lishi diaocha 侗族社會歷史調查. Bejing: Minzu Chuban She, 2009.

Du Xuncheng 杜恂誠. *Jindai Zhongguo qianye xiguan fa: Yi Shanghai qianye wei shijiao* 近代中國錢業習慣法: 以上海錢業為視角. Shanghai: Shanghai Caijing Daxue Chuban She, 2006.

Dykstra, Maura. "Beyond the Shadow of the Law: Firm Insolvency, State-Building, and the New Policy Bankruptcy Reform in Late Qing Chongqing." *Frontiers of History in China* 8, no. 3 (2013): 406–33.

———. "Complicated Matters: Commercial Dispute Resolution in Qing Chongqing from 1750 to 1911." PhD dissertation, University of California–Los Angeles, 2014.

———. "Cross-Jurisdictional Trade and Contract Enforcement in Qing China." *International Journal of Asian Studies* 16, no. 2 (2019): 99–115.

Elvin, Mark. *The Retreat of the Elephants: An Environmental History of China.* New Haven: Yale University Press, 2004.

———. "Three Thousand Years of Unsustainable Growth: China's Environment from Archaic Times to the Present." *East Asian History* no. 6 (1993): 7–46.

Elvin, Mark, and Ts'ui-jung Liu, eds. *Sediments of Time: Environment and Society in Chinese History.* Cambridge: Cambridge University Press, 1998.

Epstein, Stephan R. "Craft Guilds in the Pre-Modern Economy: A Discussion." *Economic History Review* 61 (new series), no. 1 (2008): 155–74.

Epstein, Stephan R., and Maarten Roy Prak. *Guilds, Innovation, and the European Economy, 1400–1800*. Cambridge: Cambridge University Press, 2008.

Fan Chengda 范成大. *Canluan lu* 驂鸞錄, 1175.

Fan Jinmin 范金民, Yao Yang 姚暘, and Ni Yi 倪毅. *Ming Qing shangshi jiufen yu shangye susong* 明清商事糾紛與商業訴訟. Nanjing: Nanjing Daxue Chuban She, 2007.

Fan Shuzhi 樊樹志. "Ming Qing caoyun shulue" 明清漕運述略. *Xueshu yuekan* 學術月刊 no. 10 (1962): 23–29.

Fedman, David. *Seeds of Control: Japan's Empire of Forestry in Colonial Korea*. Seattle: University of Washington Press, 2020.

Feeny, David, Fikret Berkes, Bonnie J. McCay, and James M. Acheson. "The Tragedy of the Commons: Twenty-Two Years Later." *Human Ecology* 18, no. 1 (1990): 1–19.

Foy, George. "Economic Sustainability and the Preservation of Environmental Assets." *Environmental Management* 14, no. 6 (1990): 771–78.

Freeman, Jody, and Charles D. Kolstad, eds. *Moving to Markets in Environmental Regulation: Lessons from Twenty Years of Experience*. Oxford: Oxford University Press, 2007.

Fu, Liguo, Yong-fu Yu, and Robert R. Mill. "Cunninghamia." *Flora of China*. Accessed January 8, 2020. www.efloras.org/florataxon.aspx?flora_id=2&taxon_id=108681.

Gan Xi 甘熙. *Baixia suoyan* 白下瑣言. Reprint. Nanjing xijian wenxian congkan 南京稀見文獻叢刊. Nanjing: Nanjing Chuban She, 2007.

Gatto, M. "Sustainability: Is It a Well Defined Concept?" *Ecological Applications* 5, no. 4 (1995): 1181–83.

Ge Jianxiong 葛劍雄, Cao Shuji 曹樹基, and Wu Songdi 吳松弟. *Jianming Zhongguo yimin shi* 簡明中國移民史. Fuzhou: Fujian Renmin Chuban She, 1993.

Gibson, Clark C., Margaret A. McKean, and Elinor Ostrom, eds. *People and Forests: Communities, Institutions, and Governance*. Cambridge, MA: MIT Press, 2000.

Giersch, C. Patterson. *Asian Borderlands: The Transformation of Qing China's Yunnan Frontier*. Cambridge, MA: Harvard University Press, 2006.

Guojia Linye Ju 國家林業局. "Shanmu susheng fengchan lin" 杉木速生豐產用材林. In *Zhonghua Renmin Gonghe Guo linye hangye biaozhun* 中華人民共和國林業行業標準 LY/T 1384-2007.

Haraway, Donna. "Anthropocene, Capitalocene, Plantationocene, Chthulucene: Making Kin." *Environmental Humanities* 6, no. 1 (2015): 159–65.

Hardin, Garrett. "The Tragedy of the Commons." *Science* 162 (new series), no. 3859 (1968): 1243–48.

Harvey, David. "The Future of the Commons." *Radical History Review* 2011, no. 109 (2011): 101–107.

Herman, John E. *Amid the Clouds and Mist: China's Colonization of Guizhou, 1200–1700*. Cambridge, MA: Harvard University Asia Center, 2007.

———. "The Cant of Conquest: Tusi Offices and China's Political Incorporation of the Southwest Frontier." In *Empire at the Margins: Culture, Ethnicity, and Frontier in Early Modern China*, edited by Pamela Kyle Crossley, Helen F Siu, and Donald S Sutton, 135–70. Berkeley: University of California Press, 2006.

———. "Empire in the Southwest: Early Qing Reforms to the Native Chieftain System." *Journal of Asian Studies* 56, no. 1 (1997): 47–74.

Hinton, Harold C. "The Grain Tribute System of the Ch'ing Dynasty." *Far Eastern Quarterly* 11, no. 3 (1952): 339–54.

Holling, C. S., and Gary K. Meffe. "Command and Control and the Pathology of Natural Resource Management." *Conservation Biology* 10, no. 2 (1996): 328–37.

Hostetler, Laura. *Qing Colonial Enterprise: Ethnography and Cartography in Early Modern China*. Chicago: University of Chicago Press, 2001.

Huang Yuansheng 黄源盛. *Mingchu Daliyuan Yu Caipan* 民初大理院與裁判. Taipei: Angle Publishing Co, Ltd., 2011.

Huangchao jingshi wen bian 皇朝經世文編. 120 *juan*. 1825 edition, full text from ctext.org.

Huishang gongsuo zhengxin lu 徽商公所徵信錄 (1909). In *Zhongguo huiguan zhi ziliao jicheng di yi ji* 中國會館志資料集成第一輯, edited by Wang Rigen 王日根 and Xue Pengzhi 薛鵬志, 10:173–288. Xiamen: Xiamen Daxue Chuban She, 2013.

Hunan shangshi xiguan baogao shu 湖南商事習慣報告書 (1911). In *Hunan minqing fengsu baogao shu · Hunan shangshi xiguan baogao shu* 湖南民情民俗報告書· 湖南商事習慣報告書. Reprint, Changsha: Hunan Jiaoyu Chuban She, 2010.

Inspector General of Customs. *Decennial Reports on the Trade, Navigation, Industries Etc of the Ports Open to Foreign Commerce in China and Corea and on the Condition and Development of the Treaty Port Provinces*. 4 vols. Shanghai: Statistical Department of the Inspectorate General of Customs, 1893, 1904, 1913, 1924.

Integrated Taxonomic Information System. "ITIS Standard Report Page: Cunninghamia." Accessed January 8, 2020. www.itis.gov.

Jiang Shunyuan 姜舜源. "Ming-Qing chaoting Sichuan caimu yanjiu" 明清朝廷四川采木研究. *Gugong Bowu Yuan yuankan* 故宮博物院院刊 no. 4 (2001): 24–32.

Jin Qin 金勤. "Qing mo sanda hangye zhiyi de Shangxin He mushi" 清末三大行業之一的上新河木市 no. 1 (1985): 26–28.

Jinping xianzhi 錦屏縣志 1991–2009. 2 vols. Beijing: Fangzhi Chuban She, 2011.

Kishimoto Mio 岸本美緒. "Kishū no sanrin keiyaku bunsho to Kishū no sanrin keiyaku bunsho" 貴州の山林契約文書と徽州の山林契約文書. In *Kishū Byōzoku ringyō keiyaku bunsho kaihen (1736–1950 nen)* 貴州苗族林業契約文書匯編 (1736–1950 年), edited by Daniels Christian, Yang Yougeng 楊有賡, and Takeuchi Fusaji 武内房司, 3:165–90. Tokyo: Tokyo University of Foreign Languages, 2003.

Kobayashi Takashiro 小林高四郎. "Tō Sō gajin ko" 唐宋牙人考. *Shigaku* 史學 8, no. 1 (1929): 53–101.

———. "Tō Sō gajin ko hosei" 唐宋牙人考補正. *Shigaku* 史學 8, no. 3 (1929): 165–67.

Kotenev, Anatol M. *Shanghai: Its Mixed Court and Council Material Relating to the History of the Shanghai Municipal Council and the History, Practice and Statistics of the International Mixed Court. Chinese Modern Law and Shanghai Municipal Land Regulations and Bye-Laws Governing the Life in the Settlement.* Shanghai: North-China Daily News & Herald, Limited, 1925.

Lan Yong 藍勇. "Ming Qing shiqi de huangmu caiban" 明清時期的皇木採辦. *Lishi yanjiu* 歷史研究 no. 6 (1994): 86–98.

Lee, John S. "Postwar Pines: The Military and the Expansion of State Forests in Post-Imjin Korea, 1598–1684." *Journal of Asian Studies* 77, no. 2 (2018): 319–32.

Lei Menglin 雷夢麟. *Dulü suoyan* 讀律瑣言. 1557. Reprint, Beijing: Falü Chuban She, 2007.

Li Bozhong 李伯重. "Ming Qing shiqi Jiangnan diqu de mucai wenti" 明清時期江南地區的木材問題. *Zhongguo shehui jingji shi yanjiu* 中國社會經濟史研究 no. 1 (1986): 86–96.

Li Linqi 李琳琦. "Huishang yu Ming Qing shiqi de mucai maoyi" 徽商與明清時期的木材貿易. *Qingshi yanjiu* 清史研究 no. 2 (1996): 1–9.

Li Wenzhi 李文治 and Jiang Taixin 江太新. *Qing dai caoyun* 清代漕運. Rev. ed. Beijing: Shehui Kexue Wenxian Chuban She, 2008.

Liang Cong 梁聰. *Qingdai Qingshui Jiang xiayou cunzhai shehui de qiyue guifan yu zhixu: Yi Wendou Miao zhai qiyue wenshu wei zhongxin de yanjiu* 清代清水江下游村寨社會的契約規範與秩序——以文斗苗寨契約文書為中心的研究. Beijing: Renmin Chuban She, 2008.

Liao Shengfeng 廖聲豐. *Qingdai changguan yu quyu jingji yanjiu* 清代常關與區域經濟研究. Beijing: Renmin Chuban She, 2010.

———. "Qingdai Gan Guan shuishou de bianhua yu Dayuling shanglu de shangpin liutong" 清代贛關稅收的變化與大庾嶺商路的商品流通. *Lishi dang'an* 歷史檔案 no. 4 (2001): 85–92.

Lin, Manhong. *China Upside Down: Currency, Society, and Ideologies, 1808–1856*. Cambridge, MA: Harvard University Asia Center, 2006.

Lin Hongzhuang 林紅狀. "Ming Qing ji jindai yahang yanjiu zongshu" 明清及近代牙行研究綜述. *Lishi jiaoxue* 歷史教學 no. 24 (2008): 105–108.

Liu, Dachang. "Tenure and Management of Non-State Forests in China since 1950: A Historical Review." *Environmental History* 6, no. 2 (2001): 239–63.

Liu, Kwang-Ching. "Chinese Merchant Guilds: An Historical Inquiry." *Pacific Historical Review* 57, no. 1 (1988): 1–23.

Liu, William Guanglin. "The Making of a Fiscal State in Song China, 960–1279." *Economic History Review* 68, no. 1 (2015): 48–78.

Liu Boshan 劉伯山, ed. *Huizhou wenshu di san ji* 徽州文書第三輯. Guilin: Guangxi Shifan Daxue Chuban She, 2009.

Liu Hongmo 劉洪謨. *Wuguan quezhi* 蕪關榷志, 1603.

Liu Mingguang 劉明光. *Zhongguo ziran dili tuji* 中國自然地理圖集. 3rd ed. Beijing: Zhongguo Ditu Chuban She, 2010.

Liu Peiliang 柳培良 and Fan Jingyu 范淨宇. "Nanjing shi mucai shikuang diaocha shang" 南京市木材市況調查上. *Nongye tongxun* 農業通訊 1, no. 10 (1947): 17–24.

Liu Shigu 劉詩古. "Ming mo yijiang Poyang Hu diqu 'shuimian quan' zhi fenhua yu zhuanrang: Yi 'maihu qi' he 'zuhu zi' wei zhongxin" 明末以降鄱陽湖地區"水面權"之分化與轉讓——以"賣湖契"和"租湖字"為中心. *Qingshi yanjiu* 清史研究 no. 3 (2015): 60–73.

Long Denggao 龍登高. "Diquan jiaoyi yu shengchan yaosu zuhe: 1650–1950" 地權交易與生產要素組合:1650–1950. *Jingji yanjiu* 經濟研究 no. 2 (2009): 146–56.

———. "Qingdai diquan jiaoyi xingshi de duoyang hua fazhan" 清代地權交易形式的多樣化發展. *Qingshi yanjiu* 清史研究 no. 3 (2008): 44–58.

Long Denggao 龍登高 and Peng Bo 彭波. "Jinshi diannong de jingying xingzhi yu shouyi bijiao" 近世佃農的經營性質與收益比較. *Jingji yanjiu* 經濟研究 no. 1 (2010): 138–47.

Long Denggao 龍登高, Ren Zhiqiang 任志強, and Zhao Liang 趙亮. "Jinshi Zhongguo nongdi chanquan de duochong quanneng" 近世中國農地產權的多重權能. *Zhongguo jingji shi yanjiu* 中國經濟史研究 no. 4 (2010): 18–26.

Lu Qizao 盧其慥. "Gannan mucai hangye shihua" 贛南木材行業史話. *Ganzhou wenshi ziliao di er ji* 贛州文史資料第二輯 (1986): 112–17.

Lu Yin 蘆隱. "Bo xinding shichi muma zhi yuanli yi" 駁新訂市尺木馬之原理議. *Muye jie* 木業界 1, no. 3 (1940): 12–13.

———. "Shangxin He shanmu ye wushi nian gaikuang" 上新河杉木業五十年概況. *Muye jie* 木業界 (1940): 1.4, 5–9; 2.1, 10–13; 2.2, 13–17.

———. "Wo ye laitan Longquan ma" 我也來談龍泉碼. *Muye jie* 木業界 1, no. 3 (1940): 11.

Ludwig, Donald. "Environmental Sustainability: Magic, Science, and Religion in Natural Resource Management." *Ecological Applications* 3, no. 4 (1993): 555–58.

Luo Yudong 羅玉東. *Zhongguo lijin shi* 中國釐金史. Shanghai: Shangwu Yinshu Guan, 1936.

Ma, Debin. "Law and Economy in Traditional China: A 'Legal Origin' Perspective on the Great Divergence." In *Law and Long-Term Economic Change: An Eurasian Perspective*, edited by Jan Luiten van Zanden and Debin Ma, 46–67. Stanford, CA: Stanford University Press, 2011.

Ma Min 馬敏. "Shangshi caipan yu shanghui: Lun wan Qing Suzhou shangshi jiufen de tiaochu" 商事裁判與商會——論晚清蘇州商事糾紛的調處. *Lishi yanjiu* 歷史研究 no. 1 (1996): 30–43.

Ma Min 馬敏 and Zhu Ying 朱英. *Chuantong yu jindai de erchong bianzou: Wan Qing Suzhou Shanghui ge'an yanjiu* 傳統與近代的二重變奏——晚晴蘇州商會個案研究. Chengdu: Bashu Shushe, 1993.

Malm, Andreas, and Alf Hornborg. "The Geology of Mankind? A Critique of the Anthropocene Narrative." *Anthropocene Review* 1, no. 1 (2014): 62–69.

Mann, Susan. *Local Merchants and the Chinese Bureaucracy: 1750–1950*. Stanford, CA: Stanford University Press, 1987.

Mao Qiling 毛奇齡. "Hangzhou zhihuo yi" 杭州治火議. In *Wulin zhanggu congbian* 武林掌故叢編. Vol. 9. Taipei: Tailian Guofeng Chuban She, 1967.

Margary, Augustus Raymond, and Rutherford Alcock. *The Journey of Augustus Raymond Margary, from Shanghae to Bhamo, and Back to Manwyne*. London: Macmillan and Co., 1876.

Marks, Robert. *China: An Environmental History*. 2nd ed. Lanham, MD: Rowman & Littlefield, 2017.

———. *Tigers, Rice, Silk, and Silt: Environment and Economy in Late Imperial South China*. Cambridge: Cambridge University Press, 1998.

Matteson, Kieko. *Forests in Revolutionary France: Conservation, Community, and Conflict 1669–1848*. New York: Cambridge University Press, 2015.

McDermott, Joseph P. *The Making of a New Rural Order in South China: I. Village, Land, and Lineage in Huizhou, 900–1600*. New York: Cambridge University Press, 2014.

McNeil, J. R. "China's Environmental History in World Perspective." In *Sediments of Time: Environment and Society in Chinese History*, edited by Mark Elvin and Liu Ts'ui-jung, 31–49. New York: Cambridge University Press, 1998.

Menzies, Nicholas K. *Forest and Land Management in Imperial China*. New York: St. Martin's Press, 1994.

———. "Forestry." In *Agro-Industries and Forestry*, by Christian Daniels and Nicholas K Menzies, 541–740. Science and Civilisation in China Vol. 6, Part 3. Cambridge: Cambridge University Press, 1996.

———. "Three Hundred Years of Taungya: A Sustainable System of Forestry in South China." *Human Ecology* 16, no. 4 (1988): 361–76.

Miller, Ian Matthew. *Fir and Empire: The Transformation of Forests in Early Modern China*. Seattle: University of Washington Press, 2020.

Millward, James A. *Beyond the Pass: Economy, Ethnicity, and Empire in Qing Central Asia, 1759–1864*. Stanford, CA: Stanford University Press, 1998.

Ming Qing Huizhou shehui jingji ziliao congbian di er ji: Zhongguo Shehui Kexue Yuan Lishi Yanjiu Suo cang Song Yuan Ming sandai Huizhou tudi maimai wenqi jiyao 明清徽州社會經濟資料叢編第二集: 中國社會科學院歷史研究所藏宋元明三代徽州土地賣賣文契輯要. Beijing: Zhongguo Shehui Kexue Chuban She, 1988.

Ming Qing Suzhou gongshang ye beike ji 明清蘇州工商業碑刻集. Jiangsu: Jiangsu Renmin Chuban She, 1981.

Minshi xiguan diaocha baogao lu 民事習慣調查報告錄. 1930. Reprint, Beijing: Zhongguo Zhengfa Daxue Chuban She, 2000.

Miyazawa Tomoyuki 宮澤知之. "Sodai no gajin" 宋代の牙人. *Toyoshi kenkyu* 東洋史研究 39, no. 1 (1980): 1–34.

Moll-Murata, Christine. "Chinese Guilds from the Seventeenth to the Twentieth Centuries: An Overview." *International Review of Social History* 53, no. S16 (2008): 213–47.

Moore, Jason W. *Anthropocene or Capitalocene? Nature, History, and the Crisis of Capitalism*. Oakland, CA: PM Press, 2016.

Morse, Hosea B. *The Guilds of China*. Shanghai: Kelly & Wash Ltd, 1909.

Nanjing wuzi zhi 南京物資志. Beijing: Zhongguo Chengshi Chuban She, 1993.

Negishi Tadashi 根岸佶. *Chūgoku no girudo* 中國のギルド. Tokyo: Nihon Hyōronsha, 1953.

———. *Shanhai no girudo* 上海のギルド. Tokyo: Nihon Hyōronsha, 1951.

Ni Yuping 倪玉平. *Qingchao Jia Dao guanshui yanjiu* 清朝嘉道關稅研究. Beijing: Beijing Shifan Daxue Chuban She, 2010.

North, Douglass C. *Institutions, Institutional Change, and Economic Performance*. Cambridge: Cambridge University Press, 1990.

Ogilvie, Sheilagh C. "The Economics of Guilds." *Journal of Economic Perspectives* 28, no. 4 (2014): 169–92.

———. *Institutions and European Trade: Merchant Guilds, 1000–1800.* Cambridge: Cambridge University Press, 2011.

———. "Rehabilitating the Guilds: A Reply." *Economic History Review* 61 (new series), no. 1 (2008): 175–82.

Olson, Mancur. *The Logic of Collective Action: Public Goods and the Theory of Groups.* Cambridge, MA: Harvard University Press, 1965.

Osborne, Anne. "Highlands and Lowlands: Economic and Ecological Interactions in the Lower Yangzi Region under the Qing." In *Sediments of Time: Environment and Society in Chinese History,* edited by Mark Elvin and Ts'ui-jung Liu, 203–34. New York: Cambridge University Press, 1998.

———. "The Local Politics of Land Reclamation in the Lower Yangzi Highlands." *Late Imperial China* 15, no. 1 (1994): 1–46.

Ostrom, Elinor. *Governing the Commons: The Evolution of Institutions for Collective Action.* Cambridge: Cambridge University Press, 1990.

Ouyang Tianxing 歐陽天星. "Gannan mucai hangye shihua buji" 贛南木材行業史話補記. *Ganzhou wenshi ziliao* 贛州文史資料 (1986): 166–72.

Peng Zeyi 彭澤益, ed. *Zhongguo gongshang hanghui shiliao ji* 中國工商行會史料集. Beijing: Zhonghua Shuju, 1995.

Perdue, Peter C. *Exhausting the Earth: State and Peasant in Hunan, 1500–1850.* Cambridge, MA: Harvard University Asia Center, 1987.

———. "Official Goals and Local Interests: Water Control in the Dongting Lake Region during the Ming and Qing Periods." *Journal of Asian Studies* 41, no. 4 (1982): 747–65.

Pomeranz, Kenneth. *The Making of a Hinterland: State, Society, and Economy in Inland North China, 1853–1937.* Berkeley: University of California Press, 1993.

Poteete, Amy R., and Elinor Ostrom. "In Pursuit of Comparable Concepts and Data about Collective Action." *Agricultural Systems* 82, no. 3 (2004): 215–32.

Qi Meiqin 祁美琴. "Guanyu Qingdai queguan eshui de kaocha" 關於清代榷關額稅的考察. *Qingshi yanjiu* 清史研究 no. 2 (2004): 61–70.

Qu Jian 瞿見. "Wenben yu chaoben: *Caiyun huangmu andu* de chuanchao" 文本與抄本——《採運皇木案牘》的抄傳. *Tianye yu wenxian* 田野與文獻 no. 91 (2018): 1–9.

Rajan, S. Ravi. *Modernizing Nature: Forestry and Imperial Eco-Development 1800–1950.* Oxford: Oxford University Press, 2006.

Reardon-Anderson, James. "Land Use and Society in Manchuria and Inner Mongolia during the Qing Dynasty." *Environmental History* 5, no. 4 (2000): 503–30.

Robbins, Alicia S. T., and Stevan Harrell. "Paradoxes and Challenges for China's Forests in the Reform Era." *China Quarterly* 218 (2014): 381–403.

Rowe, William T. "Approaches to Modern Chinese Social History." In *Reliving the Past: The Worlds of Social History*, edited by Olivier Zunz, 236–96. Chapel Hill: University of North Carolina Press, 1985.

———. *Hankow: Commerce and Society in a Chinese City, 1796–1889*. Stanford, CA: Stanford University Press, 1984.

———. *Hankow: Conflict and Community in a Chinese City, 1796–1895*. Stanford, CA: Stanford University Press, 1989.

———. "Ming-Qing Guilds." *Ming Qing Yanjiu* 1, no.1 (1992): 47–ins01.

Rubenstein, Daniel I. "Science and the Pursuit of a Sustainable World." *Ecological Applications* 3, no. 4 (1993): 585–87.

"Sanjiang muye jianshu" 三江木業簡述. *Qiguang yuekan* 企光月刊 3, no. 1–2 (1942): 12–17.

Schlesinger, Jonathan. *A World Trimmed with Fur: Wild Things, Pristine Places, and the Natural Fringes of Qing*. Stanford, CA: Stanford University Press, 2017.

Scott, James C. *Seeing Like a State: How Certain Schemes to Improve the Human Condition Have Failed*. New Haven: Yale University Press, 1998.

Serageldin, Ismail. "Making Development Sustainable." *Finance and Development* 30, no. 4 (1993): 6–10.

———. *Sustainability and the Wealth of Nations: First Steps in an Ongoing Journey*. Washington, DC: World Bank, 1996.

"Shanghai shi shehui ju muye shangqing diaocha" 上海市社會局木業商情調查, 1935. SHMA, S145-1-47.

Shen Xuefeng 申學鋒. "Qingdai caizheng shouru guimo yu jiegou bianhua shulun" 清代財政收入規模與結構變化述論. *Beijing shehui kexue* no. 1 (2002): 84–90.

Shi Ying 石瑩. "Qingdai Hankou de zhumu shichang jiqi guimo fenxi" 清代漢口的竹木市場及其規模分析. *Zhongguo jingjishi yanjiu* 中國經濟史研究 no. 1 (2015): 108–19.

Shiba Yoshinobu 斯波義信. *Commerce and Society in Sung China*. Translated by Mark Elvin. Ann Arbor: University of Michigan Press, 1970.

———. *Sōdai shōgyō shi kenkyū* 宋代商業史研究. Tokyo: Kazama Shobō, 1968.

Shiga Shuzo 滋賀秀三. "Family Property and the Law of Inheritance in Traditional China." In *Chinese Family Law and Social Change in Historical and Comparative Perspective*, edited by David C. Buxbaum, 109–50. Seattle: University of Washington Press, 1978.

Shin, Leo Kwok-yueh. *The Making of the Chinese State: Ethnicity and Expansion on the Ming Borderlands*. Cambridge: Cambridge University Press, 2011.

Sivaramakrishnan, K. *Modern Forests: Statemaking and Environmental Change in Colonial Eastern India*. Stanford, CA: Stanford University Press, 1999.

Songster, E. Elena. "Cultivating the Nation in Fujian's Forests: Forest Policies and Afforestation Efforts in China, 1911–1937." *Environmental History* 8, no. 3 (2003): 452–73.

Stavins, Robert N. "Experience with Market-Based Environmental Policy Instruments." In *Handbook of Environmental Economics*, 1:355–435. Amsterdam: Elsevier, 2003.

Steffen, W., J. Grinevald, P. Crutzen, and J. McNeill. "The Anthropocene: Conceptual and Historical Perspectives." *Philosophical Transactions of the Royal Society A: Mathematical, Physical and Engineering Sciences* 369, no. 1938 (2011): 842–67.

Stephens, Thomas B. *Order and Discipline in China: The Shanghai Mixed Court, 1911–27*. Seattle: University of Washington Press, 1992.

Sutton, Donald S. "Ethnicity and the Miao Frontier in the Eighteenth Century." In *Empire at the Margins: Culture, Ethnicity, and Frontier in Early Modern China*, edited by Pamela Kyle Crossley, Helen F Siu, and Donald S Sutton, 190–228. Berkeley: University of California Press, 2006.

Takeuchi Fusaji 武内房司. "Narukami to meikan no aida: Shindai Kishū Byōzoku ringyō keiyaku bunsho ni miru Byōzoku no shūzoku to funsō shori" 鳴神と鳴官のあいだ——清代貴州苗族林業契約文書に見る苗族の習俗と紛争処理. In *Kishū Byōzoku ringyō keiyaku bunsho kaihen (1736–1950 nen)* 貴州苗族林業契約文書匯編 (1736–1950 年), edited by Christian Daniels, Yougeng Yang 楊有賡, and Fusaji Takeuchi 武内房司, 3:83–120. Tokyo: Tokyo University of Foreign Languages, 2003.

Tan Qixiang 譚其驤. "Zhongguo neidi yimin shi: Hunan pian" 中國內地移民史——湖南篇. *shixue nianbao* 史學年報 no. 4 (1932).

Tang Bingnan 湯丙南. "Hankou ce mucai zhi fa" 漢口測木材之法. *Hubei sheng nonghui nongbao* 湖北省農會農報 2, no. 9 (1921): 91–93.

Tang Lixing 唐力行. "Ming Qing Huizhou mushang kao" 明清徽州木商考. *Xueshu jie* 學術界 no. 2 (1991): 43–52.

Tiffen, Mary, Michael Mortimore, and Francis Gichuki. *More People, Less Erosion: Environmental Recovery in Kenya*. Nairobi, Kenya: ACTS Press, 1994.

Totman, Conrad D. *The Green Archipelago: Forestry in Preindustrial Japan*. Berkeley: University of California Press, 1989.

Trac, Christine Jane, Amanda H. Schmidt, Stevan Harrell, and Thomas M. Hinckley. "Environmental Reviews and Case Studies: Is the Returning Farmland to Forest Program a Success? Three Case Studies from Sichuan." *Environmental Practice* 15, no. 3 (2013): 350–66.

Turner, Robert Kerry, ed. *Sustainable Environmental Economics and Management: Principles and Practice.* Chichester, UK: Wiley, 1993.

Vermeer, Eduard B. "Population and Ecology along the Frontier in Qing China." In *Sediments of Time: Environment and Society in Chinese History,* edited by Mark Elvin and Ts'ui-jung Liu, 235–79. New York: Cambridge University Press, 1998.

von Glahn, Richard. *The Economic History of China: From Antiquity to the Nineteenth Century.* Cambridge: Cambridge University Press, 2016

———. *Fountain of Fortune: Money and Monetary Policy in China, 1000–1700.* Berkeley: University of California Press, 1996.

———. "Modalities of the Fiscal State in Imperial China." *Journal of Chinese History* 4, no.1 (2020): 1–29.

Wang, Chaoqun, Lin Xue, Yuhong Dong, Lingyu Hou, Yihui Wei, Jiaqi Chen, and Ruzhen Jiao. "The Development of Chinese Fir Plantations Undergo Significant Changes in Soil Microbial Metabolic Function and Enzyme Activities." *Journal of Forest Research* 24, no. 4 (2019): 261–65.

Wang Boxin 王伯心. "Nanjing shi mucai maoyi jijia fangfa gaiyao" 南京市木材貿易計價方法概要. *Linye tongxun* 林業通訊 no. 1 (1947): 2–4.

Wang Zhen 王珍. "Tunxi shangbu yu Huizhou mushang" 屯溪商埠與徽州木商. In *Huishang shihua* 徽商史話, edited by Shiliang Zhu 朱世良, 79–80. Hefei: Huangshan Shushe, 1992.

Wang Zhenzhong 王振忠. "Taiping Tianguo qianhou Huishang zai Jiangxi de muye jingying: Xin faxian de 'Xihe Muye Zuanyao.'" 太平天國前後徽商在江西的木業經營——新發現的《西河木業纂要》. *Lishi dili* 歷史地理 28 (2013): 144–65.

Waters, Colin N., Jan Zalasiewicz, Colin Summerhayes, Anthony D. Barnosky, Clement Poirier, A. Ga uszka, A. Cearreta, et al. "The Anthropocene Is Functionally and Stratigraphically Distinct from the Holocene." *Science* 351, no. 6269 (2016): aad2622.

Watson, James L. "Anthropological Overview: The Development of Chinese Descent Groups." In *Kinship Organization in Late Imperial China, 1000–1940,* edited by Patricia Buckeley Ebrey and James L. Watson, 274–92. Berkeley: University of California Press, 1986.

Watson, Rubie S. "Corporate Property and Local Leadership in the Pearl River Delta, 1898–1941." In *Chinese Local Elites and Patterns of Dominance,* edited by Joseph W Esherick and Mary Backus Rankin, 239–60. Berkeley: University of California Press, 1990.

Wing, John T. *Roots of Empire: Forests and State Power in Early Modern Spain, c. 1500–1750.* Leiden: Brill, 2015.

Wong, R. Bin. "Taxation and Good Governance in China, 1500–1914." In *The Rise of Fiscal States: A Global History 1500–1914,* edited by Bartolome

Yun-Casalilla, Partick K. O'Brien, and Franciso Comin Comin, 353–77. Cambridge: Cambridge University Press, 2012.

Worster, Donald. *American Environmentalism: The Formative Period, 1860–1915*. New York: John Wiley & Sons, Inc., 1973.

Wu Chuanjun 吳傳鈞. "Nanjing Shangxin He de mushi: Changjiang zhongxia you mucai jisan de zhongxin" 南京上新河的木市——長江中下游木材集散的中心. *Dili* 地理 6, no. 2–4 (1949): 37–44.

Wu Zhonglun 吳中倫, ed. *Shanmu* 杉木. Beijing: Zhongguo Linye Chuban She, 1984.

Wuliao jiazhi zeli Databases: Prices and Wages in Public Construction in the Qing Dynasty. Distributed by Geschichte Chinas, Ruhr-Universität Bochum. www.ruhr-uni-bochum.de/gpc/datenbanken.html.

Xing, Pei, Qibin Zhang, and Patrick J. Baker. "Age and Radial Growth Pattern of Four Tree Species in a Subtropical Forest of China." *Trees* 26, no. 2 (2012): 283–90.

Xing'an huilan 刑案匯覽. 60 *juan*, GJK.

Xu Bin 徐斌. *Zhidu, jingji, yu shehui: Ming-Qing liang Hu yuye, yumin, yu shuiyu shehui* 制度、經濟與社會: 明清兩湖漁業、漁民與水域社會. Beijing: Kexue Chuban She, 2018.

Xu Guangqi 徐光啟. *Nongzheng quanshu* 農政全書, 1639.

Xu Tan 許檀. "Qingdai qianqi de Jiujiang Guan jiqi shangpin liutong" 清代前期的九江關及其商品流通. *Lishi dang'an* 歷史檔案 no. 1 (1999): 86–91.

Xue Yunsheng 薛允升. *Dulü cunyi* 讀律存疑. 1905. Reprint, Taipei: Chinese Materials and Research Aids Service Center, 1970.

Yang Xiangjun 楊湘鈞. *Diguo zhi bian yu guatou zhi lian: Shanghai Huishen Gongxie quanli guanxi bianqian yanjiu* 帝國之鞭與寡頭之鏈——上海會審公廨權力關係變遷研究. Beijing: Beijing Daxue Chuban She, 2006.

Yang Yougeng 楊有庚. "Qingdai Qian dongnan Qingshui Jiang liuyu muhang chutan" 清代黔東南清水江流域木行初探. *Guizhou shehui kexue* 貴州社會科學 no. 8 (1988): 48–53.

Yang Yusheng 楊玉盛. *Shanmu lin ke chixu jingying de yanjiu* 杉木林可持續經營的研究. Beijing: Zhongguo Linye Chuban She, 1998.

Yin Qing 蔭青. "Jiangxi zhi mucai ye" 江西之木材業. *Jingji xun kan* 經濟旬刊 4, no. 7 (1935): 1–16.

Ying'an 英安. *Caiyun huangmu andu* 採運皇木案牘, ca. 1781. National Science Library at the Chinese Academy of Sciences, Beijing.

Yu Xintuo 俞新妥. "Shanmu de hunnong linye" 杉木的混農林業. *Shengtai xue zazhi* 生態學雜誌 10, no. 2 (1991): 25–28.

———. *Shanmu zaipei xue* 杉木栽培學. Fuzhou: Fujian Keji Chuban She, 1997.

Zeli bianlan 則例便覽. 49 *juan*, GJK.

Zelin, Madeleine. "Chinese Business Practice in the Late Imperial Period." *Enterprise and Society* 14, no. 4 (2013): 769–93.

———. "Eastern Sichuan Coal Mines in the Late Qing." In *Empire, Nation, and Beyond: Chinese History in Late Imperial and Modern Times*, edited by Joseph W Esherick and Wen-Hsin Yeh, 105–22. Berkeley: University of California Press, 2006.

———. "The Firm in Early Modern China." *Journal of Economic Behavior & Organization* 71, no. 3 (2009): 623–37.

———. *The Merchants of Zigong: Industrial Entrepreneurship in Early Modern China*. New York: Columbia University Press, 2005.

———. "The Rise and Fall of the Fu-Rong Salt-Yard Elite: Merchant Dominance in Late Qing China." In *Chinese Local Elites and Patterns of Dominance*, edited by Joseph W Esherick and Mary Backus Rankin, 82–109. Berkeley: University of California Press, 1990.

Zhan Mingduo 詹鳴鐸. *Wo zhi xiaoshi: Xin faxian de huishang xiaoshuo* 我之小史——新發現的徽商小說. Edited by Wang Zhenzhong 王振忠. Hefei: Anhui Jiaoyu Chuban She, 2008.

Zhang, Meng. "Financing Market-Oriented Reforestation: Securitization of Timberlands and Shareholding Practices in Southwest China, 1750–1900." *Late Imperial China* 38, no. 2 (2017): 109–51.

———. "Frontier Timber in Southwest China: Market, Empire, and Identity." In *The Cultivated Forest: Trees and People in Asian History*, edited by Bradley Camp Davis, Brian Lander, John S. Lee, and Ian M. Miller. Seattle: University of Washington Press, forthcoming.

———. "Timber Trade along the Yangzi River: State, Market, Environment, and Frontier, 1750–1930." PhD dissertation, University of California–Los Angeles, 2017.

———. "Timber Trade Organizations in Shanghai: Institutions, Enforcement, and Dispute Resolution, 1880–1930." *International Journal of Asian Studies* 14, no. 2 (2017): 143–70.

Zhang Chuanxi 張傳璽, ed. *Zhongguo lidai qiyue huibian kaoshi* 中國歷代契約會編考釋. Beijing: Beijing Daxue Chuban She, 1995.

Zhang Haipeng 張海鵬 and Wang Tingyuan 王廷元, eds. *Ming Qing Huishang ziliao xuanbian* 明清徽商資料選編. Hefei: Huangshan Shushe, 1985.

Zhang Yingqiang 張應強. "Cong Guazhi 'Yishi Yongzun' shike kan Qingdai zhonghou qi de Qingshui Jiang mucai maoyi" 從卦治《奕世永遵》石刻看清代中後期的清水江木材貿易. *Zhongguo shehui jingji shi yanjiu* 中國社會經濟史研究 no. 3 (2002): 53–59.

———. *Mucai zhi liudong: Qingdai Qingshui Jiang xiayou diqu de shichang, quanli, yu shehui* 木材之流動: 清代清水江下游地區的市場、權力與社會. Beijing: Sanlian Shudian, 2006.

Zhang Yingqiang 張應強 and Hu Teng 胡騰. *Xiangtu Zhongguo Jinping* 鄉土中國 錦屏. Shanghai: Sanlian Shudian, 2004.

Zhang Yingqiang 張應強 and Wang Zongxun 王宗勳, eds. *Qingshui Jiang wenshu di er ji* 清水江文書第二輯. 10 vols. Guilin: Guangxi Shifan Daxue Chuban She, 2009.

"Zhejiang zhi mucai" 浙江之木材. *Zhong wai jingji zhoukan* 中外經濟週刊 no. 219 (1927): 11–16.

Zhenxun Muye Gonghui baogao lu 震巽木業公會報告錄, 1925. SHMA, S145-1-7.

Zhou Lin 周琳. "Bianshang yihuo haishang: Cong zhongjie maoyi jiufen kan Qianlong zhi Daoguang shiqi Chongqing de guanya zhi" 「便商」抑或「害商」——從仲介貿易糾紛看乾隆至道光時期重慶的「官牙制」. *Xin shixue* 新史學 24, no. 1 (2013): 59–106.

Zhuang Lunyi 莊綸裔. *Lu xiang gongdu* 盧鄉公牘. 4 *juan*, GJK.

INDEX

Note: Page numbers in *italics* refer to maps, figures, and tables.

N

R

S

U

V

W

X

Y

Z

CULTURE, PLACE, AND NATURE

Studies in Anthropology and Environment

Timber and Forestry in Qing China: Sustaining the Market, by Meng Zhang

Consuming Ivory: Mercantile Legacies of East Africa and New England, by Alexandra C. Kelly

Mapping Water in Dominica: Enslavement and Environment under Colonialism, by Mark W. Hauser

Mountains of Blame: Climate and Culpability in the Philippine Uplands, by Will Smith

Sacred Cows and Chicken Manchurian: The Everyday Politics of Eating Meat in India, by James Staples

Gardens of Gold: Place-Making in Papua New Guinea, by Jamon Alex Halvaksz

Shifting Livelihoods: Gold Mining and Subsistence in the Chocó, Colombia, by Daniel Tubb

Disturbed Forests, Fragmented Memories: Jarai and Other Lives in the Cambodian Highlands, by Jonathan Padwe

The Snow Leopard and the Goat: Politics of Conservation in the Western Himalayas, by Shafqat Hussain

Roses from Kenya: Labor, Environment, and the Global Trade in Cut Flowers, by Megan A. Styles

Working with the Ancestors: Mana and Place in the Marquesas Islands, by Emily C. Donaldson

Living with Oil and Coal: Resource Politics and Militarization in Northeast India, by Dolly Kikon

Caring for Glaciers: Land, Animals, and Humanity in the Himalayas, by Karine Gagné

Organic Sovereignties: Struggles over Farming in an Age of Free Trade, by Guntra A. Aistara

The Nature of Whiteness: Race, Animals, and Nation in Zimbabwe, by Yuka Suzuki

Forests Are Gold: Trees, People, and Environmental Rule in Vietnam, by Pamela D. McElwee

Conjuring Property: Speculation and Environmental Futures in the Brazilian Amazon, by Jeremy M. Campbell

Andean Waterways: Resource Politics in Highland Peru, by Mattias Borg Rasmussen

Puer Tea: Ancient Caravans and Urban Chic, by Jinghong Zhang

Enclosed: Conservation, Cattle, and Commerce among the Q'eqchi' Maya Lowlanders, by Liza Grandia

Forests of Identity: Society, Ethnicity, and Stereotypes in the Congo River Basin, by Stephanie Rupp

Tahiti beyond the Postcard: Power, Place, and Everyday Life, by Miriam Kahn

Wild Sardinia: Indigeneity and the Global Dreamtimes of Environmentalism, by Tracey Heatherington

Nature Protests: The End of Ecology in Slovakia, by Edward Snajdr

Forest Guardians, Forest Destroyers: The Politics of Environmental Knowledge in Northern Thailand, by Tim Forsyth and Andrew Walker

Being and Place among the Tlingit, by Thomas F. Thornton

Tropics and the Traveling Gaze: India, Landscape, and Science, 1800–1856, by David Arnold

Ecological Nationalisms: Nature, Livelihood, and Identities in South Asia, edited by Gunnel Cederlöf and K. Sivaramakrishnan

From Enslavement to Environmentalism: Politics on a Southern African Frontier, by David McDermott Hughes

Border Landscapes: The Politics of Akha Land Use in China and Thailand, by Janet C. Sturgeon

Property and Politics in Sabah, Malaysia: Native Struggles over Land Rights, by Amity A. Doolittle

The Earth's Blanket: Traditional Teachings for Sustainable Living, by Nancy Turner

The Kuhls of Kangra: Community-Managed Irrigation in the Western Himalaya, by Mark Baker

CPSIA information can be obtained
at www.ICGtesting.com
Printed in the USA
BVHW070350260522
638164BV00003B/5

9 780295 748870